Register for Free Membership to

solutions@syngress.com

Over the last few years, Syngress has published many best-selling and critically acclaimed books, including Tom Shinder's *Configuring ISA Server 2004*, Brian Caswell and Jay Beale's *Snort 2.1 Intrusion Detection*, and Angela Orebaugh and Gilbert Ramirez's *Ethereal Packet Sniffing*. One of the reasons for the success of these books has been our unique **solutions@syngress.com** program. Through this site, we've been able to provide readers a real time extension to the printed book.

As a registered owner of this book, you will qualify for free access to our members-only solutions@syngress.com program. Once you have registered, you will enjoy several benefits, including:

- Four downloadable e-booklets on topics related to the book. Each booklet is approximately 20-30 pages in Adobe PDF format. They have been selected by our editors from other best-selling Syngress books as providing topic coverage that is directly related to the coverage in this book.

- A comprehensive FAQ page that consolidates all of the key points of this book into an easy-to-search web page, providing you with the concise, easy-to-access data you need to perform your job.

- A "From the Author" Forum that allows the authors of this book to post timely updates and links to related sites, or additional topic coverage that may have been requested by readers.

Just visit us at **www.syngress.com/solutions** and follow the simple registration process. You will need to have this book with you when you register.

Thank you for giving us the opportunity to serve your needs. And be sure to let us know if there is anything else we can do to make your job easier.

SYNGRESS®

SYNGRESS®

Skype Me!

From Single User to
Small Enterprise and Beyond

Michael Gough, SkypeTips.com

Salman Abdul Baset • Joshua Brashars • Larry Chaffin
Michael Cross • Dan Douglass
Michael Sweeney

FOREWORD
BY BILL CAMPBELL
SKYPE JOURNAL

KEY	SERIAL NUMBER
001	HJIRTCV764
002	PO9873D5FG
003	829KM8NJH2
004	94533D3VG5
005	CVPLQ6WQ23
006	VBP965T5T5
007	HJJJ863WD3E
008	2987GVTWMK
009	629MP5SDJT
010	IMWQ295T6T

PUBLISHED BY
Syngress Publishing, Inc.
800 Hingham Street
Rockland, MA 02370

Skype Me! From Single User to Small Enterprise and Beyond

Transferred to Digital Printing 2009.

ISBN: 1-59749-032-6

Publisher: Andrew Williams
Acquisitions Editor: Gary Byrne
Technical Editors: Michael Goughand
                   Salman Abdul Baset
Technical Proofreader: Neil Lindsey

Page Layout and Art: Patricia Lupien
Copy Editor: Darlene Bordwell
Indexer: Rich Carlson
Cover Designer: Michael Kavish

Distributed by O'Reilly Media, Inc. in the United States and Canada.
For information on rights, translations, and bulk purchases contact Matt Pedersen, Director of Sales and Rights, at Syngress Publishing; email matt@syngress.com or fax to 781-681-3585.

Author Dedication:

For my daughter, for without her I would have never known
how wonderful and rewarding being a father could be.

To all those that helped in this project by testing, reviewing and contributing,
thank you!

A Word from the Author:

Skype is an ever moving target with updates and new products being released
all the time. As you read this book you may find that Skype or a product has
been updated with a newer version. Know that even though Skype may look
different, or a product was updated, the features or content still applies. Just find
the equivalent item in the new version and go with the flow. There are many
products, both software and hardware we did not cover or that came out after
we completed the book. We will update **www.skypetips.com/
web_pages/skype_me.html** with any updates to the book or feedback we
receive so that you can have access to the latest information.

We hope you enjoy the book and it helps you understand the world of Skype
and how you can use the latest in Voice technology over the Internet to communicate with your family and friends and explore the many options Skype has
to offer to improve your communication experience and make life a little more
fun and cost effective.

Syngress Acknowledgments

Syngress would like to acknowledge the following people for their kindness and support in making this book possible.

Syngress books are now distributed in the United States and Canada by O'Reilly Media, Inc. The enthusiasm and work ethic at O'Reilly are incredible, and we would like to thank everyone there for their time and efforts to bring Syngress books to market: Tim O'Reilly, Laura Baldwin, Mark Brokering, Mike Leonard, Donna Selenko, Bonnie Sheehan, Cindy Davis, Grant Kikkert, Opol Matsutaro, Steve Hazelwood, Mark Wilson, Rick Brown, Tim Hinton, Kyle Hart, Sara Winge, Peter Pardo, Leslie Crandell, Regina Aggio Wilkinson, Pascal Honscher, Preston Paull, Susan Thompson, Bruce Stewart, Laura Schmier, Sue Willing, Mark Jacobsen, Betsy Waliszewski, Kathryn Barrett, John Chodacki, Rob Bullington, Kerry Beck, and Karen Montgomery.

The incredibly hardworking team at Elsevier Science, including Jonathan Bunkell, Ian Seager, Duncan Enright, David Burton, Rosanna Ramacciotti, Robert Fairbrother, Miguel Sanchez, Klaus Beran, Emma Wyatt, Chris Hossack, Krista Leppiko, Marcel Koppes, Judy Chappell, Radek Janousek, and Chris Reinders for making certain that our vision remains worldwide in scope.

David Buckland, Marie Chieng, Lucy Chong, Leslie Lim, Audrey Gan, Pang Ai Hua, Joseph Chan, and Siti Zuraidah Ahmad of STP Distributors for the enthusiasm with which they receive our books.

David Scott, Tricia Wilden, Marilla Burgess, Annette Scott, Andrew Swaffer, Stephen O'Donoghue, Bec Lowe, Mark Langley, and Anyo Geddes of Woodslane for distributing our books throughout Australia, New Zealand, Papua New Guinea, Fiji, Tonga, Solomon Islands, and the Cook Islands.

Lead Author
and Technical Editor

Michael Gough is host and webmaster of www.SkypeTips.com, which was launched in January 2005 and receives more than 100,000 hits per month, and www.VideoCallTips.com, which receives more than 30,000 hits per month. Michael writes articles on Skype and related issues. He also explains Skype's options and instructions to users so that they can practically apply Skype at home and in the workplace. Michael also evaluates products used with Skype and provides feedback to the vendors on features and improvements to help drive the direction of Skype-related products. Michael is also the host and webmaster for the Web site www.VideoCallTips.com, which is focused on helping people understand how to make video calls to family and friends, and maintains ratings of the many video call solutions available.

Michael's full-time employment is as a computer security consultant with 18 years' experience in the computer technology field. Michael works for a Fortune 500 company, where he delivers security consulting services to their clients. Michael also presents for his company at many trade shows and conferences and works with associations and groups, advising agencies like the FBI on Skype security and the Center for Internet Security on wireless security.

Technical Editor

Salman Abdul Baset is a first-year Ph.D. student in the computer science department at Columbia University. His areas of research include multimedia and peer-to-peer networks, ubiquitous computing, network security, reverse engineering/hacking of programs, and privacy. He holds an M.S. in Computer Science from Columbia University and a B.S. in Computer System Engineering from Ghulam Ishaq Khan Institute of Engineering Sciences & Technology in Pakistan.

Contributing Authors

Joshua Brashars is a telecommunications specialist in San Diego, CA. Joshua spends most of his time tinkering with voice-over-IP applications and the rest of his time working with Secure Science Corporation, breaking things apart. Joshua would like to thank his family, friends, Johnny Long, Lance James, and all of his hacker friends for their undying support.

Larry Chaffin (CISSP, PMP, JNCIE, MBCP, CWNP, NNCSE, NNCDE, CCNP, CCDP, CCNP-WAN, CCDP-WAN) is the CEO/Chairman of Pluto Networks and the Vice President of Advanced Network Technologies for Plannet Group. He is an accomplished author; he cowrote *Managing Cisco Network Security* (ISBN: 1-931836-56-6) and has also been a coauthor/ghost writer for 11 other technology books for VoIP, WLAN, security, and optical technologies. Larry has more than 29 vendor certifications such as the ones already listed, plus Cisco VoIP, Optical, Security,

VPN, IDS, Unity, and WLAN. He is also certified by Nortel in DMS Carrier Class Switches along with CS100'S, MCS5100, Call Pilot, and WLAN. Many other certifications come from vendors such as Avaya, HP, IBM, Microsoft, PeopleSoft, and VMware. Larry has been a Principal Architect around the world in 22 countries for many Fortune 100 companies designing VoIP, Security, WLAN, and optical networks. His next project is to write a book on Nortel VoIP and a new security architecture book he has designed for VoIP and WLAN networks.

Michael Cross (MCSE, MCP+I, CNA, Network+) is an Internet Specialist/Computer Forensic Analyst with the Niagara Regional Police Service (NRPS). He performs computer forensic examinations on computers involved in criminal investigation. He also has consulted and assisted in cases dealing with computer-related/Internet crimes. In addition to designing and maintaining the NRPS Web site at www.nrps.com and the NRPS intranet, he has provided support in the areas of programming, hardware, and network administration. As part of an information technology team that provides support to a user base of more than 800 civilian and uniform users, he has a theory that when the users carry guns, you tend to be more motivated in solving their problems.

Michael also owns KnightWare (www.knightware.ca), which provides computer-related services such as Web page design, and Bookworms (www.bookworms.ca), where you can purchase collectibles and other interesting items online. He has been a freelance writer for several years, and he has been published more than three dozen times in numerous books and anthologies. He currently resides in St. Catharines, Ontario, Canada, with his lovely wife, Jennifer, his darling daughter, Sara, and charming son, Jason.

Dan Douglass (MCSE+I, MCDBA, MCSD, MCT, Brainbench .Net Programmer Job Role) is the Special Projects Manager with a cutting-edge medical software company in Dallas, TX. His latest venture is as President/Owner of a new technology firm, Code Hatchery. He currently provides software development skills and internal training and integration solutions, as well as peer guidance for technical skills development. Dan's specialties include enterprise application integration and design; HL7, XML, XSL, C++, C#, JavaScript, Visual Basic, and Visual Basic.Net; database design and administration; Back Office and .NET Server platforms; Network design, including LAN and WAN solutions; all Microsoft operating systems; and Mac OS X, FreeBSD, and Linux. When he has free time, Dan teaches programming, database design, and database administration at a prominent Dallas university. Dan is a former U.S. Navy Nuclear Submariner and lives in Plano, TX, with his very supportive and understanding wife, Tavish.

Dan wishes to extend special thanks to his mother-in-law, Sue Moffett, for all her love and support through the years.

Michael Sweeney (CCNA, CCDA, CCNP, MCSE, SCP) is the owner of the Network Security consulting firm Packetattack.com. Packetattack.com's specialties are network design and troubleshooting, wireless network design, security, and analysis. The Packetattack team uses industry-standard tools such as Airmagnet, AiroPeekNX, and NAI Sniffer. Packetattack.com also provides digital forensic analysis services.

Michael has been a contributing author for Syngress for the books *Cisco Security Specialist's Guide to PIX Firewalls* (ISBN: 1-931836-63-9), *Cisco Security Specialist's Guide to Secure Intrusion Detection Systems* (ISBN: 1-932266-69-0), and *Building DMZs for Enterprise Networks* (ISBN: 1-931836-88-4). Through PacketPress, Michael has also published *Securing Your Network Using Linux* (ISBN: 1-411621-77-8).

Michael has recently joined the ranks of "Switchers" where he is not using two OS X Macs full-time in security work and day-to-day activities. He keeps a running blog on his misadventures and discoveries about Apple, OS X, and Macs in general at hackamac.packetattack.com.

Michael graduated from the University of California, Irvine, extension program with a certificate in communications and network engineering. Michael currently resides in Orange, CA, with his wife, Jeanne, and his three daughters, Amanda, Sara, and Olivia.

Foreword Contributor

Bill Campbell is the Technical Editor of the Skype Journal (www.SkypeJournal.com). He authored the first Skype API Guidebook (being published in 10 languages) for the Skype Development Community. As CEO of Qzoxy Software Inc., he developed the first Presence Server for managing online user status. As the inaugural member of the Skype Developer Program, he continues to be one of a handful to test all new Skype products. About a third of his career was spent as a manager at the Hewlett-Packard Company. Fifteen years ago, Bill founded the PTCompany, www.theptcompany.com, which specialized in business process reengineering and project management tools. Bill and his team provide consulting services to help corporations define their Skype strategies or to develop products around the Skype API. Bill lives in Kelowna, British Columbia, Canada.

Contents

Foreword

You are going to love *Skype Me! From Single User to Small Enterprise and Beyond*. Here's why: Michael Gough knows his stuff. Michael has also completed a remarkably difficult project around a remarkably cool product, Skype.

Michael is a busy guy. I have no idea where he found time to write a book. He delivers consulting services to clients of a Fortune 50 company where he works. He's been at it for 18 years. On the side, he is a Computer Security Consultant, presenting at conferences, working with associations and groups, and advising agencies such as the FBI. Michael knows Skype. He is the man behind the hot Web sites www.SkypeTips.com and www.VideoTips.com. These sites are filled with helpful advice, product reviews, stories, and articles that make the hundreds of thousands of visitors get a richer experience from the Skype application.

What's remarkable about this book? A few months ago Michael first shared his idea in a message to me: "I am going to write a book to help home users, super users, small businesses, and large corporations understand Skype." I studied the outline. A few days later I sent a message back to him: "Michael, it can't be done." But I ate crow as I read the completed manuscript.

Michael has covered all that you need to know about Skype. His book will sweeten your Skype experience. It contains basic information for early adopters as well as technical tips for power users.

What's cool about Skype? What makes Skype such a remarkable product? How can it possibly reach out to touch individuals in such a wide spectrum from users in the home to a large corporation? The short answer is simplicity.

Skype's simple, subtle user interface hides a deep layer of rich functionality. It's so simple that my mom can use it. In fact, "Can mom use it?" is a question asked by members of the Skype development team every day. Skype is an application that even after over two years of daily use continues to "wow" me. Let Skype wow you, too.

Let this book help you quickly discover the hidden delights inside the Skype application.

—*Bill Campbell*
Technical Editor, Skype Journal
www.SkypeJournal.com

Part I: Getting Started with Skype

Chapter 1

An Overview of Skype

Subjects in this chapter:

- **What Is All the Hype about Skype?**

- **What Are VoIP, Voice Chat, or Voice Calls?**

- **Skype Architecture (Basic/Advanced)**

- **Peer-to-Peer Technology (Basic/Advanced)**

- **Peer-to-Peer Conferencing (Basic/Advanced)**

- **Skype Options (Basic)**

- **Skype Security (Basic)**

What Is All the Hype about Skype?

So what is all this hype about Skype, anyway? Skype is the fastest-growing communication application on the Internet. According to the article "Intel Working with Skype" that appeared on Australian IT on August 30, 2005, Skype has roughly 54 million users and as of that month accounts for 46 percent of all North American voice traffic carried over the Internet. Many refer to Skype as an instant-messaging (IM) application. Think of Skype as more of a voice call application that also provides IM features. IM allows you to type quick messages to your list of contacts and send them instantly. What Skype adds to IM is the ability to talk, in real time, with your contacts in addition to typical IM functions. More important, the quality of the audio, features, and options available for Skype users gives Skype the advantage over the rest of the IM products. Skype has made Internet telephony, or Voice over IP (VoIP)—in other words, voice calls over the Internet—available to everyone, geeks and nongeeks alike. For geeks, and you know who you are, Skype is just plain cool.

Skype has grown at an incredible rate. According to Skype.com, in the approximately two years it has been available, it has been downloaded over 155 million times and has approximately 54 million users and around 2 million paid subscribers as of August 2005. Skype has brought VoIP into homes and is used by just about every demographic group, from children to grandparents. Everyone who uses IM loves Skype because it lets you not only type messages but actually talk to people as well as you can on a regular telephone call.

The computer industry loves Skype so much that they have rushed to develop products that exploit Skype's capabilities. Skype allows you to not only use it when you are at your computer, but additional options and add-ons allow you to use it just like a regular telephone. Unlike most of the other IM voice solutions, with Skype you do not have to be sitting in front of your computer to use it if you employ an advanced option. Skype is not just for the experienced computer user; it's also for the average person. Once you understand how you can use Skype just like a telephone in your home or office, the more you will start using it as a regular addition to your communication utilities.

What Are VoIP, Voice Chat, or Voice Calls?

Voice over IP or VoIP (pronounced *Voyp*) involves using the Internet or a local area/wide area network (LAN/WAN) to transmit voice calls versus the way the telephone companies do it using a dedicated system. Companies use enterprise-quality VoIP solutions to allow telephones to use the same data network that its computers are connected to. Internal calls within a company are routed over the internal LAN/WAN instead of going out to the public switched telephone network (PSTN) or local telephone company for every call. This saves companies significant money, since all internal company calls are then free.

Besides just the cost savings that you would have when you bypass the PSTN, VoIP allows companies to converge networks. *Converging a network* means that the phone and computer will share the same network connection, thereby allowing companies to save money on network drops, equipment, and staff to support the second network. So, by converging the two networks, you lose one network altogether, reduce staff, and save the company money.

VoIP for the Home User

VoIP also includes solutions such as Vonage, AT&T CallVantage, Time Warner Digital Phone, and almost every local telco in the nation. The systems offered to home users either use a network cable connection from your local cable provider or a digital subscriber line (DSL) from your local telco. Both of these solutions provide a data network back to the local company to offer VoIP service to the home user. These networks are not peer-to-peer (P2P) networks, as Skype is, since the calls stay connected through a central server. (We look at this process later in this chapter.)

Understanding the Basics... To Pay or Not to Pay for VoIP

The only real reason to pay for VoIP from your local provider is if you want a certain amount of defined uptime on your system and access to a service department. If you can live with a problem every so often and want to save some money, go with Skype. Face it—how many times does the local cable or telco come to your house to fix something anyway?

Voice Chat

Voice chat is commonly thought of as using applications like IM to "chat" audibly with your contacts. In the past, the quality of these solutions was inferior to that of a traditional telephone call, but the price was right——*free!* Most IM solutions available today (MSN, AIM, Yahoo!) offer some form of voice chat capability. These applications require you to sit in front of your computer to perform a voice chat with your contacts, and the quality is often inferior to that of a telephone call.

Skype is the first application to take what can be called a voice chat to a whole new level, called a *voice call.* First, the quality of Skype's audio is superior to any other solutions. Second, Skype is very network friendly, so little is required to make Skype work in your environment. Third, the options for voice calls within Skype are very effective. Fourth, the add-ons available for Skype make this application useful to anyone from novice to expert computer user.

Skype Architecture (Basic)

Skype is unique in the way that it communicates between users. Skype allows users to communicate using what is called *peer-to-peer (P2P) networking*. For example, the typical Skype architecture can be used to establish a voice call between two users, Bob and Alice.

Bob starts off by logging into Skype (1). The Skype server authenticates Bob and logs him in (2). Now Bob wants to call Alice, so he initiates a Skype voice call (3), and the connection is direct from Bob's computer to Alice's computer via the Internet. The voice call is not routed through a central server, as many solutions are. This improves performance and allows for a more secure voice call. An intermediate computer, known as a supernode, will assist with Jordan's computer finding Clyde's computer, but once this is done, the voice call connection is established directly between Jordan's computer and Clyde's computer. In addition, the connection (3) is completely encrypted with Advanced Encryption Standard (AES) 256-bit encryption and is unique for every call Bob makes.

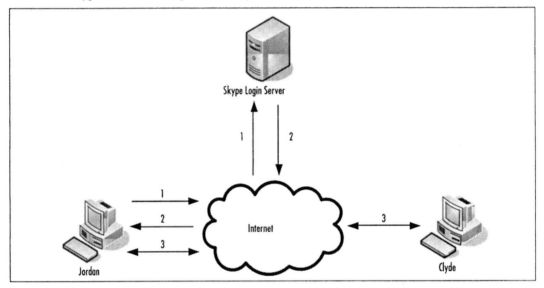

Peer-to-Peer Technology (Basic)

Skype uses P2P technology to improve the quality of the application. P2P allows for direct communication with all parties involved, which improves performance and eliminates delays in the voice call as well as allowing for Skype to be a secure solution by connecting only the users involved, not running the connection through a server.

A P2P voice call is first started by both users connecting to the Internet (1). Users can connect many different ways, such as through a corporate LAN/WAN, cable modem, DSL, or even wirelessly.

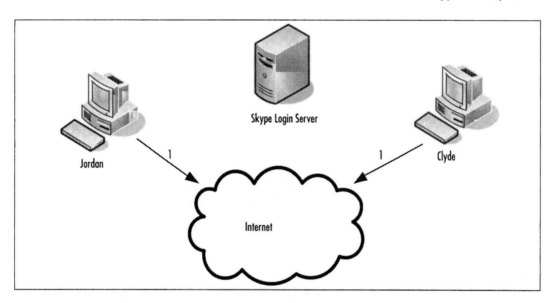

The users use TCP ports to connect to the Skype login server (2) via the Internet. The connection is secured using 256-bit AES encryption. The symmetric AES keys that are negotiated between the server and client are handled using 1536- and 2048-bit RSA.

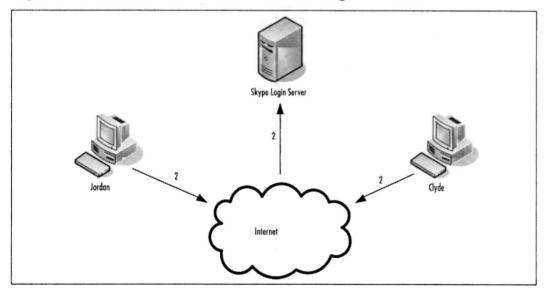

The client registers, tells the login server where the call recipient is located, and gives all other information needed to register and broadcast to other clients via the server.

For Jordan to make a connection to Clyde, his computer must search the Internet (3) using the help of intermediate Skype systems (supernodes) in the Internet 'cloud', and Clyde's system must also update those same systems (3) to make Clyde's presence known. Information is passed from other clients and supernodes at this point to help complete the call.

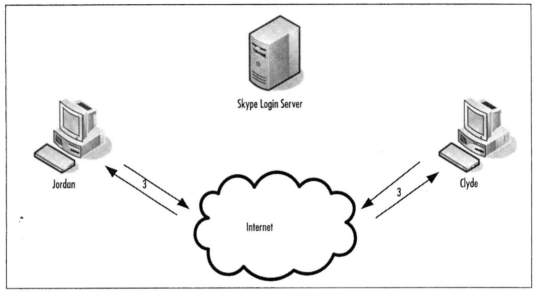

The picture below depicts the direct (P2P) connection that has been established between Jordan and Clyde (4). In other chapters we will discuss how other clients can and will allow calls go through their systems in order for you to complete your call, but this diagram represents the basics of how the calls are made.

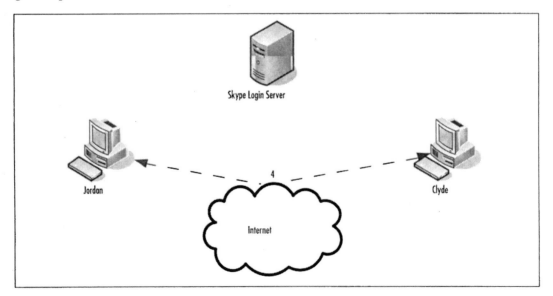

Peer-to-Peer Conferencing (Basic/Advanced)

Skype also allows users to bring conferencing to the mix with its P2P network. Let's show you how a P2P conference call is made. (This topic is covered in more depth in a later chapter.)

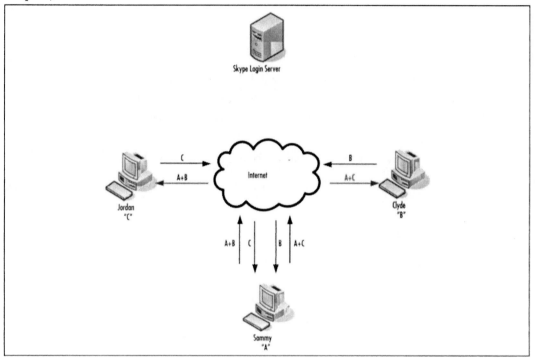

1. Sammy acts as a mixer, mixing his own packets with those of Clyde and sending to Jordan and vice versa.

2. The Skype user who has the most powerful computer and the fastest connection to the Internet should be used as the conference host and mixer.

3. A two-way call will consume approximately 36Kbps of bandwidth.

4. A three-way call will consume approximately 54Kbps of bandwidth.

Tweaking the Technology... Voice Networks of Different Scale

With the number of file-sharing programs and now Skype, P2P networks have proven that they can be scaled to handle large-scale connections around the world. They have tweaked the technology to bring voice to the masses where only data once was.

Skype Options (Basic)

Skype is not your typical IM application. By adding superior quality voice capabilities and features to support the voice call option, Skype is the leader in the IM application space. Most IM applications have the following features:

- Chat
- File transfer
- Block users

Many IM products have more features, but the aforementioned ones are rather common to all IM applications. Skype adds voice capability, along with many features that further enhance the voice call experience, enabling Skype to be a more feature-rich and practical solution than it's competitors.

Skype has some advanced features that we cover in a later chapter, but the following is the list of basic features Skype offers:

- Chat
- Multiuser chat
- Voice calls
- File transfers
- Block users
- Multiuser voice calls (conference calls)
- Send your contacts to another user

Skype offers several other administrative features to help you with your experience. These are covered in more detail later in the book:

- Manage events
- Manage your advanced features or services
- Import your contacts from a vCard
- Export your contacts to a vCard
- Manage your blocked users
- Manage your call list
- Search for Skype users
- Review recent chats

- Edit your profile
- SkypeOut
- SkypeIn

Skype Security (Basic)

One of the questions people often ask about Skype is, "Is Skype secure?" If you are talking over the Internet on just about any possible subject from the events of your day to mergers and acquisitions, security of your voice call and IMs becomes a concern to some users or corporations. Of course, casual conversation on cordless and cell phones can be listened to on scanners someone makes at home with parts from a local electronics store, and your home telephone can be tapped very easily. More modern cordless phones offer rotating security codes so it makes it harder to eavesdrop, but it is still possible. Furthermore, people can just listen to anyone's conversation at a public location, since we use cell phones just about every-where and discuss practically everything as though we were in a private location.

Questions about Skype security arise from the fact that it uses the Internet to carry voice traffic. The Internet, the big unknown cloud that carries all kinds of data and now voice calls over a public network, has the potential to be "overheard" at any point along the transmission path. So should you be concerned? The answer is simple: It depends. It depends on what you are discussing and whether you care that what you say is overheard by total strangers. Most of us will automatically say "I care—I don't want anyone listening to my voice calls." This is why a secure solution, such as Skype, is a good fit for the privacy-con-scious person or organization. Email, which has become widely accepted, has no inherent encryption. This makes it insecure unless extra measures are undertaken to sign and encrypt data independently, but this is a topic for another discussion.

Skype uses 256-bit AES to encrypt every session between users. More important, this encryption changes each time you contact someone via IM, file transfer, or a voice call. So if some malicious person managed to capture all the data and decrypt your AES key, it would be worthless for the next call you make with Skype. Cracking the AES key would take someone roughly 20 years, so it's not very probable. The U.S. Government uses AES to encrypt sensitive data, so it must be pretty secure.

Tweaking the Technology... Skype Security and the Enterprise

Larger corporations that are very security conscious want to know exactly how an application, in this case Skype, performs its magic before they'll certify Skype for use within the corporate enterprise. More on how Skype uses AES encryption is included in Chapter 11.

Evidence suggests that Skype's implementation of encryption has been well thought out and that this qualifies it to be the most secure IM and voice call application on the Internet today. While the precise details of how Skype manages the AES keys or executes the encryption, it is fairly safe to say the manner in which the keys are rotated, that the probability of anyone hacking into a Skype session is extremely low and therefore of negligible concern.

Chapter 2

Installing Skype

Solutions in this chapter:

- Requirements to Make Voice Calls (Basic and Advanced)

- Connection Types

- Testing Your Existing Setup

- Installing Skype for Windows

- Installing Skype for Pocket PC

- Installing Skype for Apple

- Installing Skype for Linux

Requirements to Make Voice Calls (Basic and Advanced)

The first place to start in making voice calls is to make sure your system or systems are capable of performing good voice calls. A few minimum requirements should be met to guarantee that your experience will be a good one.

The following are Skype-recommended minimum requirements to perform voice calls, categorized by the type of equipment you'll be using.

Personal Computer (PC)

To take advantage of all the advanced features of Skype and to experience the best sound quality possible, Skype recommends the following configuration:

- A personal computer (PC) running Windows 2000 or Windows XP
- 1GHz processor minimum
- 256MB RAM
- 30MB free space on your hard drive
- Full-duplex sound card
- Headset (defined as having both headphones and a microphone)
- A high-speed Internet connection (cable, DSL, wireless, or other)

If your PC is five years old or less, it will most likely perform just fine. Though Skype specifies you can use Windows 2000 or Windows XP, we recommend that you use the latest version of the operating system and stay current within five years for support and security reasons. So our recommendation is to use:

- Athlon, Celeron (>500MHz), Pentium III, or better
- Microsoft Windows XP

Understanding the Basics... What Version of Windows to Use

We recommend using Windows XP rather than Windows 2000 and keeping your operating system current within three to five years. We also recommend keeping your system current with Windows Updates.

We make these additional recommendations because of the additional features you can perform with Skype. We will expand on how you can talk and listen to Skype voice calls in Chapter 8, "Hardware Add-ons for Skype." Skype recommends a headset (USB or one that connects to a full-duplex PC sound card), but there are other options you can consider in lieu of a headset:

- Headphones of any kind with a separate noise-canceling microphone

- Externally powered speakers (that plug into the wall) along with a noise-reduction microphone

Understanding the Basics...
What to Use for a Microphone and Speakers?

A headset/microphone combination works the best for Skype calls. You may also use external speakers and a "noise-canceling microphone" combination for Skype calls; these will work just as well, though you will need to adjust the speakers' volume to reduce feedback.

PC Laptops

If you have a laptop, it might have both speakers and a built-in microphone. This will work, but if you find the voice quality unsatisfactory, you can add a headset or headphone/noise-canceling microphone combination that you can throw into your laptop bag. Such a device will work much better for Skype calls with most laptops. Some laptops have speakers and no built-in microphone, so you can add a noise-canceling microphone, a headset, or a head-phone/noise-canceling microphone combination. None of these devices will break the bank.

Apple Devices

If you are one of the nearly 10 percent of computer users who have Apple or Mac machines, you will also have minimum system requirements. We suggest the following for a good Skype voice call experience:

- Apple G3, G4, or G5 or better

- 600MHz or better

- 256MB of RAM

- A 30GB or larger hard drive

- Audio and video (included with Apple systems)

- Mac OS 10.3 (Panther) or later

Apple Laptops

If you have a PowerBook or iBook, it might have both speakers and a built-in microphone. This will work, but if you find the quality to be unsatisfactory, you can add a headset/noise-canceling microphone that you can throw in your laptop bag. Such a device will work much better for Skype calls. Some laptops have speakers and no built-in microphone, so you can add a noise-canceling microphone, a headset, or a headphone/noise-canceling microphone combination. None of these devices will break the bank.

Pocket PC

Many of us use a personal digital assistant (PDA), and these devices may be capable of using the Pocket PC (PPC) version of Skype. The following is the recommended configuration:

- Windows Mobile 2003 for Pocket PC
- 400MHz processor
- Wireless (WiFi) enabled
- Wired headset/microphone preferred
- Bluetooth headset profile (optional)

If you are in the market for a new Pocket PC device, some work better than others. The main thing to look for is that they work well without a headset. If Skype works well without a headset, Skype will work even better with a headset.

Headsets

Many Pocket PC devices work much better with a headset because the built-in microphone and speaker are too close together and work poorly in many cases or are located in the wrong positions on the device to act like a telephone. Adding a headset/microphone will significantly improve the quality of a Skype call on a Pocket PC device.

Understanding the Basics... Pocket PC Quality Tip

Setting the volume one setting down from maximum will reduce the echo in a Skype call.

Bluetooth Headsets

Many people like to use Bluetooth headsets with their cell phones. If your Pocket PC device is capable of using a Bluetooth headset, you might want or prefer a wireless

Bluetooth headset over a wired headset. Be sure to check with the device manufacturer to ensure it supports a Bluetooth headset profile.

Linux

Linux has the same requirements as a personal computer, since it uses the same hardware, with the exception that you are using one of the many Linux distributions instead of Windows. For Skype, the same requirements apply as for the PC in that we recommend that you use the latest version of your Linux distribution.

Skype packages are available for the following distributions of Linux:

- SuSe version 9 and newer
- Fedora Core 3 or newer
- RPM for Mandrake 10.1 or newer
- Debian
- Dynamic binary tarball (requires Qt 3.2)
- Static binary tarball (compiled with Qt 3.2)

Connection Types

You may use many types of Internet connections with Skype. This section takes a look at the options to help you decide which ones to use. The following connection types are covered:

- Local area network (LAN) connection
- Wireless (WiFi) connection
- Dialup modem

LAN-Based Connections

The most popular way to connect using Skype is using a LAN-based connection. Here we cover two types of LAN-based connection:

- Home high-speed connection
- Work LAN connections

A Word about Upload and Download Speed

In dealing with high-speed Internet connections, it is important to understand that there are two speeds:

- **Upload speed** The speed at which you send data
- **Download speed** The speed at which you receive data

Generally speaking, the download speed will always be significantly faster than the upload speed with a cable modem or telephone company digital subscriber line (DSL) offering. Skype works pretty well with either a cable modem or DSL connection, but if the upload speed is low, you could run into voice call quality issues. You will find this issue when you're staying in hotels, for example, or in WiFi hotspots, because many people are sharing the same broadband connection at one time.

The typical speeds for residential available high-speed Internet or broadband connections are:

- **Cable modem** 4Mbps download, 250Kbps upload
- **Standard DSL** 1.5Mbps download, 128Kbps upload
- **Satellite** 500Kbps download, 56Kbps upload

Home High-Speed Connections

To clarify terms, we use the term *broadband* to describe any high-speed Internet connection available for your home. You may already have or be planning to get a broadband Internet connection like those offered by your cable television provider or telephone company. These are the two primary connection types available to the residential home user and, in many cases, small business owners as well. In addition you may have the option of Satellite or the newer 3G Broadband offered by your Cell Phone carrier or Wi-Max (802.16) wireless broadband connection. In Europe and many other countries and just starting here in the United States your Cell Phone carrier offers a high-speed broadband option for laptops that uses a PC Card to connect to the Cell Phone companies high-speed data network. This option is mostly marketed to laptop users and not recommend for the home user. Contact your Cell phone company for more information on their high-speed broadband offerings for laptops.

We will not cover Wi-Max as it is still a few years away for most of us, just know it is coming for those people that cannot get DSL, Cable or 3G service. Wi-Max is not widely available and is a fairly new option in the Broadband space. Wi-Max is best described as a "Wireless Broadband" or a very fast and strong signal wireless that will go long distances for users that can not get DSL, Cable or other forms of broadband access. WiMax will be able to provide users with a fast Broadband connection when a Broadband connection from your Cable Television provider or Telephone company is not available, but it will take a few years to be readily available to home users.

We do not recommend satellite broadband connections, since the upload speed is not much faster than a dialup connection and they are more costly. To enjoy good-quality Skype calls, you need a good broadband connection, so check out your available options and select the fastest, most cost-effective solution you can find. The faster the connection, the better. In the United States, a cable modem provides the best download and upload speeds, but options for DSL from your telephone company could rival those of your cable provider. Whatever your decision, be sure to get faster than the following specs to take full advantage of Skype and the software add-ons available for it:

- Download speed greater than 1Mbps
- Upload speed greater than 128Kbps

Your provider may offer faster solutions, but in the United States these tend to be the basic offerings. Europe and other countries have many more options, and in Russia, 10Mbps download and upload fiber connections are available—very fast indeed. So be sure to check with your broadband provider to inquire about both minimum upload and download speeds. Again, the faster the connection, the better. You might want to add some options to Skype that will benefit greatly from the fastest connection you can get, such as adding video to your Skype call to have a fully functional video call between two users. (We cover video calls using Skype in the section titled "Making Video Calls with Skype" in Chapter 8.)

Testing Your Broadband Connection Speed

Many "speed-test" sites on the Internet will rate the speed of your Internet connection. The main thing to look for is that the speed test shows you both the upload and the download speeds. Many, if not most, of the speed-test sites will show you only throughput or the download speed. With Skype, your biggest concern will be the upload speed. You can find several speed-test locations at the following URL, which includes many locations world-wide: www.dslreports.com/stest.

Work LAN Connections

In the workplace, we commonly hear the term *LAN*, which stands for *local area network*. This network is much faster than what you can have at home because businesses or corporations purchase very fast Internet connections so that they can handle the traffic requirements to meet their business needs.

A LAN has many more complexities than a home connection, and these could affect your Skype voice calls. At this point all you need to know is that there is a difference between a LAN and your home connection; we cover this topic in more detail in Chapter 13.

Wireless-Based Connections

Wireless technology, often referred to as *Wi-Fi*, offers us the freedom to roam. We can use it in our home, workplace, or any public hotspot. A *hotspot* is a location that has wireless access for free or as a pay service. These locations include:

- Airports
- Hotels
- Coffee shops
- Public WiFi such as hotspots offered by towns and cities
- Internet cafés
- A person's home

In our home, wireless technology becomes popular because we can sit anywhere in our home and have access to Internet for e-mail, IM, or Skype calls. Wireless technology also becomes useful for handheld devices such as a Pocket PC or a wireless Skype phone.

The one concern about wireless connections that you should be aware of is the speed and impact of wireless networks on the throughput of a Skype voice call. There are three basic types of wireless access:

- 802.11a
- 802.11b
- 802.11g

802.11a

The 802.11a standard is not so popular a solution as 802.11b or 802.11g, and it is not available for Pocket PC devices. The largest users of 802.11a are businesses. The speed is nice at 54Mbps, but it's more costly than 802.11b and 802.11g.

802.11b

The 802.11b standard is the most popular version of Wi-Fi, but it's not so fast as 802.11a or 802.11g. It is compatible with 802.11g devices; wireless routers you purchase that can handle 802.11g will also be downward compatible with 802.11b. The 802.11b speed is only

11Mbps—far slower than the other two options. 802.11b is also the least expensive and older of the wireless solutions.

802.11g

The 802.11g standard is fast becoming the most popular version of Wi-Fi because it is fast and compatible with 802.11b clients that may already have built-in Wi-Fi cards, such as laptops. This allows a user to implement a faster version of wireless technology, but not have to replace the older, widely available and widely used 802.11b devices. The 802.11g speed is 54Mbps, which as fast as 802.11a. These features make it the best option for a wireless connection.

Many vendor-specific features promote boosting performance in 802.11g wireless routers that further increase the throughput for your Skype calls and video, if you choose to use this option with Skype.

Understanding the Basics... Wireless Recommendation

If you are looking to use wireless technology in your home or small business, 802.11g is the best option. This cost-effective solution provides options for better security, faster and better throughput, and compatibility with older 802.11b clients. It will be perfect for Skype calls and video.

For more information on wireless, read *The Wireless Internet Explained* by John Rhoton.

Modem-Based Connections

According to Nielsen/NetRatings Inc.'s *NetSpeed Report* of September 2005 (www.nielsen-netratings.com/pr/pr_050928.pdf), as of the first quarter of 2005 in the United States, broadband Internet surpassed dial-up modem Internet connections for the first time. Dial-up is a technology that is on its way out, being replaced with higher-speed connections such as broadband for home and business.

As far as whether Skype will work over a dial-up connection, it will, but it will be a poor-quality call. If both users are using a modem, the Skype call will be terrible at best. Also, if a modem is all you have, the closer you can get to the maximum dial-up speed, which is 56Kbps, the better. The slower the modem connection, the worse the Skype call quality will be.

Recommendation

Modems and dial-up connections are a dying technology. Consider upgrading to a broadband connection if you want good-quality Skype calls. We generally do not recommend dial-up connections when using Skype.

Understanding the Basics... Using a Modem

Modems do not perform well with Skype and its many add-ons.

Testing Your Existing Setup

If you have not already used a voice chat or voice call solution, the first order of business is to test your existing setup to make sure it will work as expected.

Windows

The first thing that needs to be checked is whether your system can record and play an audio file. If you know you have a sound card, you can move on to testing your record and playback ability. If you do not know whether you have a sound card, go to the "Check That You Have a Sound Card" section to see if you have a sound card installed.

The test in the next section will help you determine whether your sound card is functioning properly for a Skype call.

Testing Your Audio Capability

Windows comes with a utility called Sound Recorder that allows you to record and play short audio clips. This utility can also be used to make sure your microphone records and that your speaker plays an audio clip. To make sure your sound card and microphone/headset combination or sound-canceling microphone/external speakers work properly, record and play a sound clip.

Find **Sound Recorder** in the **Programs** menu under **Accessories | Entertainment**.

Open **Sound Recorder**, press the **red record** button, and speak into your microphone.

Once you record a clip, play it back. If you can hear your test clip, your system is working properly. If you did not hear your sound clip, check your settings and sound card connections. Also check to make sure your microphone is not muted.

- Microphone = pink connection
- Headphone/speaker = green connection

Mute is a tricky item. It is supposed to be muted in Sound Controls. It is a tricky setting so images would be confusing. This is why I used the Sound Recorder as the option to test recording.

Check That You Have a Sound Card

To check that you have a sound card, open **Control Panel**, select the appropriate **Sound** icon, and open the next window.

Select and open the **Sounds and Audio Devices** icon.

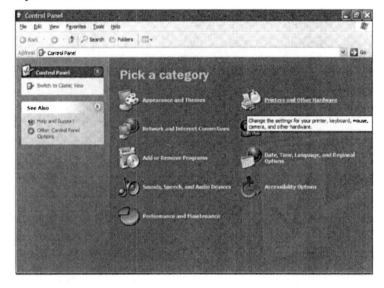

Select and open the **Sounds, Speech and Audio Properties** icon.

In the next screen, select the **Sounds and Audio Device** icon.

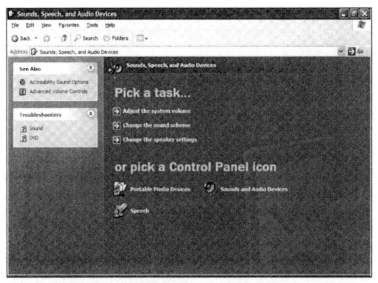

Now select the **Audio** tab to see the sound card settings.

The listed device should be your sound card. If there is no device listed in the Sound playback or Sound recording boxes, you probably do not have a sound card installed, or the drivers for the sound card are not loaded. Check with your PC manufacturer and/or sound card company to fix this issue.

Apple

Apple PowerBooks and iBooks come with integrated microphones and speakers, so there's not much to worry about in terms of testing. Apple G3, G4, and G5 computers come with sound cards, so all that you'll need is the addition of a headset/microphone or microphone and speaker combination. Make sure the mic is not muted.

Linux

The application to test your sound card on Linux varies based on the flavor of Linux you're using. Be sure to test the recording and playback capability with the appropriate recording application that comes with your flavor of Linux.

Pocket PC

The Pocket PC is designed to take memos, so many have built-in microphone and speakers. They might not work very well, but they are often included. Many Pocket PC devices use a special 4C connector that is not the same as the connections used for cell phones or your PC. These have four connectors, and only special headsets or adapters can be used in a headset/microphone combination. You can read an article about these special 4C connectors at www.skypetips.internetvisitation.org/articles/pocketPC.html.

Some Pocket PC devices also have Bluetooth, but for a device to use Bluetooth headsets, a headset profile must be included with the device.

Be sure to check the vendor's specifications before purchasing a Pocket PC so that you understand what it can and cannot do. You might also want to test the device for two weeks before purchasing it to thoroughly test Skype with the device. Be sure that, if you are purchasing the device new, you ascertain the return policy for the model you are looking to purchase so you have ample time to test it with Skype.

Installing Skype for Windows

The first step in installing Skype is to download it. To download the latest version of Skype for Windows, go to the following URL: www.skype.com/download/.

Select the **Windows** icon. You will be taken to the main download page, which provides you with the latest requirements and other information.

If you want the latest step-by-step download and installation instructions, Skype provides a download guide at the following URL: www.skype.com/help/guides/.

Now let's get started. Open the file you just downloaded and you will be presented with the following screen:

Select your language and click **Next**. You will then see the following screen:

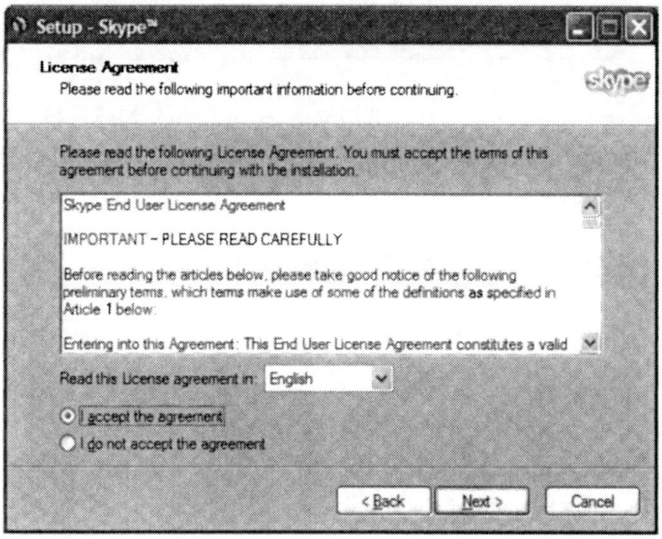

Read the End Users License Agreement (EULA). Be sure you understand it completely, and if you agree to its terms, select **Next**.

Tweaking the Technology... Corporations Beware

If you are installing Skype at or for your company, be sure to check with your management to be sure you are not in violation of company policy.

When you select **Next**, you will be presented with the following screen:

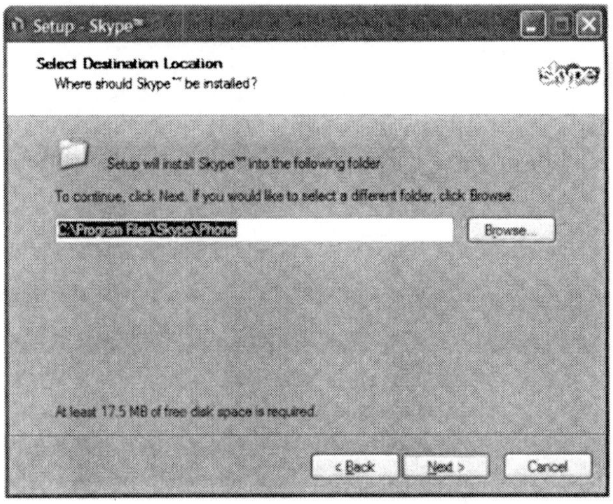

Select the directory you want to install Skype to and click **Next**. Unless you know that you want to install Skype to another directory or location, just accept the default, since this choice will work for most everyone.

After Skype installs, you will be presented with the following screen:

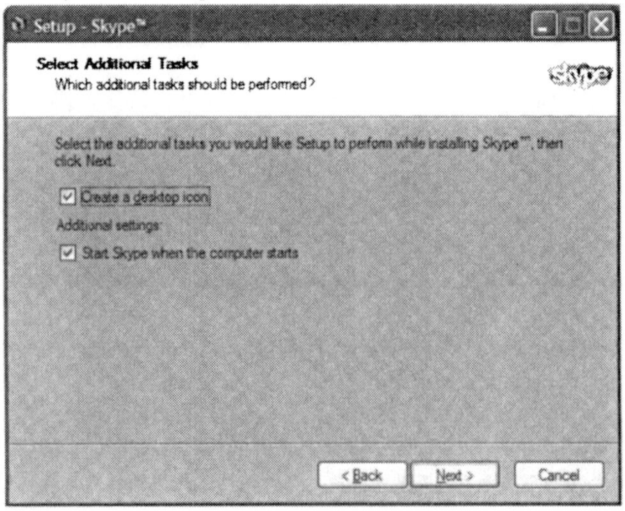

We suggest that you leave both these options selected, since you will most likely want a desktop icon for Skype and to launch Skype when you first start your computer. Select **Next** once you make your selection.

After Skype is installed, you will then be prompted as to whether you want to start Skype. Click **Finish**.

If you have never installed Skype before, you will be presented with the Create a new Skype Account screen.

If you already have a Skype name, select the [Existing Users - Log in to Skype] tab. If this is the first time you are using Skype or you want to create a new Skype user, fill out the screen and be sure to select this check box after you have read the EULA:

> *☐ Yes, I have read and I accept the Skype End User Licence Agreement

Skype usernames can include the underscore (_) or period (.) characters to help you create a unique name. Here are some examples:

- michaelgough

- michael.gough

- michael_gough

Select **Next** to create the account. If the name is already taken, you will be prompted with some examples. Select your own option and continue with registration. You will then be prompted with the following screen to enter your personal information:

Fill out the screen with your personal information. You may leave this information blank if you do not want your profile to show this information about you.

You may optionally include an email address in your profile, but it will not be displayed to others. This is a privacy feature designed to prevent unscrupulous spammers from harvesting email addresses using Skype. But those who know your complete email address will be able to use it to search for you (no partial searches using an email address are possible). Most often this feature is used by friends who know your email address, but not your Skype name. You also have the opportunity to decide whether you want Skype to send you e-mail about new features and other Skype-related information. We will leave this decision up to you.

When you're finished, select **Next**. If the name you chose is taken, you will see the following screen:

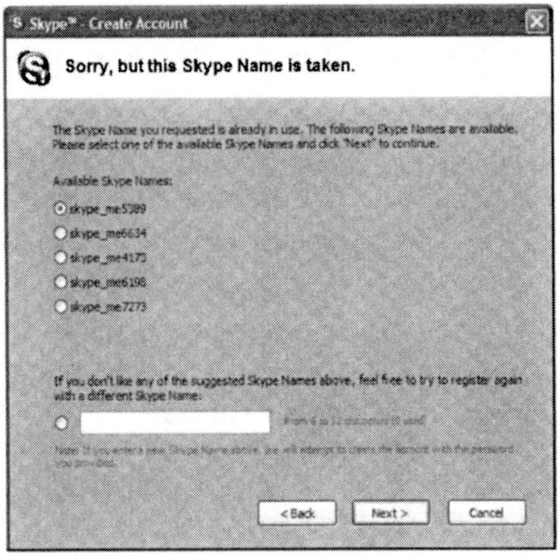

You can let Skype choose a similar name for you, but we suggest you try another name combination. Consider using the underscore and period to help make your username unique. Then click **Next**.

When the name is successfully registered, Skype will log the user in. Now Skype is ready to use, and you will see the following screen:

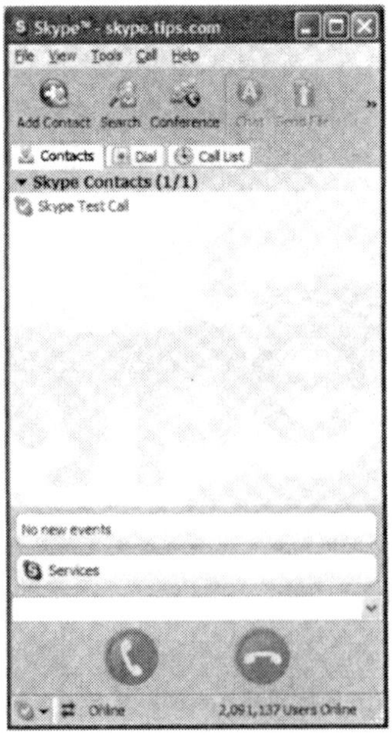

Now you are ready to add contacts and start using Skype. (You'll learn more about this in the section of Chapter 3 titled "Adding or Searching for Contacts."" Skype adds the user Skype Test Call for you so you can make your first test call. We will discuss making a test call in Chapter 3.

Skype also now has a Getting Started Wizard that will appear once Skype successfully logs into your account. You can use this guide as additional assistance to get started using Skype.

If you do not want to see this wizard every time you start Skype, just select the Do not show this wizard at startup check box, and the Getting Started Wizard will be disabled.

Installing Skype for Pocket PC

The first step in installing Skype is to download it. To download the latest version of Skype for Pocket PC, go to the following URL: www.skype.com/download/.

Select the **Pocket PC** icon and it will take you to the main download page. The page provides you with the latest requirements and other information.

If you want the latest step-by-step download and installation instructions, Skype provides a download guide at the following URL: www.skype.com/help/guides/.

Downloading Skype for the Pocket PC

There are three ways to download and install Skype and prepare for installation to the Pocket PC. One is to download Skype directly to your Pocket PC that has a WiFi Internet connection. The second is to download the SkypeForPocketPC.exe file to your computer when you have docked and synchronized your Pocket PC and launch the installer from your computer. The third is to download the SkypeForPocketPC.cab file to your computer, copy it to your Pocket PC, and start the Skype installation from your Pocket PC.

Download Directly to the Pocket PC

If this option is available to you, doing a direct download is the best way to install Skype for the Pocket PC. Select the **Cab installer for handheld device** from the Skype Pocket PC download page. If you download Skype directly to your Pocket PC, the download utility will ask if you want to **Open file after download**. Make sure this choice is selected and start the download. Pocket PC .cab files will automatically install when launched, so all that will be left to do is open the Skype application, which will be found in the **Programs** folder of your Pocket PC.

Follow the instructions in Chapter 3 for signing up as a new user and adding users to Skype.

Download to Your Computer and Launch the Skype Installer

If you select the **Download Skype for Pocket PC** installer to your computer, you will first need to connect your Pocket PC to your docking cradle and establish a connection. Once you are connected to your Pocket PC with ActiveSync, you will see the following screen.

Select **Next** and you will be taken to the following End User License Agreement screen:

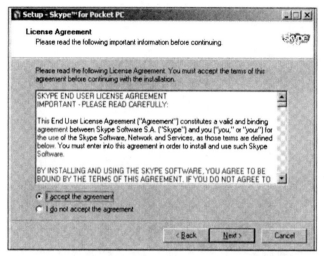

Make sure you read and understand the EULA, and then select **I accept the agreement**. Then click **Next**. You will see the following screen. Go ahead and accept the defaults to install the Pocket PC Skype installer.

You will then be taken to the next screen. Select **Install** to continue.

Once the Skype installer is completed, you be prompted to select **Finish** to launch the Pocket PC installer from your computer.

Setup - Skype™ for Pocket PC   _□×

Completing the Skype™ for Pocket PC Setup Wizard

Setup has finished installing Skype™ for Pocket PC on your computer.

Click Finish to exit Setup.

www.skype.com

[Finish]

At this time the Skype installer will start the process of coping files and installing Skype onto your Pocket PC device.

If your Pocket PC device does *not* support Skype, the following screen will appear:

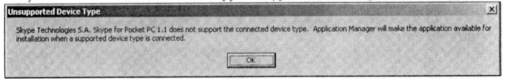

This means that your Pocket PC does not meet the minimum system requirements to run Skype.

Download to Your Computer
and Copy the Installer to Your Pocket PC

If you download the Skype cab installer for Pocket PC device to your computer first, you will need to connect your Pocket PC to your docking cradle and establish a connection. Once you are connected to your Pocket PC with ActiveSync, you will see the following screen. We are connected as Guest in this example.

Select the  icon to open a folder on your Pocket PC. Just drag the SkypeForPocketPC.cab file onto your Pocket PC device.

Once the file is copied, go to your Pocket PC and double-click the **file** icon, and it will install Skype to your Pocket PC device.

All that will be left to do is open the Skype application, which you'll find in the **Programs** folder of your Pocket PC.

Follow the instructions in Chapter 3 to sign up as a user and add users to Skype.

Understanding the Basics...
Pocket PC and Skype Compatibility Tip

If you have a Pocket PC and are unsure whether it is capable of running Skype, simply run the SkypeForPocketPC.exe installer, and it will tell you during the installation whether your device is capable of running Skype.

Installing Skype for Mac OS X

The first step in installing Skype is to download it. To download the latest version of Skype for Mac OS X, go to the following URL: www.skype.com/download/.

Select the **Mac OS X** icon and it will take you to the main download page. The page provides you with the latest requirements and other information.

If you want the latest step-by-step download instructions, Skype provides a download guide at the following URL: www.skype.com/help/guides/.

When you download Skype you will see the Skype [S] icon. The screen will prompt you to drag the icon into the **Applications** folder, and Skype will then be ready to use.

You will see the Skype [S] icon on the Mac Dashboard at the bottom right of the screen

Once Skype is installed, you are ready to log in or sign up as a new user. The main Skype screen looks like the following:

Refer to Chapter 3 for more on how to do this. The Windows version is used for the examples in this book because it is the most widely used version, so if you're a Mac user, keep in mind that some screens and features available in Windows might not be available for the Mac OS X version.

Installing Skype for Linux

The first step in installing Skype is to download it. To download the latest version of Skype for Linux, go to the following URL: www.skype.com/download/.

Select the **Linux** icon and you will be taken to the main download page. The page provides you with the latest requirements and other information.

Linux Installation Options

There are several options for installing Skype onto Linux. Since there are several flavors of distributions of Linux, you will need to select the package that is right for your configuration. The following is a list of Skype packages available for various Linux flavors:

- SuSe version 9 and newer

- Fedora Core 3 or newer

- RPM for Mandrake 10.1 or newer

- Debian

- Dynamic binary tarball (requires Qt 3.2)

- Static binary tarball (compiled with Qt 3.2)

The easiest way to install the Linux version is to use one of the install packages that are already compiled and available for SuSe, Fedora, Mandrake, or Debian. If you are using RedHat Linux, you may use the Fedora RPM package for RedHat as well.

Installing a Precompiled Skype for Linux Package

Installing the precompiled Skype for Linux packages is straightforward. Like any package, once you download the package you simply double-click the **package** icon and it should launch the package installer.

RPM Version

Follow these steps to install the RPM version:

1. Open a console.

2. Log on as superuser or root.

3. Find the location where you saved the RPM.

4. Enter the following command:

   `rpm -U skype-version.rpm`

   where *skype-version.rpm* is the name of the file you downloaded, such as *skype-1.2.0.11-fc3-i586.rpm*.

Once the package is installed, open Skype from the appropriate menu location. For Fedora you will find it under Applications | Internet | Skype.

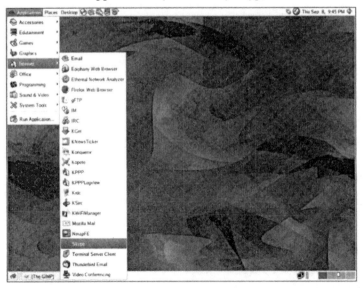

Once Skype is installed, you are ready to log in or sign up as a new user. Chapter 3 describes in more detail how to do this. The Windows version is used for the examples in this book because it is the most widely used version, so if you're a Linux user, keep in mind that some screens and features available in Windows might not be available for Linux versions.

Here is a screenshot of the Fedora for Linux installation.

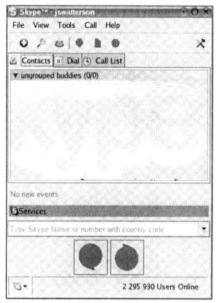

Generic Tarballs

If you cannot use one of the existing compiled installations, you can use the regular UX tarball option to install Skype. There are two versions of binary tarball:

- Dynamic binary tarball (requires Qt 3.2)
- Static binary tarball (compiled with Qt 3.2)

If you are already familiar with using tarballs, go ahead and install Skype onto your Linux distribution.

Here are the steps for installing the tar version of Skype:

1. Open a console

2. Find the location where you saved the tar.bz2 file

3. Enter the following command:

```
tar xjvf skype-version.tar.bz2
```

where *skype-version.tar.bz2* is the name of the file you downloaded, such as *skype-1.2.0.11.tar.bz2* or *Skype_staticQT-1.2.0.11.tar.bz2*. Skype is then unpacked to the current directory. Note that this does not require root privileges. If you cannot log in as a superuser, use the Static binary tarball.

Chapter 3

Getting Started Using Skype

Solutions in this chapter:

- Signing Up As a User
- Adding or Searching for Contacts
- Starting a Chat
- Making a Test Call
- Making Your First Call
- Inviting Others to Join Skype
- Setting Your Status
- Advanced Settings

Signing Up As a User

We covered signing up as a new user during the installation process, but you might want or need to create multiple users or accounts at a later time. For example, you might want one account for you and another account for someone else in your household. Maybe you have a computer and a laptop, so you want to have a different account for each. Whatever your need, you can create and use multiple accounts in Skype.

After Skype has logged you in, you will be presented with the following screen:

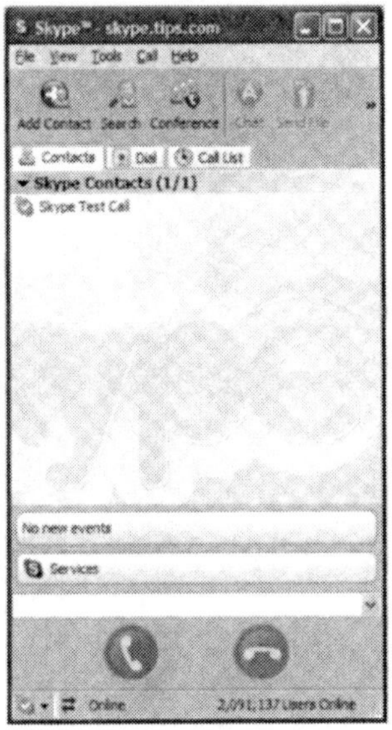

To create an additional account, select the **File** menu, and then select **Log in as a New User...**, as the following image indicates.

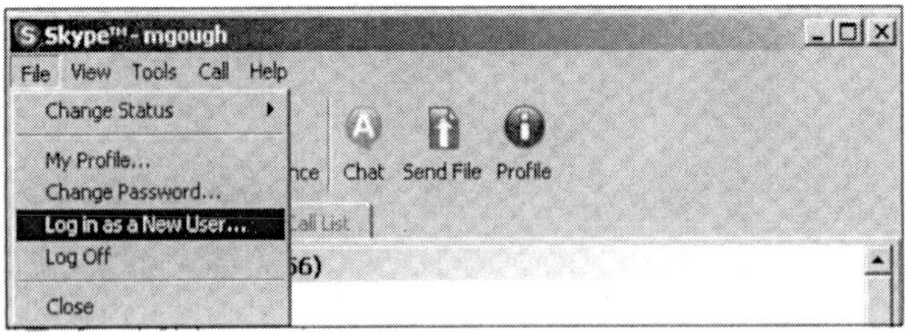

You will then be presented with the same screen you saw when you first signed up for your Skype account.

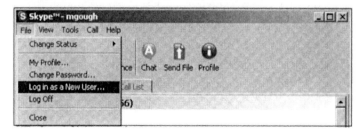

Select the **New Users – Create a Skype Account** tab. As we covered in Chapter 2 when you first signed up, create a new Skype name for yourself and follow the prompts. Once you are successful in creating a new account, Skype will log on the new user for you.

Switching between Users

If you have more than one user on your system, you will want to switch between these users from time to time. To switch between users you have created or allow any users who want to use their Skype accounts on your computer, select the **File** menu and then select **Log in as a New User...**, as the following image indicates.

You will then be presented with the following screen:

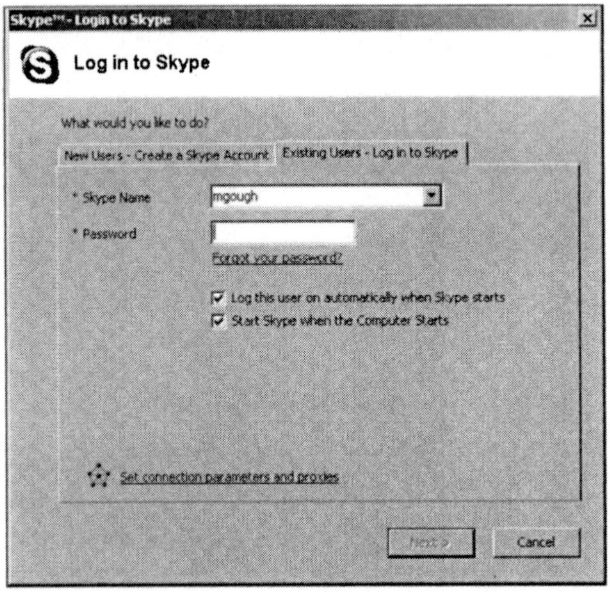

Select the **Skype Name** drop-down box, and you will see a list of all users who have logged in to the computer.

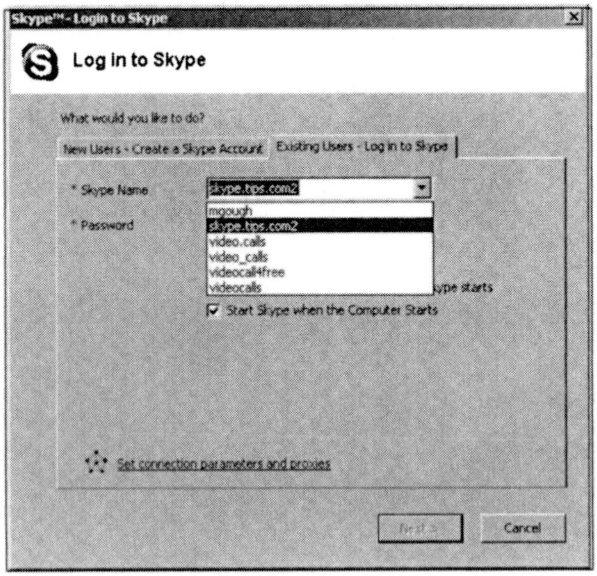

Select the user you want to log on, enter the correct password, and select **Next**.

Do not worry about the *Set connection parameters and proxies* link just yet. This is an advanced option that we'll cover later.

You will then be presented with the main Skype screen showing the user you selected is logged in.

Adding or Searching for Contacts

Now that you are up and running, you will want to add Skype users or search for Skype users with whom you want to communicate. You can verbally ask people you know for their Skype names, send them an e-mail, or search in the Skype directory for them. You can add users two ways: via Add a Contact for a known Skype name or by searching the Skype directory for users.

Adding Contacts

There are two ways two add contacts. One is to click the 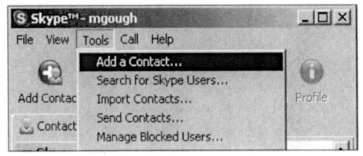 icon or choose **Add a Contact** from the **Tools** menu.

Select one of the two options to add a user, and you will be presented the following screen.

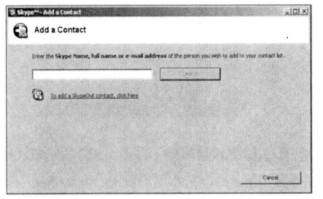

Enter the Skype name that you want to add and press the [Search] button.

You will then be presented with the results of your search to validate the user you want to add.

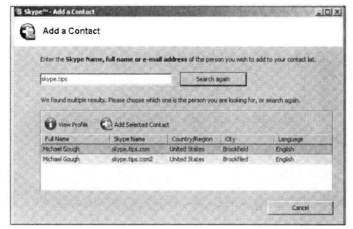

If more than one user is listed in the results, select one of them. At this point you may view the user's profile or just add the selected contact. You may also double-click the user's name and you will be presented with the following screen:

This screen will show you the contact's short profile so that you can verify that he or she is the person you want to add. You can click either the **Close** or, if you want to add the contact, click the **Add Contact** button.

Once you add the contact, you will be presented with the following screen.

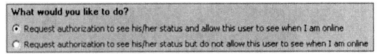

You can send the contact a message letting him or her know who you are. I left the default message on the screen, but you may type anything you like in the message window.

You are then presented two choices for requesting authorization. Every time you ask a Skype user to add you to their contact list requires the user's authorization.

What would you like to do?
- Request authorization to see his/her status and allow this user to see when I am online
- Request authorization to see his/her status but do not allow this user to see when I am online

When the other user accepts the default authorization request, you will each be able to see the Online status of one another.

For more privacy, you can ask a contact to add you but not let them know when you are online. This is appropriate when you want to make calls to a person but not let them know every time you are online.

Understanding the Basics... Request Authorization

We recommend leaving the default selection when you request authorization and let your contact see when you are online, unless you desire more privacy and do not want to be disturbed.

After you send the request for authorization, you will be returned to the search result screen. Go ahead and close the window to return to the main Skype screen.

Your new Skype contact has been added and now will show up in your contact list as grayed out until the user approves your request for authorization. Your new contact will see the following screen to authorize you:

Once the contact approves you, the icon next to the user will turn green, showing you that you have been approved and added to the other user's contact list.

Go ahead and repeat the steps we just described to add to your contact list all the people for whom you know their Skype contact names.

Understanding the Basics... Advertise Your Skype Name

You can add your Skype name to your e-mail signature so that anyone you normally communicate with will see you have a Skype name and can add you to their contact lists:

```
Skype = mgough
```

Searching for Contacts

If you do not know your contact's Skype name, you can search the Skype directory for contacts using a simple search or and advanced search. Searches rely on the information a user adds to his or her profile. If your contact does not fill in all the profile entries, you will have difficulty locating that person.

Basic Search

There are two ways to start a basic search. One is by selecting the [Search] icon; the other is from the **Tools** menu.

Select one of the two options to add a user, and you will be presented with the following screen:

Type the term you want to search for into the Search text box. You can search for three information items in the main Search box:

- User's Skype name
- User's full name
- User's e-mail address

Fill in what you want to search for and select the [Search] button, and your results will be returned. In the following screen I searched for SkypeTips, to return my username.

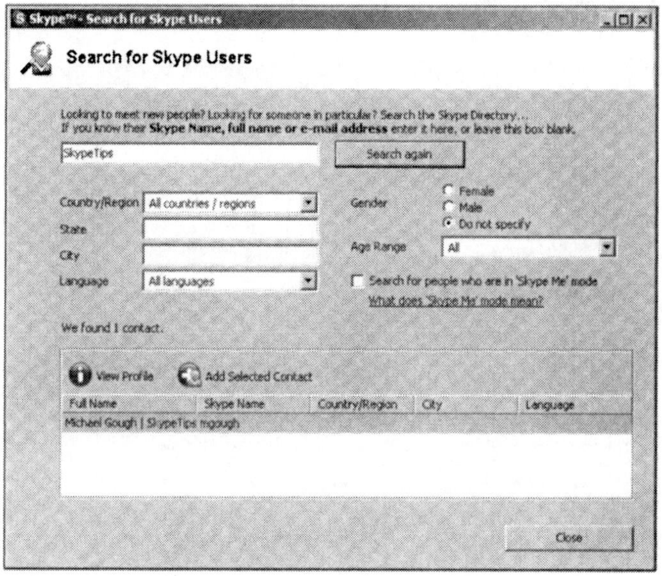

Advanced Search

If the basic search does not locate the user you are looking for, you can use additional information items to search for a user:

- State
- City
- Language
- Gender
- Age range

Do not worry about SkypeMe mode at this time; we'll cover that a little later.

You can now search for a contact by any of the criteria shown on this screen. Keep in mind that you can only search for information the user has entered into his or her profile. If the user did not input a city, for example, you will not be able to locate him or her based on city.

You may also use the wildcard (*) option to search for all items, but it is not completely effective. The wildcard option will return some interesting results. In the following screen, I typed in **M* Gough**. This returns the names of anyone whose first name starts with M and whose last name or Skype name is *Gough*.

Use the various search options to find the Skype users you are looking to add to your contact list.

Starting a Chat

One of Skype's main features that you will use often is the Chat or IM feature. You will just say "Hi" or ask if someone is available for a voice call using the Chat option.

Before we start to explain how to start a Chat, we first need to discuss the selection of a contact in your list. Until now your contact list looked something like this.

When you select a contact in your list, the view will change to expand that user's information.

The Contact name expands to include some basic profile information about the user. At this point, you can also right-click on the user name to get a menu of actions.

To start a chat, find the contact you want, select the **name** with a single mouse click, and initiate the chat using one of two methods: Select the [icon] icon at the top of the screen or right-click with your mouse on the **contact name**, and select [Start Chat...]. We will discuss how to adjust the Skype Options settings later in this chapter, but if you make the default for double-click a contact to Start Chat, you will also be able to initiate a chat by double-clicking your **contact's name**. Most IM tools such as MSN, Yahoo!, AIM, and others all use double-clicking to start a chat, so you will want to change this so that when you double-click a **contact** in your list it opens a Chat window and does not call your contact.

Once the Chat window is open, you can start typing your message, use emoticons, change the text, and invite other contacts to your chat.

Notice the [lock] icon in the bottom-right corner. This lock icon indicates that the chat session between contacts is encrypted with 256-bit AES encryption.

From within the Chat window you can also initiate the following actions by clicking these icons:

- [icon] Add a contact to your chat (multiparty chat)

- [icon] Set the topic of your chat

- [icon] Quit the current chat

-  Call your contact

- Send your contact a file

You can also view a contact's profile by selecting the profile icon from the side of the Chat window.

Making a Test Call

Now that Skype is installed and you have added one or more contacts, it is time to make your first test call. Skype provides a test user called Echo123 that is added when Skype is installed.

Select the **Echo123** contact and you will see the following screen:

Click the icon to call **Echo123**, or right-click the **contact name** and select Call This Contact . To solicit an inbound test call from **Echo123** right-click the contact name and select Start Chat… In the Chat window type 'call me' and click the **Enter** button. Once connected, **Echo123** greets you with a message that explains how you may leave a short test voice message, just like an answering machine. Once you complete your 10-second message, it will be played back to you so that you'll know whether Skype is working properly. If you hear your message played back, you are good to go and are ready to make your first Skype voice call to a real contact!

You are now ready to make your first Skype voice call to a real contact!

Making Your First Call

Now that you have completed the system test, you are ready to start talking with your family, friends, and colleagues.

Select a **contact** and either double-click the **contact's name** or use the  icon to initiate the call. When you call someone and that person does not answer, you will get a busy signal or voicemail. Once a contact answers, you can do the following within a call:

- ▪   Chat
- ▪   Call another contact or make a conference call
- ▪   Send your contact a file
- ▪   View their profile
- ▪   Put the call on hold
- ▪   Mute or unmute the microphone

When you initiate a call to one of your contacts and they answer, you will see a screen that resembles the following:

Expand the Skype window by selecting the right side of the window and dragging the window wider to the right to expose two additional icons. You should see the following screen.

Notice that you now have two more icons for putting the call on hold and muting the call.

In the bottom left corner of the screen, you should see the 🔒 icon. This lock indicates that the voice call session between contacts is encrypted with 256bit AES encryption.

Putting a Call on Hold

You can place the call on hold so that you can answer another call or attend to a task by selecting the ![Hold] icon. You might want to do this to answer another call or to initiate a conference call, or for any other reason. To take the call off hold, select the ![Hold] icon.

Muting and Unmuting the Microphone

You can mute and unmute the microphone by selecting the ![Mute] icon. You might want to do this to reduce feedback if you are using a microphone and external speakers, if you are just listening to a conference call, or if someone is talking to you in person and you do not want your call participants to hear what is going on. To unmute the microphone, select the ![Mute] icon again.

Hanging Up the Call

Either party can end the call by selecting the ![Hangup] hangup icon.

Inviting Others to Join Skype

Since not everyone you know has or uses Skype, you might want to invite your family, friends, and colleagues to learn and use this great tool. Of course, you can ask them verbally or send them an e-mail, but Skype offers an automated way that will also provide the invitee a link via which he or she can download Skype. To do this, select **Share Skype with a Friend** from the **Tools** menu.

This choice launches your browser and takes you to the Skype Web site, where you can invite users to download and start using Skype via an e-mail Skype sends.

Share Skype With A Friend

It's how babies are made and it's also good for your karma. It lets you talk to all your friends and family through the Internet for free.

Send a message to a friend and give them your Skype Name. You can also attach a gift like a viral or a souvenir to the email if you want to be extra nice.

Your Name

Your Skype Name
skype_me_too

Your Message
Hi, check out this thing called Skype. If you get on it too, we can talk to each other for free.

Friend 1's Email

Friend 2's Email

Send to more friends

You can also send your family, friends, and colleagues an e-mail that contains a URL to the Skype download page, but the Skype invitation page makes it easy for you to invite users and get them familiar with the Skype Web site.

Setting Your Status

To let others online know your status (whether you're online or off), use the Current Status setting. You set your status by selecting the **drop-down box** indicated by the 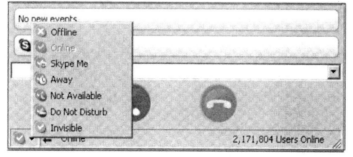 icon in the bottom-left corner of the Skype screen.

No new events

Offline
Online
Skype Me
Away
Not Available
Do Not Disturb
Invisible

Online   2,171,804 Users Online

You can also set your status from the **Task Bar** icon in the bottom-right corner of your screen.

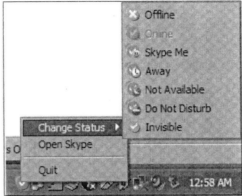

You are presented with seven status options:

- Offline
- Online
- Skype Me
- Away
- Not Available
- Do Not Disturb
- Invisible

Offline

The Offline status setting will let your contacts know that you are no longer online. Because you are physically disconnected from the Skype network at this point, they cannot send you chat messages or call you.

- Indicates that you are offline
- Contacts see you as offline
- You cannot be contacted via chat or voice calls

Online

The Online status setting changes your status back to normal online status and available for all features.

- Indicates that you are available and online

- Contacts can see that you are online

- You can be contacted via chat and calls

Skype Me

The Skype Me status setting makes you available for random chat, and anyone can call or chat with you *without authorization*. This setting overrides the authorization requests, so make sure that you really want this status setting because it means that anyone at any time can contact you from searches in the Skype directory. Privacy is basically disabled while this status setting is selected.

- Indicates that you are available and taking any calls from anyone, without authorization

- Contacts can see you are online and you can be "Skyped"

- You can be contacted via chat and calls

Understanding the Basics... Skype Me Status

Be careful using the Skype Me status option because it means that anyone can contact you any time, without authorization.

Away

The Away status setting tells your contacts that you are "away" and not at your computer to answer calls or chat. All features still work with this status setting enabled. This setting can be set manually and is automatically set to Away after you have not used your computer for a short period of time—five minutes by default. The status setting will return to Online once computer activity is sensed, only when it was automatically set by inactivity.

- Indicates that you are away from your computer for a short period of time

- Contacts can see you are online but away

- Automatically changes back to Online when computer activity is sensed

- You can be contacted via chat and calls

Not Available

The Not Available status setting tells your contacts you unavailable and not at your computer to answer calls or chat. All features still work with this status setting enabled. This setting can be set manually and is automatically set to Not Available after you have not used your computer for a long period of time—20 minutes by default. The status setting will return to Online once computer activity is sensed, only when it was automatically set by inactivity.

- Indicates that you have been away for a long period of time

- Contacts can see that you are online but are not available

- Automatically changes back to Online when computer activity is sensed

- You can be contacted via chat and calls

Do Not Disturb

The Do Not Disturb status setting tells your contacts that you should not be disturbed. However, your contacts can still contact you, and chats and calls will still come through. You will not hear ringing for incoming calls, and you must manually change this status setting when you want your contacts to know that you are available again.

- Contacts can see that you are online, but the status is Do Not Disturb

- You can make outbound contacts

- You can be contacted

Invisible

The Invisible status setting makes it look as though you are offline (even though you are not). You can still be contacted when your status is set to Invisible.

- Contacts see you as offline

- You can make outbound chats or calls

- You can be contacted

Basic Options

Now that you are up and running with Skype, we can explore the options available to better configure and customize Skype to your personal preferences. The following are the options that you can configure to meet your needs:

- General settings

- Privacy

- Notifications

- Sound alerts

- Sound devices (advanced)

- Hotkeys

- Connection (advanced)

- Advanced

- Voicemail (advanced)

We will not cover all these settings in this chapter, since we are only covering the basic settings at this point. The advanced settings are covered later in the book. To access the Skype Options settings, select the **Tools** menu, then select **Options**.

You will be presented with the list of options in the **General Options** tab.

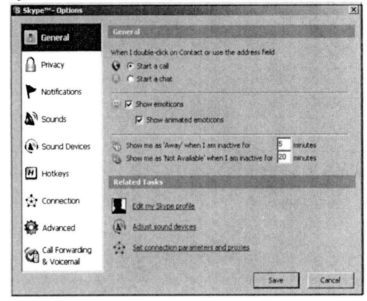

Save and Cancel Buttons

If you change a setting, you must do one of two things: Click the [Save] button to save your changes, or click the [Cancel] button to cancel your changes. You only have to click the Save button once after you have completed changes to any and all Option screens. If you click the Cancel button on any screen prior clicking the Save button, you will lose all changes since the last save. Some changes require you to restart Skype, so just follow the prompts.

General Options

The General options tab allows you to set the following items:

- Double-click on a contact or use the address field

- Show emoticons

- Show me as away after X minutes

- Show me as not available after X minutes

Under Related Tasks, you will see:

- Edit your profile

- Adjust your sound devices

- Set connection parameters and proxy

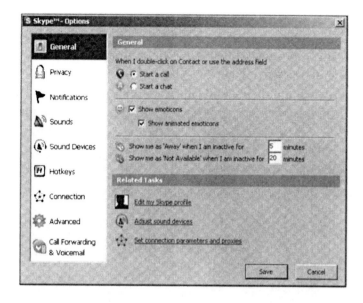

When I Double-Click a Contact Name, What Happens?

By default, when you double-click your mouse a contact name, Skype calls that contact. You might find that this is not the best option, because every time you double-click a user name accidentally, you will call that contact and then have to cancel the call. We recommend you change this setting to Start Chat. Then you can call your contact from within the Chat window by selecting the [icon] icon, as we discussed in Chapter 2.

If you are an MSN, Yahoo!, AIM, or other IM user, you might find it convenient to set Start Chat as your default.

Understanding the Basics... General Options

We recommend that you set the **Double-Click** option to:

When I double-click on Contact or use the address field
- ○ Start call
- ● Start chat

Show Emoticons

Emoticons are the cute little animated icons that appear in your Chat window when you select one of them from the menu. They help convey your feelings in an instant message. You will want to enable this setting unless you do not prefer to use emoticons.

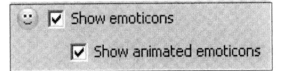

Understanding the Basics... General Options

We recommend you set the **Emoticons** option to:

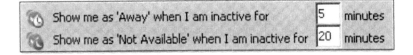

Show Me As...

There are two status settings that are automatic when you stop using your computer for a period of time. Skype will automatically set your status to one of the following:

We covered what these two settings mean in Chapter 2. If you want to adjust these settings so other users do not think you are away or not available after the default period of time, you may set these to your desired state. If you set the Away value to 0 it will disable both these features.

Understanding the Basics... General Options

We recommend you set the **Show me as** option to:

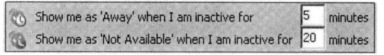

Show me as 'Away' when I am inactive for   5   minutes

Show me as 'Not Available' when I am inactive for   20   minutes

Related Tasks: Editing Your Skype Profile

Skype lists several items that are related in the Related Tasks area. For the General tab, the following are listed.

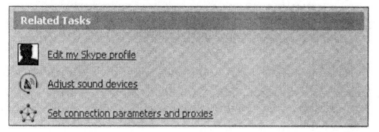

We cover only editing your profile here, since *Adjust sound devices* and *Set connection parameters and proxies* are advanced settings we cover in the "Advanced Settings" section of Chapter 6.

The one related task that appears in the General tab is the ☐ Edit my Skype profile settings. This is where you add more information about yourself that you want published in the Skype directory. Most of the information you enter here is public information, so take care not to enter information you do not want others to know about you.

When you select the [Edit my Skype profile] option, you will be presented with the following screen:

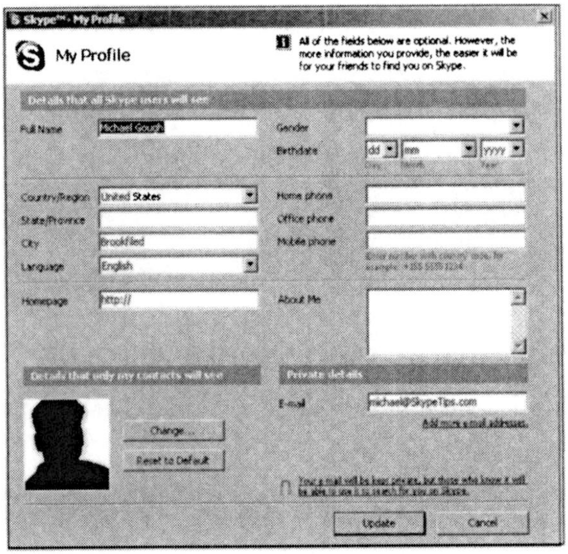

As you can see by my profile, I choose to share very little information with the public. I prefer that people contact me through my Web site or send me e-mail. This way I can limit the number of people looking for other Michael Goughs in the world or people who think they know me but whom I don't remember.

What you put in here will be your personal preference. You can use the Full Name field to list something additional about you. Notice in the following screen that I have modified my Full Name to include my SkypeTips.com Web site. Changes to your profile are made available as soon as you click the Update button, but it will probably take a bit longer for this information to propagate throughout the network.

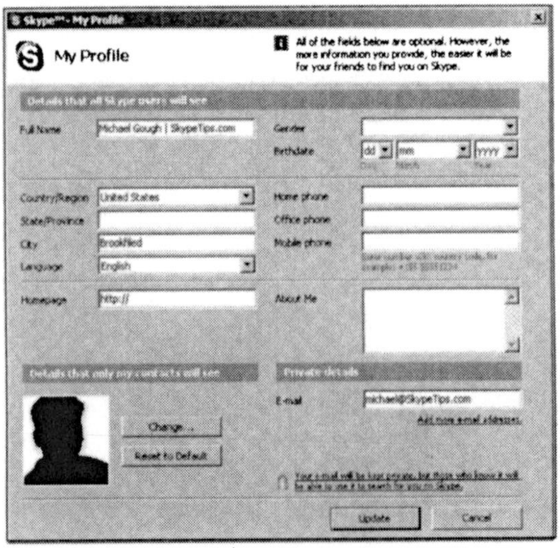

This is what your contacts will see when they select your name (Chapter 6 explains in detail how to use the fields in this dialog box):

This way you can customize what your contacts see next to your name on their contact list, or in my case my SkypeTips.com Web site.

Privacy Options

The Privacy Options tab allows you to set the following items:

- Allow calls from
- Allow chat from
- Allow SkypeIn calls from (advanced)
- Keep Chat History

Under Related Tasks, you will see:

- Manage blocked users
- Manage other programs' access to Skype (advanced)

If people do a search and find you in the Skype directory, these settings will control what they can do upon selecting you as a new contact. The following is a list of possible settings:

- Anyone can call or chat

- Only people from my contacts list can call or chat

- Only people whom I have authorized can call or chat

It is important that you understand the differences among these three settings so that you make the best choice for your situation. The three settings have different meanings in terms of the way people can chat and call you. Do you want anyone to initiate a chat or call you before or after authorization, or do you want only people in your contacts list to be able to chat or call you?

Anyone Can ...

If this option is selected, anyone can send a chat message or call you after they send you a request for Authorization. However, also be aware that they can chat and call you *before* you authorize them, as a part of asking you for authorization. Others can use this setting to explain to you who they are and why you should authorize them.

Only People from My Contacts Can ...

If this option is selected, only people you have added to your contacts can send a chat message or call you. Users will be alerted that you are "not a contact" in their main Skype window if they attempt to chat or call you. If you are privacy conscious and do not want to be contacted by a user until you add that user to your contact list, this is the best setting to choose. Also, if you once authorized a contact and later removed the person from your contacts list, that user will be unable to chat to or call you. When a contact sends you a request for authorization, the chat and call features will be disabled.

Only People Whom I Have Authorized Can ...

If this option is selected, potential contacts cannot chat or call you before you have authorized them and added them to your contacts. Users who have never been authorized will be alerted that they are "not authorized to call" you in their main Skype window if they attempt to chat to or call you. If you delete a previously-authorized user from your contact list with this option set, the user will still be able to contact you unless you block the user. If you delete a contact from your contact list with this option set, the user may still chat to or call you.

Understanding the Basics... Privacy Options

Here's a brief summary of the privacy options:

- For the most privacy, enable **Only people from my Contacts can...**
- For good privacy, enable **Only people whom I have authorized can...**
- For the least privacy, enable **Anyone can...**

Allow Calls From

This setting is where you set who can call you.

Understanding the Basics... Privacy Options

We recommend you set the **Allow Calls** option to:

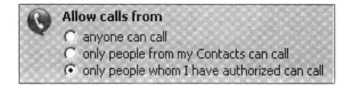

Allow Chat From

This is where you set who can chat with you.

Understanding the Basics... Privacy Options

We recommend you set the **Allow Chats** option to:

> **(A) Allow chats from**
> - ○ anyone can start chat
> - ○ only people from my Contacts can start chat
> - ◉ only people whom I have authorized can start chat

Keep Chat History

If you chat with your contacts, you might close the chat window and later want to remember what you chatted about. Skype gives you the option of saving your history for each chat for the following lengths of time:

- No history

- Two weeks

- One month

- Three months

- Forever

You may select whatever option you feel is best, but we would recommend changing this setting only after you understand Skype better and when you know that you do not want to save the chat history forever. Chat histories are stored unencrypted on users' machines.

Understanding the Basics... Privacy Options

We recommend you set the **Keep chat history for** option to **Forever**.

> Keep chat history for [forever ▼]   [Clear History]
>
> no history
> ...ed Tasks   2 weeks
>   1 month
> Manage blocked users 3 months
>   forever

Related Tasks

In the Related Tasks area, Skype lists several items that are related. For the **Privacy** tab, the following items are listed.

We cover only *Manage blocked users* here. *Manage other programs' access to Skype* is an advanced setting that we cover in the "Advanced Settings" section of Chapter 6.

Blocked Users

To access and manage your list of blocked users, use the **Related Tasks** area of the **Privacy** tab.

If there are Skype users that you no longer wish to contact you for any reason, you can block them by adding them to your Blocked Users list. They will not be able to see your online status, even if this had been previously authorized, and you will disappear from their contact list until you remove them from your Blocked User list. This tab is where you manage the list.

You may block a user when you right-click his or her name in your contacts list. You can also access this list from within a chat window by selecting the ⟩⟩ icon.

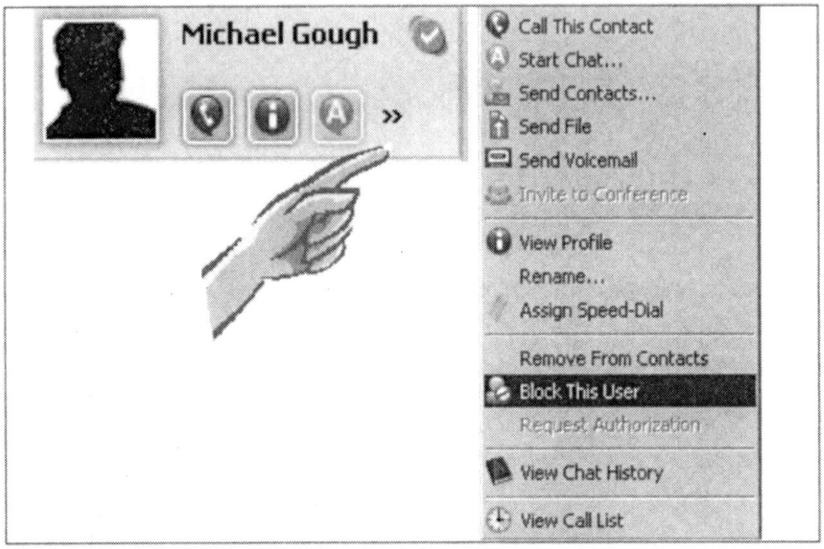

Notification Options

The Notification options tab allows you to display a notification if another Skype user does one of the following:

- Comes online

- Calls you

- Starts a chat with you

- Sends you a file

- Requests authorization

- Sends you contacts

- Leaves you a voicemail (advanced)

or to display messages for:

- Help/Tips

Only the *Comes online* setting is annoying when it's set. As users come and go, the notification pops up in the bottom-right corner of your screen and can be very active, since it will also notify you regarding users' status change from Away, Not Available, and others. We recommend leaving the other settings on by default so you know when an event happens.

Understanding the Basics... Privacy Options

We recommend you set the **Comes online** option to:

Related Tasks

In the Related Tasks area, Skype lists several items that are related. For the **Notification** tab, the following are listed:

Related Tasks

Configure sound alerts

Configure sound alerts is an advanced setting that we cover in the "Advanced Settings" section of Chapter 6.

Tasks Bar Icon

When an event has happened that you missed, the 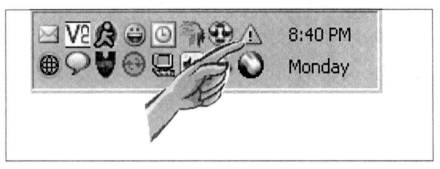 icon in the Windows Task Bar will flash with a caution icon like this ⚠ . This notifies you that you have a missed call.

Events

Skype notifies you of any events in the main Skype window, such as missed calls or if someone has left you voicemail message.

Within your main Skype window, you will see a message in the **Event** window:

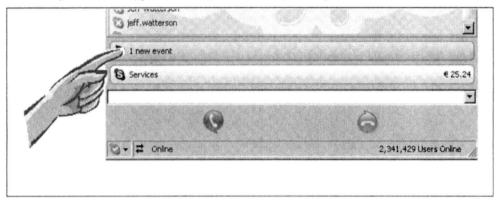

This message will tell you how many events you have. To check an event, simply select the yellow tab and it will expand to show you the specific events from each user.

> ⚑ 2 new events
>
> 🕓 1 Missed Call
>   MG Cell
>
> 📧 1 new voicemail
>   Michael Gough

You'll see if you have a missed call or someone has left you voicemail (more on that in the "Voice Mail" section of Chapter 6). When you select the specific event, it will take you to all the events related to that contact.

Here you can listen to your voicemail or delete the event by selecting the trash [trash icon] icon. Here you can listen to your voicemail or delete the event by selecting the trash icon. Caution should be exercised when clicking on the trash icon, to avoid inadvertently deleting event items.

Sound Alerts

The Sound Alerts option allows you to set the sounds that play for certain events. Next to each option are three icons:

- [icon] Play the sound
- [icon] Select a different sound file
- [icon] Reset the sound to Skype default

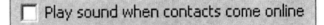

The default sounds are a good place to start, but if you tend to change sounds to your liking, feel free to customize Skype to play sounds the way you want.

Understanding the Basics... Privacy Options

We recommend you deselect the **Play sound when contacts come online** setting:

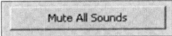

You may also choose **Mute All Sounds** and rely solely on the visual alerts to let you know what Skype is doing. We do not recommend this choice, however, as you could just as easily mute your sound card or turn off your speakers if you do not want Skype to make sounds as you use it.

Hotkeys Options

Many users still like to use the keyboard to control certain functions of their computer. Skype allows you to set several hotkeys for the following actions:

- Answer call

- Ignore call

- Reject/hang up call

- Focus Skype

- Search for Skype users

- Mute microphone

If you want to use hotkeys, you first have to enable them by selecting the **Enable global hotkeys** check box.

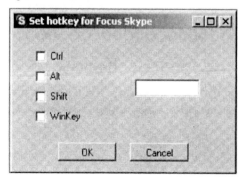

After you enable the hotkeys, you can set or change them to what you want. First, set the hotkey combination you want. Select the Change Hotkey button and you will be prompted with the following screen:

Fill in the hotkey combination you want to use. In the following example, we will set Focus Skype to **Alt + S**.

Now when you press the **Alt + S** key combination, the main Skype window will appear.

Now you must select the [Enable Hotkey] button to activate your setting.

Understanding the Basics... Hotkeys

Be sure to test your hotkey combination to see whether any of the applications you normally use have the same combination you want to set for Skype.

While in Chat, Pressing Enter Will …

When you use chat, the default action when you press **Enter** is to send the chat message to your contact. If you like, you can change this action so that when you press **Enter**, you only create a new line in your message instead of sending the message. If you do this, you can send the message either by using your mouse to click the **Enter** icon in the chat window, or you can use the **ALT+S** keystroke combination.

Understanding the Basics...
While in Chat, Pressing Enter Will...

We recommend leaving the default to **Enter** sending the chat message:

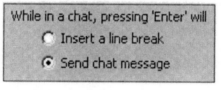

Chapter 4

Basic Features of Skype

Solutions in this chapter:

- Selecting or Changing Your Language
- Understanding Skype's Status Icons
- Using Chat or Instant Messaging
- Handling File Transfers
- Making Voice Calls
- Managing Contacts
- Importing Contacts

Selecting or Changing Your Language

If you install Skype and later decide you want to use a different language, you can do so by selecting from the Main menu **Tools** and then **Select Language**.

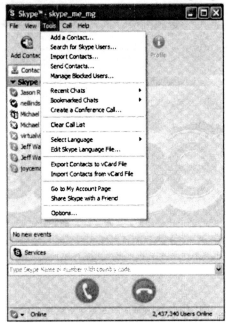

You can select one of the many languages Skype supports to set your preferred language.

You can edit the Skype Language file, a topic that's covered in "Advanced Options" in Chapter 6.

Understanding Skype's Status Icons

When you log on to Skype, you will see several different icons in the main Contacts window These icons indicate information about each user's status. The following is a list of the various status indicators you will see in the main Contacts window.

- Online
- Not Available
- Away
- Do not disturb
- Calls are being forwarded
- Offline
- Offline with Voice Mail active
- Pending Authorization

Each of these icons tells you each Skype user's status.

Online

Users with the icon are online and available for all features of Skype.

Not Available

Users with the icon have been away from their computer for an extended period of time but are available for all features of Skype.

Away

Users with the icon are away from their computer for a short period of time and available for all features of Skype.

Do Not Disturb

Users with the icon are announcing that they would prefer not to be contacted. However this status indicator, in and of itself, does not actually prevent contact from others.

Calls Are Being Forwarded

Users with the ⬚ icon have Call Forwarding enabled and available for all features of Skype. If you send a file or chat message, the user will not receive it until the next time he or she launches Skype. If you place a voice call to this user, you will reach that user on the telephone or the user to whom they forwarded their account.

Offline

Users with the ⬚ icon are probably genuinely offline, and this makes them unavailable for all features of Skype, but they may also have made themselves Invisible, in which case they can still be contacted if you try. If a user's Privacy Setting permits it, and you send a file or chat message when they are actually offline, they will not receive it until the next time they are online, and this may not occur until the next time they launch Skype. If you place a call to this user, Skype will ring them until it is convinced that they are genuinely offline, invisible or until the user answers.

Offline with Voice Mail

Users with the ⬚ icon are apparently offline as indicated above, and most of the time this means that they are unavailable for all features of Skype. After a preset number of rings (15 by default) you will be directed to his or her voicemail to leave a message.

Pending Authorization

Users with the ⬚ icon have not yet authorized you and this *only* means that you cannot yet see their online status. It does not prevent you from contacting them in any way unless they have elevated their Privacy Option from the default setting (which is to allow chats and calls from anyone).

Using Chat or Instant Messaging

Skype has a very nice chat or IM client that allows you to carry on not only one-on-one chats but also multiuser chats. IM or Chat is the most basic of options for Skype, but it will also be the most used, next to the voice call feature, of course.

Setting the Double-Click Option to Start a Chat

The first order of business we recommend is setting your double-click option to **Start a Chat**. Refer to Chapter 3, "Basic Options," where we discuss setting Skype to default on double-click to start a chat. Setting Skype to **Start a Chat** on double-clicking a contact name will align with what most of us are used to with other IM products, since this is what happens when you double-click a username in MSN, Yahoo!, AIM, and other IM solutions.

Understanding the Basics...
Setting Double-Click to Start a Chat

We recommend setting double-clicking a user to **Start a Chat** as your default setting, to match what other IM applications do.

Hiding the User Information

One option that you can adjust is the Chat window itself. You have the capability to hide the user information in the right side of the Chat window to make your Chat window larger. To do this, just select the ⊙ icon to hide the user information:

To bring back the user information, simply select the ⊙ icon.

Starting an Instant Message or Chat

Instant messaging is fairly straightforward; only a few things need to be pointed out so that you know what can be done in a chat session and your options in a chat session:

- Chat history

- Set a topic for the chat session

- Emoticons

- Changing the font

- Inviting more users to a chat

Chat History

The maximum amount of chat history that is stored is controlled by your choice of an appropriate time interval under Privacy Options as discussed in Chapter 3, "Basic Options", and we previously recommended that the default setting (forever) be initially left unchanged.

If you want to change this setting, go to the **Tools** menu, select **Options**, and select the **Privacy** tab to change the setting.

You can also view the entire history of each Contacts chat by selecting the ⟫ icon to access the menu and then selecting **View Chat History**.

An alternate method for displaying the entire Chat History (that is, since the last time it was purged), is to right-click on a specific user in the Contact list, and then to select View Chat History from the menu, as shown below.

Either method for viewing the chat history will open your Web browser and display the entire history of your chats with the particular contact selected. This is shown on the next page.

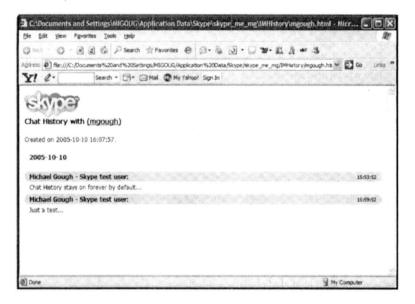

Understanding the Basics... Chat History

We recommend that you *not* use Chat History when you use a public or shared computer, because your messages will remain and anyone who uses the machine after you will be able to view them. On these systems, set Chat History to **No History**.

Deleting Chat History

If you want to change how long you store chat history or delete all of it, go to the menu **Tools** and then **Options**, and then choose the **Privacy** tab. You will see the Clear History button.

If you right-click with your mouse anywhere in the upper part of the chat window where chat messages are logged, you will see another menu that gives you a few more options:

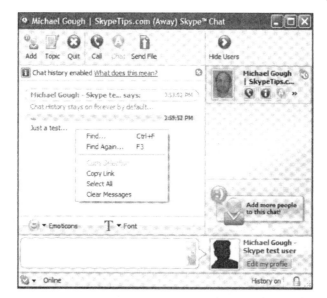

You can **Find** a word or words within the chat conversation and **Find Again** for additional occurrences of the word or words you are searching for. You can **Copy Link** a Web link or URL to paste into a document or into your browser, and you can **Clear Messages**, which clears all your chat history for this chat session but will not clear it from Chat History.

Setting a Chat Topic

If you are openly chatting with one or more of your contacts you might want to set a *chat topic*. This allows you send a notice to every user in the chat session as to the topic of the current discussion. You set the chat topic by selecting the icon and then typing in the topic you want to set. In the following example, we typed in **Skype Video** as the topic:

Once we press **Enter**, we see the topic appear in our chat window and the windows of all other users who are in the chat as well.

The message will scroll off the Chat Window, but you will still see the topic on the topic bar:

Also note the little 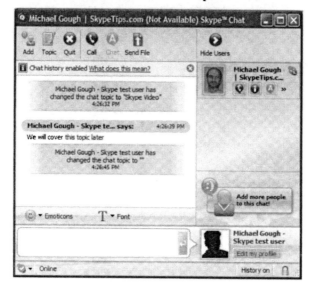 icon that indicates you can set a bookmark for the chat topic, to use it use later.

To clear the topic, just click the topic word and the text box appears. Then simply delete the text in the box and press **Enter** to clear the chat topic, or click on the paper/pencil icon to the left of the text box.

You will then see in the Chat window that the topic is cleared.

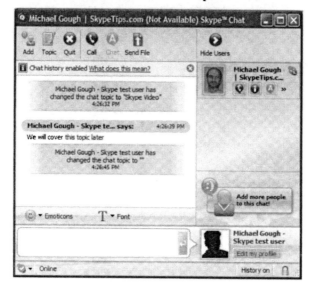

Recent Chats

If you ever want to view the details of the **ten** most-recent chats you have had with your contacts, you can do so by selecting **Tools | Recent Chats** and selecting the user whose chat you want to view.

You will then see the last chat session for the contact you selected.

Bookmarked Chats

If you ever want to go back and view the chat topic you bookmarked, you can select **Bookmarked Chats** from the **Tools** menu and select the user you were chatting with.

Another easy way to keep track of a group working together on a project and their discussions is by using *multichat*. It is a good way to keep an open forum for any project you are working on. You can find the chat using the Main menu **Tools** option and then **Bookmarked Chats**.

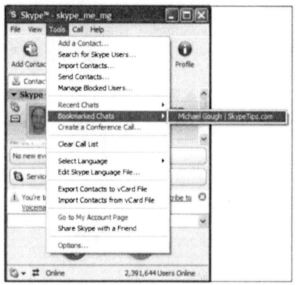

You will then see the Chat window appear with the history of the bookmarked chat.

Using Emoticons

Another chat option is to use what are called *emoticons*. These little icons allow you to express emotions quickly and in an animated way, to make the chat more fun and to better get your point across and possibly prevent misunderstandings. To access the emoticons, select the little yellow ☺ ▾ Emoticons icon. This will bring up the selection of emoticons available for you to use in your chat.

These little emoticons are animated (i.e. they move around) if you accept the default setting under General Options. Unfortunately we cannot depict this animation in this book, so experiment with them in your Chat window to help them make your chats more entertaining.

Changing the Font

Another chat feature is the ability to change the font within your chat window. Do this by selecting the ⟨T ▾ Font⟩ icon. This brings up the Font screen for you to select various options.

Play around with the fonts you like to make your chats more interesting.

Inviting More Users to a Chat

One of the nice features of Skype Chat is the capability to invite literally hundreds of contacts to a chat session. Chat takes up little bandwidth, so you could invite as many users as you want without too much impact on your Internet connection. However, it should be obvious that if you have too many of your contacts in a chat session, it could get pretty hard to follow the conversation.

To create a multiuser chat, first start a chat with one of your contacts, as we have already discussed. There are two ways to invite more users to a chat session. You can either select the ⟨icon⟩ icon or, on the right side of the Chat window in the User bar, click **Add more people to this chat!**.

Once you select one of these two options, you will be presented with the following screen to add more contacts to your chat session.

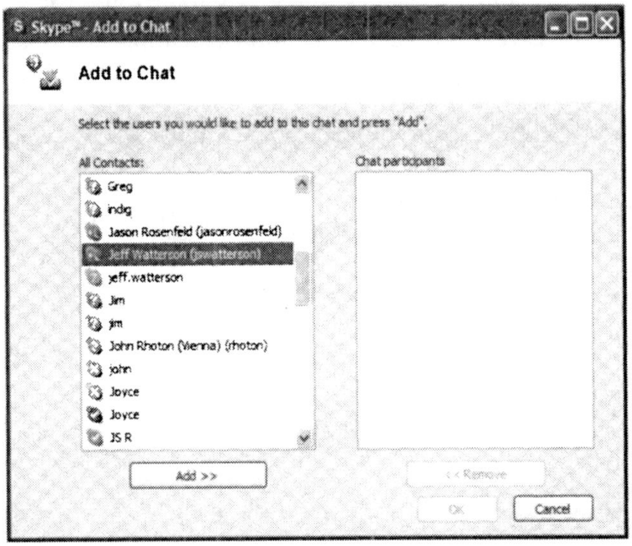

Just select one or more users and select the **Add** button to add that contact's name to the list of chat participants.

Once you add one or more users to the list, click the **OK** button to add the users to your chat session.

Now all three Skype contacts in this example are able to chat with one another. Also notice that their contact information shows up in the User Information bar on the right side of the window. Remember, you can hide the user information by selecting the ⊙ icon. Any user can end the chat by selecting the ⊗ icon. If the person who initiated the multiuser chat session quits, then all users are disconnected from the chat session. Anything you can do in single-user chat you can do in multiuser chat.

Handling File Transfers

File transfers are very popular in the IM space; IM is used by most everyone to send files to one or more users. Skype allows you to send a file to one or more users.

Understanding the Basics... Accepting Files via IM

A word of warning: *Never* accept computer files via any IM client software from users you do not personally know. Preferably such files should be sent via e-mail where ISP- and computer-based virus scanners can search for any potential viruses. Files received directly via IM can also be scanned on an individual basis after they have been received. Particular attention should be given to .EXE, .BAT, .CMD, .VBS, or any other file type that is 'executable'.

There are several ways to send a file to a contact on Skype:

- In a chat

- In a call

- By itself

You can send one or more files, but if you send multiple files, Skype will queue them up one at a time and send them one by one.

Sending a File in a Chat

While Skype does not yet support transferring a complete folder by just selecting the folder name, you can select multiple files to be sent in a single batch. Files queued in this fashion will be sent sequentially. It is also possible to queue files one at a time, and they can be transmitted concurrently to one or more recipients, albeit each at slower speed. You can perform file transfers by selecting files directly (e.g. from Windows Explorer), and in both a single-chat or multi-chat session. To send a file in a single-person chat, select the icon in the main Chat window:

Once you select the icon, you will presented with the following screen to browse for a file to send:

Browse to the location of the file or files that you want to send.

Select a file or files and click the **Open** button to start the transfer. You will now be presented with a screen that indicates you are sending a file. The contact or contacts you are sending the file to must accept the file to start the transfer.

Sending a File Directly from Windows Explorer

My favorite way to send one of more files to my Skype contacts is to do it by selecting the file directly and using the Send To option, then selecting one or more of my Skype contacts to send the file to. Begin by locating a file using Windows Explorer (or similar program), and then right-click the filename to bring up the Windows context-sensitive menu. Select **Send To** and then select **Skype**, as the following screen indicates:

You will be prompted to choose the Skype contact you want to send the file to.

You will then see the typical File Transfer status window.

Notice the check box **Close this dialog box when download completes.** You will want to select this option so that you do not need to close each File Transfer window unless you want to be alerted to the completion of the download.

If you do not select the box to close the complete window, you will be presented the following screen when the file transfer completes.

Note the little icon that indicates that your file transfer was encrypted.

Understanding the Basics... Close the File Transfer Check Box When Download Completes

It is a good idea to select the **Close this dialog box** when download completes option when you're sending a file.

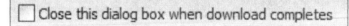

Sending Files to Multiple Contacts

When you are in a multiuser Chat window, you will notice that the icon changes to .

The file transfer works the same way as a single-user file transfer. Each user needs to accept the file transfer to receive the file or files that you want to send them. You will see a File Transfer window for each user in the chat session.

If you do not select **Close this dialog box when download completes**, you will see a File Transfer Complete box for each user who successfully downloads the file you are sending.

Sending a File in the Main Contacts Window

You can send files from the main Contacts window by first selecting the contact's name and then selecting the icon.

You can also right-click a user in the main Contacts window and select Send File from the window that opens.

Sending a File While in a Voice Call

While in a voice call with one or more contacts, you can also initiate a file transfer by selecting the  icon.

When you are in a voice call, file transfers will be throttled back to reduce bandwidth usage and make sure the quality of your voice call does not suffer.

Understanding the Basics...
Sending Files While in a Voice Call

When you send files while in a voice call, the file transfer speed will be dramatically less to make sure it does not interfere with the voice call quality. It is recommend that you send only small files while you're in a voice call.

Relayed File Transfers

Except while voice calls are also in progress, file transfers will be fairly quick as long as there is a direct peer-to-peer (P2P) connection between the two computers. If you get the following screen when you're sending a file, it means that your file is being relayed through one or more computers to get to the person you are sending it to.

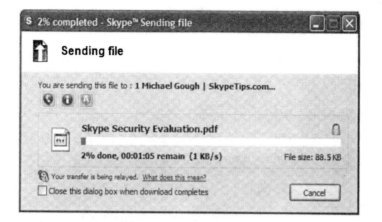

When you are receiving a file and see the following screen, you know the file you are receiving is being relayed and progress will be slow.

A relayed file transfer will occur whenever there is a corporate firewall in place or the user does not have a P2P-friendly DSL/cable router.

We cover more ways to show how Skype is connecting and if relays are being used in Chapter 6.

If you get the Relayed File Transfer message, you are better off sending the file via e-mail unless the file is very small. There is no way to control this behavior except to do testing with your various contacts and discover which contacts can perform direct file transfers and which cannot.

Users with older DSL/routers that are not P2P friendly or other firewall solutions that are not P2P friendly will suffer relayed file transfer issues and will also have relayed voice calls! More about relayed voice calls and file transfers in Chapter 6.

Making Voice Calls

Skype's best features is the voice call. Voice call is the feature that has led to the Skype explosion and its success as the third leading IM product and the leader in the voice call client space.

There are several ways to start a Skype voice call. From within a Chat window, you can select the 🖳 icon, or from the User Information bar, you can select the 🖳 icon.

From the main Contacts window, you can select a user and then click the big 🖳 icon. This will probably be the manner in which you will call your contacts most of the time. Optionally you can right-click on a contact and select Call This Contact from the menu.

When we discussed setting the double-click option to **Start a Chat**, you might not have opted to do this. If you left the Skype default unchanged, you can and double-click the user's name in the Contact list to start a Skype call. You can even type the user's Skype name in the Skype command window (just above the call and hang-up icons) and then call by pressing the Enter key.

When you place the call, the screen will change to reflect the fact that a call is in progress.

Once your contact answers, you will see the following screen to indicate that the call has been connected and that a voice session has begun. Notice the Call Duration timer in the middle of the screen.

At this point, you can commence a high-quality voice call with your contact.

There are several things you can do during a voice call. You can mute your microphone, place the call on hold, and of course, disconnect the call. You can also start a chat if you wish, and this can be handy if you wish to send your contact a Web link, for example, or otherwise need to clarify something in writing.

Conference Calls

Skype allows not only single one-on-one voice calls but also multiuser or conference calls for up to five people. Our home broadband connections only support only so many calls before we run into delays and quality suffers. So, in very rough terms, if a typical Skype call takes 50Kb per voice call, then adding four more users might push the total up closer to 200Kb. You upload speed might be less than this; a general rule of thumb is not to send or receive more data than your slowest connection, to keep a consistent quality in your voice call. This is where knowing your Internet connection speed, as we discussed in Chapter 2, comes in handy and helps you understand how to best use your broadband connection and maintain good-quality calls. And the user who has the fastest broadband connection should generally act as the host in a conference call.

There are two ways to create conference calls. One is to add additional contacts to an existing call; the other is to create a conference call from scratch.

Add a Contact to an Existing Call

To add a user to a voice call that's already in progress, you need to switch to the **Contacts** tab in the main Skype window and select a user.

Then click the  icon to add the selected contact to the already existing voice call. You will then see the name of the user being called added to your original voice call.

The user at the bottom is you, and the users along the top are the people you called. Remember, if you disconnect from the call, all users will disconnect. The person who originated the voice call must stay connected to maintain the conference call, so be sure to plan who will initiate the call. You can, however, daisy-chain multiple users into a voice call—in other words, the person you call adds a friend, and then that friend adds another friend and so forth. Just about any combination will work, but when the person who initially called hangs up his or her call, all users that person called will be disconnected.

Managing Contacts

There are many ways to manage your Skype contacts. Two major ways are:

- Sending contacts
- Importing contacts

Sending Contacts

Sending one or more of your contacts to another Skype user is a handy option. For example, if you have two or more computers in your home, or if you have a laptop, and therefore might use separate accounts let people know when you are on the road, the ability to send contacts from one Skype user to another can be handy.

Also, if your family or friends have a contact you do not have, they can send you that contact's information. For example, one of your family members could send you another family member's contact information, saving you the trouble of searching for the user.

You can send one or more of your contacts to any user. From the Main menu, select **Tools** and then select **Send Contacts**, or select one of your contacts on the main Contacts window or from within a Skype call.

Use the right-click menu and select **Send Contacts**. You will then be presented the following screen to select to contacts you want to send.

Select the contacts you want to send, and click the **Add** button to add those people to the list. Then click the **Send** button to send your contacts.

Once the contacts are sent, you will see the following screen, indicating the status—telling you whether the sending of your contacts was successful or not.

Importing Contacts

Skype has a tool that will help you import contacts from several sources. To access the Import Contacts tool, select the **Tools** menu and select **Import Contacts**.

This will bring up the Import Contacts Wizard.

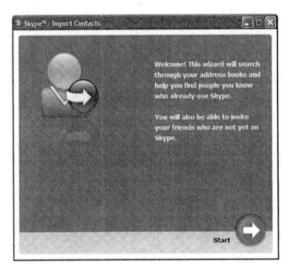

Select **Start** and the Import Contacts Wizard will list the address books that Skype can import from. In the following example we will look at our Microsoft Outlook contacts.

The Import Contacts Wizard will then advise you on how to allow access to your address book to import the contacts you want. On this screen you will see all the address books from which Skype supports importing contacts . Select the ones you want to attempt an import from and select **Next**.

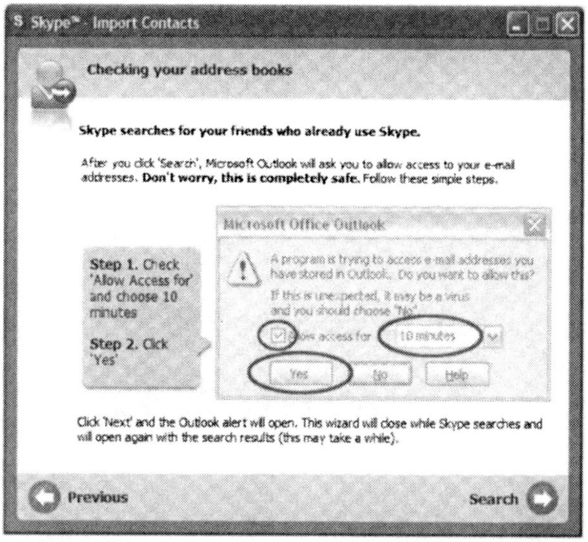

If Microsoft Outlook is not already open, you will be presented with the following screen.

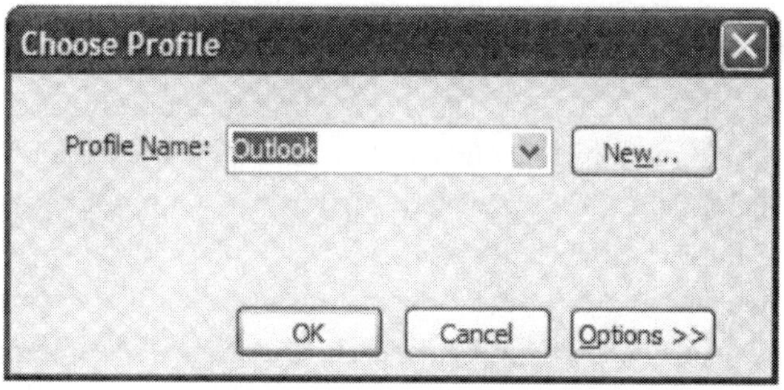

Go ahead and open Microsoft Outlook and allow Skype to access Microsoft Outlook for **10 minutes**, and click the **Yes** button.

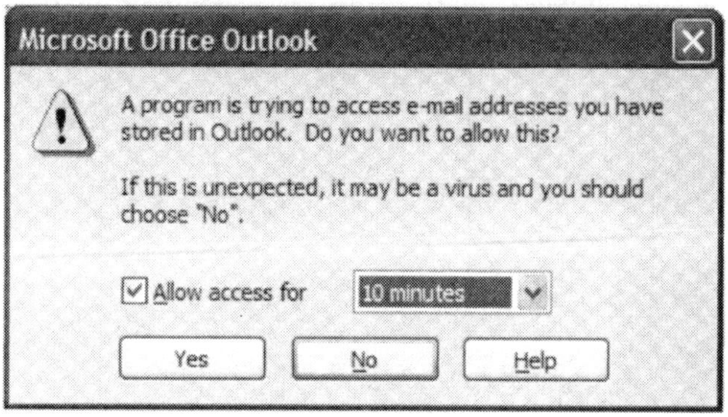

The Import Contact Wizard will search Microsoft Outlook for contacts that it recognizes have Skype usernames. The tool will look up the information in your address book and compare the information to the Skype user database. This process will take some time to complete as it compares users. Once it is complete, you will be presented with the following screen:

Of more than 200 entries in my Microsoft Outlook address book, Skype found only one user who matched Skype's database. This is because the address book I selected was my work e-mail address book, and most of us would not or should not sign up with Skype using our work e-mail address. You might have better luck with your personal e-mail address book for the Import Contacts Wizard.

It should be noted that the Import Contacts tool is not all that accurate at matching your address book contacts with Skype contacts. It is easier to invite users to join Skype through your e-mail signature, another IM client, or **Share Skype with a friend** from the Skype **Tools** menu.

You can, however, invite the users from your address book to join Skype when you select Next from the previous screen. You will be presented with the following screen:

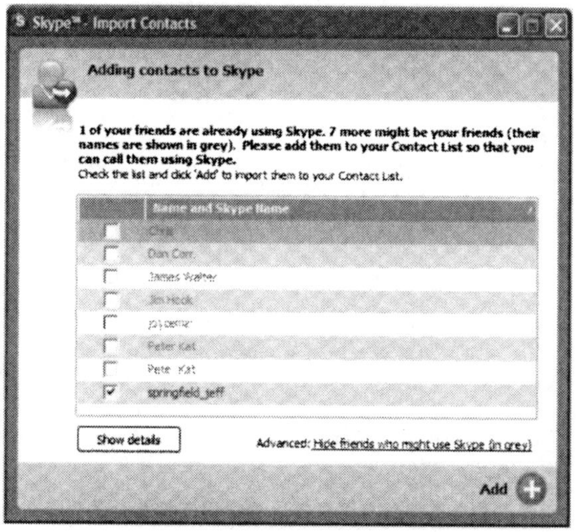

In this screen you can add users Skype thinks it has matched to your contact list. Once you add the users from this list, you will be presented with the following screen to invite users in your address book to use Skype via an e-mail invitation, similar to the "Share Skype with a friend" option under the Tools menu.

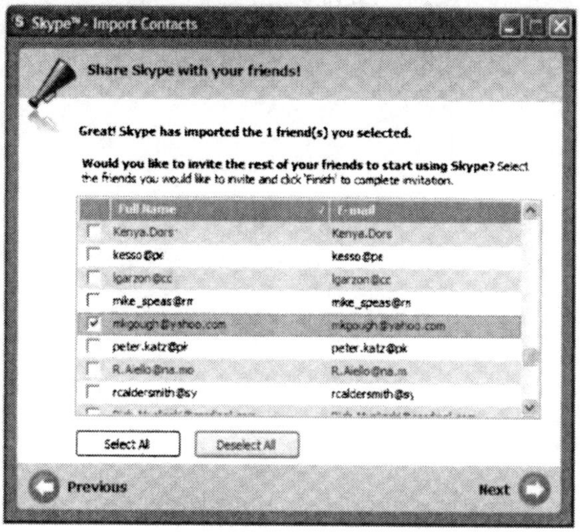

Select all the users you want to invite to use Skype, and select **Finish** to send them invitations to use Skype.

You will then be presented with the following screen to customize the message you want to send to the users invite.

Customize the message, making sure to add your name so people know who you are, and then press **Next**. You will be presented with the following screen that indicates that your Import Contacts Wizard is complete.

Select **Finish**. You are now done importing and inviting contacts, and you'll see the following screen:

Click the **Yes** button to close the window and return to the main Skype Contacts window.

Understanding the Basics... Importing Address Books

Unless you know that many of the users in your e-mail address book have Skype accounts, do not use the Import tool, because it is time consuming and not all that accurate.

Chapter 5

Common Uses for Skype

Solutions in this chapter:

- Talking with Family and Friends for Free or Low Cost

- Lower-Cost Long Distance

- Alternative to Plain Old Instant Messaging

- Running Multiple Instances of Skype on One System

- Making Video Calls with Skype

Talking with Family and Friends for Free or Low Cost

The obvious use for Skype is to call family, friends, and colleagues for free. Here are a few of the many uses for Skype voice calls:

- Family members living in different cities

- Family members overseas

- Family members abroad on active military duty

- Empty nesters when the children go away to school

- Family in elder care facilities or senior centers

- People who travel and phone home

We refer to a call between at least two computers as a "Skype-to-Skype" call. With the addition of SkypeOut, an advanced feature we cover in Chapter 6, you can make calls not only to computers but also to any landline telephone or cell phone.

To use Skype to reduce your telephone bill, you have to get your family, friends, and colleagues to start using Skype. You might want to point out to them how they too can lower their local and long distance telephone bills. An article I wrote in March 2005 on how Skype allowed me to lower my telephone bill by as much as 60 percent is posted on my Web site at http://skypetips.internetvisitation.org/articles/replacing_local_phone_service_with_Skype.html.

Many of us do not sit at our computer or want to sit at our computer to communicate with everyone we know using Skype, so you might be thinking, "Yeah, Skype is cool, but I am *not* going to go to the computer every time I want to make or receive a phone call." In Chapter 7, we will discuss how you can make Skype calls from any phone in your home and not have to be sitting in front of your computer.

Before you go out and cancel your local and or long distance telephone service, however, we need to mention three major limitations to Skype. We recommend Skype to *supplement*, not replace, your local telephone service, for these reasons:

- Skype cannot dial 911 emergency services.

- Skype cannot dial 411 services.

- Skype cannot do faxing.

You may be saying, "I don't really use these services, so can I use Skype to replace my local telephone provider?" We can't recommend that you do that, but theoretically the answer is yes, you can. But you then accept all risks relating to not being able to call 911 and have emergency services dispatched to your home.

e911 Service

e911 service is the same as the 911 service that you dial on a landline telephone, with the exception that it is dialed from a VoIP solution, thus the *e* prefix.

In the United States, Vonage was sued because its e911 service was not able to directly connect to the 911 emergency service and pass the location or physical address of the call onto the emergency services provider. This caused the United States to change the laws and force VoIP providers to comply with direct e911 services so that this would not happen to any new customers.

Skype does not have to comply with this law yet in the United States, since it is not considered a true telephone service provider. I'm not sure why they are not considered a provider, since you could theoretically use Skype for everything except the three types of call listed previously. I would venture to guess that in the future Skype will be required to comply with U.S. regulations on e911 services.

So we will leave it up to you to decide how to best mix Skype and your local phone service or that of other VoIP providers like Vonage, but one thing is for certain: Skype can easily replace your long distance telephone provider!

411 Information Directory

To a large extent, the availability of an assortment of inexpensive, often free, Web-based services has eliminated the need to use a regular phone to access traditional information service and 411 directory assistance, particularly in the home. However, when on the road, it is still sometimes necessary to solicit directory assistance. Here in Wisconsin, I can dial 1-262-555-1212 from my cell-phone or using SkypeOut to connect with the traditional phone company's information directory service. Even if you do not yet have a SkypeOut account, Skype may be used to call most tool free numbers, also entirely for free.

Skype and Faxes

One function that is widely requested is the ability to send faxes over a SkypeOut or SkypeIn call. Unfortunately, you cannot do this with the current Skype version. One day there will likely be service providers that will figure this out and offer something that works with Skype. But for now, if you need to send and receive faxes, you need to keep your local telephone service or sign up for one of the Web-based fax solutions such as eFax. You can also look at using another VoIP provider, such as Vonage, AT&T Call Vantage, or Time Warner Digital Phone, to send and receive faxes, since these providers can handle them.

Understanding the Basics... Skype Limitations

- Does not allow you to dial 911 services.
- Does not allow you to dial 411 services.
- Does not allow you to send faxes.

Lower-Cost Long Distance

SkypeOut is a service you can buy that allows you to use your computer to call anyone who has a regular telephone or cell phone at rates that may be less expensive than you are paying now. This cost savings is especially true for local and long distance calls you make from your home telephone. We examine the details of the SkypeOut service in Chapter 6.

Cell Phones

Cell phones have plans that provide you unlimited calling for some period of minutes. Many come with free long distance calling as a part of the calling plan, so Skype might not be cheaper than your cell phone service in many cases. Since cell phones have limited minutes, though, SkypeOut could be cheaper in the long run based on the cell phone minutes you use if they exceed your cell phone calling plan.

SkypeOut Primer

After registering for SkypeOut and then purchasing credits (in Euros, U.S. Dollars, British Pounds, or Japanese Yen) you have the ability to make calls from your computer to landline and mobile telephones. Think of SkypeOut as being identical to buying a telephone calling card, but better. So far we have not discussed the details of how to make Skype calls from anywhere other than your computer, but know you can if you get the right hardware add-on for Skype. If you could call Skype users for free and make normal telephone calls to any telephone number using SkypeOut, all from your existing telephone, you would be very interested, would you not?

SkypeOut gives you the ability to dial any phone number from the Skype client at your computer. All we need to do now is get Skype to work without you having to sit at your computer but instead on the telephones you already have in your home, and do it easily. Then it would be very practical to use Skype to lower your long distance calling charges and make long distance calls similarly to the way you do now. More on how we will accomplish this task in Chapter 7.

Alternative to Plain Old Instant Messaging

We all have heard of and probably used one of the many IM applications like these (data marked with an asterisk is based on information from Lehman Brothers, comScore Media Metrix):

- **MSN Messenger** 178.2 million users worldwide*

- **Yahoo! Instant Messenger** 78.8 million users worldwide*

- **AOL Instant Messenger** 30 million users worldwide*

- **ICQ** 29.2 million users worldwide*

- **iChat** Only for Apple Mac users; it is compatible with AIM

- **GAIM for Linux**

- **IRC** Internet Relay Chat

- **Trillian** Supports ICQ, IRC, AIM, Yahoo! and MSN chats

- **GoogleTalk** The newest player

- **Skype** 50 million worldwide users as of August 2005; growing by 150,000 users daily

Skype does almost everything these other solutions do as far as instant messaging, but as we stated in the beginning, Skype has voice capability, which takes IM to another level. Skype is clearly the fastest-growing IM application and soon will be in third place in terms of users worldwide, behind Yahoo! Instant Messaging, probably by the end of 2005. With the additions coming to Skype for Video, for example, Skype will soon rival Microsoft MSN Messenger in number of users globally.

You do not have to run just one IM application, of course. Many of us have AIM, MSN, Yahoo! and Skype all running so that we are as connected as we can be, since everyone uses something different and you want to be able to chat with all your contacts on whatever application they have. The nice thing is that all these IM solutions play well with one another and do not cause any issues when running at the same time, so go ahead and fill up your taskbar or dashboard with IM icons.

As a matter of fact, I use Skype with MSN Messenger at the same time with my daughter and family, but more on why I do this in the section titled "Making Video Calls with Skype" in Chapter 9.

Running Multiple Instances of Skype on One System

Skype tends to be a one-user-per-computer type of solution. Many people have one computer in our home but more than one Skype user in our home, so how do you run Skype so two or more users can use the same computer and receive chat or, more important, voice calls?

Windows XP is what we recommend as the optimal operating system. With Windows XP comes an option to open an application and run that application as a different user from the one who is currently logged on. This allows you to have two instances of Skype running at the same time, in effect having two users able to accept Skype calls on the same computer.

Unless you set up different sound devices, however, you will be able to accept or make only one Skype call at a time. We discuss more on setting up multiple sound devices in Chapter 7.

Tweaking the Technology...
Running Multiple Instances of Skype on One System

It is important to note that this is considered a hack and is not supported by Skype.

Make Sure You Have Multiple Users

The first order of business is to make sure you have more than one user on your computer or you add one. To check this for Windows, open **Control Panel** and select the **User Accounts** icon. Here is the Control Panel Category view:

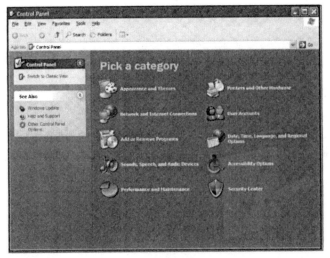

Here is the Control Panel Classic view:

In the default Category view for Windows XP, select **User Accounts** and you will be presented with the following screen:

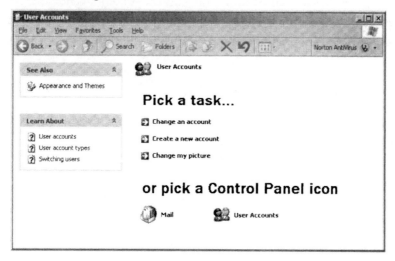

Select **User Accounts** at the bottom to see a list of users that exist on your computer.

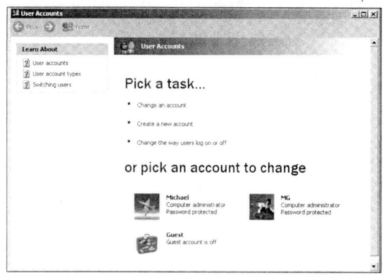

Next, look to see that you have more than one user on the system. Note that you cannot consider Guest an account you can use. The Guest account should be disabled at all times. In the following example we have two users, Michael and MG. Michael is my primary account, so I'll use MG as the account with which to launch the second instance of Skype.

Adding Another Windows User

If you need to add another user to try the multiple instances of Skype, select the **Create a new account** option in the User Accounts screen:

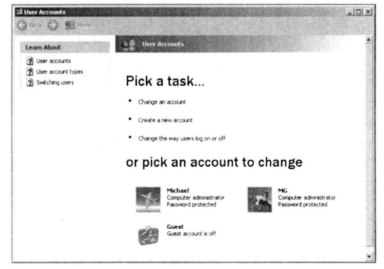

You will be presented with the following screen to add a username:

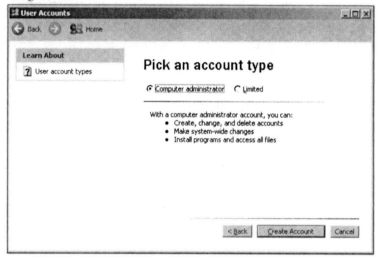

Type the name **Skype user** in the text box and select **Next**. You will then be presented with the following screen:

If you are going to use multiple users, we suggest setting up the user as a computer administrator. Then select the **Create Account** button.

You will now see that you added the user we called "Skype user" to your list of users.

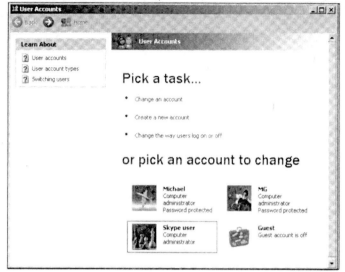

Before you go any further, you should always set a password for any account that is an administrator to protect it from being easily misused. Select the new user you created and you will be presented with the next screen:

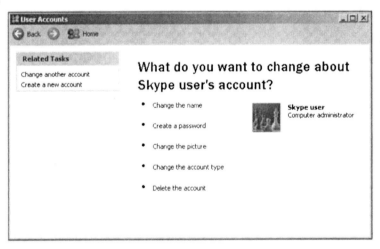

In this window you can create a password or, once a password is assigned, change the password. You can also change the account type to a nonadministrator after you finish testing your multiuser Skype configuration, to better restrict the account from misuse.

Launching Skype with *Run As*

You need to launch the second instance of Skype by finding Skype in your Program menu, right-clicking on the **Skype** menu icon, and selecting **Run As**.

You may also do this from your Skype desktop icon:

Once you select [Open / Run as...], you will then be presented the following screen:

You need to select 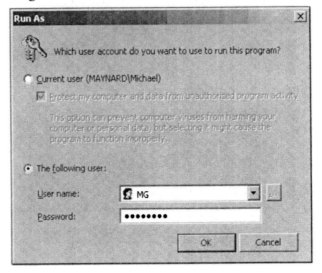 to select a different user than the one who is already logged on to Windows. You will be presented the following screen once you've selected **The following user**:

Enter your second username. In this example it is MG. Then select **OK** to continue. Skype will launch and provide you the following screen:

Enter your second username and password and click **Next** to continue. You will then have two instances of Skype running at the same time as two different users ready to answer or make Skype calls.

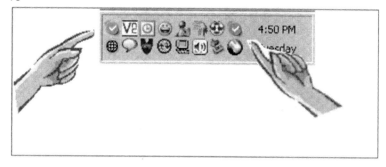

So What Can I Do with Two Instances of Skype?

For starters, for each instance of Skype you can have different settings. The most important of these settings is the Sound Devices. You can set up Skype#1 to use your telephone and Skype#2 to use your computer sound card. This way, each user can make and receive Skype calls and not interrupt the other user. Here, Skype#1 has Sound Devices using the Actiontec Internet Phone Wizard:

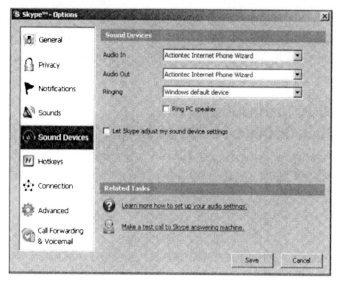

Whereas here, Skype#2 has Sound Devices using the Creative Sound Card:

How we have multiple devices is covered more in Chapter 7, but for now accept that it is possible and can work for you if you need or want to have multiple instances of Skype running at the same time.

A word of warning: Running multiple instances of Skype will increase the demand on your computer and of course your broadband connection and may affect performance and the quality of the Skype call. Do not expect it to work perfectly all the time. Remember, this is still considered a hack.

Tweaking the Technology...
Running Multiple Instances of Skype on One System

Running multiple instances of Skype will put more demand on your computer and broadband connection and may affect performance and quality of the Skype calls.

Of course you can also send files and do chat, but since two parties are using one computer, this may be cumbersome for the users trying to share a computer.

Practical Application of Running Multiple Instances of Skype

So what practical reasons would we have for running multiple instances of Skype? For starters, if you have children, they most likely monopolize your home computer. By running multiple instances of Skype, you can still make and receive voice calls using your cordless telephone connected to a Gateway device, as I do, to make and receive Skype, SkypeOut, and SkypeIn calls anywhere you have a cordless phone extension. We go into more detail on how to use gateways in Chapter 7.

Do not run multiple instances of Skype with the same Skype user account. Be sure to use different Skype account names for this feature to work effectively.

Internet Speed Tests

You can go one of several Web sites to run a speed test to find out your Internet speed. Be sure to select a site that will provide you both the upload and download speeds. There are several sites worldwide to select from, including www.dslreports.com/stest and www.Internetfrog.com.

Part II: Taking Skype to the Next Level

Chapter 6

Advanced Features of Skype

Solutions in this chapter:

- Advanced Settings
- Advanced Architecture
- Advanced Peer-to-Peer Technology
- SkypeOut
- SkypeIn
- Other Advanced Features

Advanced Settings

As you have learned in the previous chapters of this book, Skype has a number of settings and configurations that affect its functionality and usefulness for your needs. In the sections that follow, we look at a number of advanced settings that you can adjust in Skype that affect the program's startup, how calls are processed, and the way chats appear and function, as well as other settings that can impact the way you and your computer work with Skype. In addition, we discuss a number of command options that you can manually type and add to shortcuts, giving you more power in terms of the way you work with Skype. We cover the following topics in this section:

- Advanced profile settings

- Configuring sound alerts

- Sound devices

- Connection settings

- Advanced settings

- Command-line options

Advanced Profile Settings

Skype allows you to search for and talk with people you know or those you might like to meet. Skype also provides a way to share information about yourself online. People who use Skype can search for others who meet certain criteria, such as name, gender, age, language, and location that they provide in My Profile. My Profile is a dialog box that allows you to enter information about yourself. As we will see, some of this information is available to anyone who decides to search for and/or view your profile; other information is available to only Skype users that you have authorized to view your online status.

To view your Skype profile, click the **File** menu in Skype and then click the **My Profile** menu item, or click the **Tools** menu and then click **Options**, and then on the **General** settings under Related Tasks, choose **Edit My Skype Profile**. A dialog box similar to the following screen will appear. When opening this for the first time, you might be surprised to find that some of the information is already filled out. The details provided in these fields are obtained from information you provided when you set up your Skype account, but you can modify or delete any data appearing in these fields at any time.

The My Profile dialog box provides different levels of access to information that others can view. As shown in the previous figure, there are three categories, which we discuss in the sections that follow:

- Details that all Skype users will see
- Details that only can be viewed by Skype users that you have authorized to see your online status
- Private details

Details That All Skype Users Will See

Details that all Skype users will see contains information that anyone using Skype can view. Anyone talking or chatting with you in Skype can view the information by right-clicking your avatar and choosing **View Profile** from the menu that appears. Also, anyone searching Skype for people to chat with or call can view this information, partially through their search results or by right-clicking your name in the search results and choosing **View Profile** from the menu that appears.

Personalizing Skype

As we discussed earlier in this chapter, Skype provides the ability to disclose information about yourself to others on the Internet, allowing others to discover who you are (or claim to be) as a person. This makes Skype a great method for meeting new people. You can view the interests, age, location, gender, and other facts of another person before starting a conversation. This allows you to find people who share common interests or hobbies that you share or want to discuss.

My Profile is separated into three categories to disclose different areas of information to everyone or only a select few on the Internet. These categories are:

- **Details that all Skype users will see** This option means that everyone on the Internet can view this section's information using Skype.

- **Details that will be seen only Skype users that I have authorized to view my online status.** This option includes a picture you can set.

- **Private details** Email addresses are never viewable, but they can be used to find you if the user searching for you knows the complete email address. The e-mail addresses are kept private and unavailable for anyone to view using Skype.

Details that all Skype users will see contains information that is revealed to anyone searching for other Skype users. For example, while searching for user information, you could right-click a name in the search results, select **View Profile** from the menu that appears, and see profile information for that user.

You can and will want to manipulate the information that you place inside your profile to share some additional information about yourself, more than the field name indicates. For example, Michael Gough has modified his Full Name field to **Michael Gough | SkypeTips.com,** and this is how all his contacts or anyone who searches for him will see him. In addition, he advertises that he has a webcam and uses Video4IM, by placing **webcam & Video4IM** in the City field so that users who select his name will see more information than the field's name leads you to believe. Later we'll discuss the reason that Michael does not provide the name of the city he lives in. The following screen is an example of Michael's contact information.

All Michael wants anyone to know is that he is in Wisconsin, so the City field can be used for other practical information that other Skype contacts can see. Similarly, you will want to decide what normal information you want to include in your profile and what additional information you can manipulate into the available fields. For example, if you wanted everyone in your company using Skype to advertise your company name, you could add the company name to the Full Name field, such as **Joe Skyper | My Company**.

This would allow people to know that this is a work account and not a personal account. Feel free to use the fields, not just the way they are labeled, but also for what you want or need your profile to show.

Understanding the Basics... Update Your Full Name in Your Profile to Show More about You

You can add more than your name to your Full Name profile entry. Add your company name, Web site URL, or any other unique piece of information for your contacts to see.

Providing Information Without Compromising Personal Privacy

Because Skype allows you to make personal information about yourself available to others on the Internet, you should be careful how much you reveal about yourself. Of the three sections in My Profile, the **Details that all Skype users will see** is the one you should be most concerned about because anyone can view this information. You should carefully consider the information you include in your profile.

Your profile includes fields that allow you to enter information that could be used for identity theft, for example. If you include your full name, birth date, gender, location, and other information of a personal nature, unscrupulous people viewing the information could utilize this data to gain further information about you and possibly use it for illegal activity. Even worse, a predator, stalker, or other dangerous persons could view the information and put you in physical or emotional jeopardy. For example, since areas to advertise your phone numbers are available to view in Skype, a person could begin harassing you by calling the work, home, or mobile phone number that you made available.

A Word about Privacy

Whenever you use the Internet, you should always be concerned what information you post or provide publicly, such as a profile for any IM client—and that includes Skype. Think of it this way: Share as little information as you need or want based on your desired privacy state. In the Skype profile example shown several pages ago, the last name is not specified. I prefer to show it in my profile because I want to be sought out for my efforts with Skype and video calls. I also do not list the city I live in—only the state and country. I would strongly recommend that you never list any personal information about your children, and if your children are using any IM clients, check their profiles to be sure that they do *not* share any personal information about themselves. This is your responsibility as a parent.

If you represent a company, you will also want to limit the information that is shared about your employees and your company. The simplest rule to follow when entering information in your profile is: Include only the absolute minimum information about yourself, and avoid any information that allows anyone to find exactly where you live.

For example, you know my Web site, you know my country, and you know I live in Wisconsin, but that is all I would ever share in my profile except my custom information, such as that I have a webcam and use Video4IM, which appears in my City field.

Avoid listing the following information in your profile as a general rule unless you are absolutely sure you want people to know and find this information:

- Your home address

- Any phone numbers

- City

- Birth date

- The address of where you work

- Private information such as driver's license data, Social Security number, or identity card info

If you want to make a phone number available for others to call, you should consider getting a SkypeIn number. This allows people to call a phone number that will send calls to the Skype program on your computer. If you want to take the calls on your home, work, or mobile phone, the SkypeIn number is still an option. Since calls to a SkypeIn number can be forwarded to another phone number (such as your landline or mobile phone), people calling this number would be unaware of where the call is actually connecting.

In terms of other information, you can be nonspecific or alter the information slightly so it is not entirely correct. The Gender drop-down list, for example, allows you to enter your gender as male, female, or blank. By leaving it blank, you are not being specific about whether you are male or female, which can reduce the number of sex chat requests you receive or messages from people who are looking to talk to a specific gender. As we mentioned earlier, other fields can be modified, allowing you to enter information that is customized, incomplete, or nonspecific. For example, the Birthdate drop-down lists allow you to enter the day, month, and year of your birth, which advertises your birth date and age to others. If you do not want this information made available, simply do not fill out the date information, or enter an incorrect month or day so that people viewing the information would then see your correct age but still have inaccurate data on you.

You should also avoid giving directions to where your personal information is available. The profile allows you to enter a homepage, which people can then visit. In visiting your homepage, a person might be able to find your full name, work information, or other details that you specifically left out of your Skype profile for privacy reasons. If this is the case, you might want to enter the URL of a Web site that does not belong to you but that reflects your interests. For example, if you enjoy reading books, you might enter the Web site of your favorite author or publishing company. In doing so, you provide a possible topic for chat without providing details about you or your family. The other alternative, of course, is to simply leave the field blank if you do not have a Web site or do not want to provide that information to strangers.

Other Ways Your Profile Allows People to Know You

Since the fields in your profile can be modified to include whatever information you want, you can provide tidbits about yourself that can inspire conversation with others. The Full Name field does not necessarily need to contain your first and last name, so you can modify this field to include other data. You could enter such things as your first name and a brief message about your interests or some alias that is more revealing about your personality. For example, entering **Michael—avid comic book collector** says much more about a person than merely his name and allows people to find him if they search for a particular hobby or shared interest.

Another area of the profile that allows you to share information about yourself is the About Me field. Here you can provide a list of topics you would like people to know about and possibly chat about some of the things you are interested in—things you do not want to talk about online, a joke you find funny, or anything else you would like to say to others.

You can enter whatever you like in this field, but you should avoid entering detailed personal information, as we have already mentioned.

My Profile Fields

- **Full Name** Enter your name as anyone will see it. This is the short line that shows up in Skype—for example, Michael Gough | www.SkypeTips.com.

- **Gender** You can enter your gender to indicate male or female, or leave it blank (recommended).

- **Birthdate** You can enter your birth date, but unless you are absolutely sure you want to give that information out, avoid filling in this field, or provide false data that still gives your age.

- **Country/Region** This is fairly harmless information that will help others generally locate you and understand what part of the world and time zone you are in.

- **State/Province** Fill in this field to let people know roughly where you live and what time zone you are in.

- **City** Recommend staying away from entering information in this field unless you are absolutely sure that you want or need to post this information. Use this field to enter something about yourself—for example, webcam & Video4IM, or a hobby or interest.

- **Language** This will help people understand what language they need to speak to be able to communicate with you.

- **Home Phone** Avoid entering this information unless you are absolutely sure that you want to share it with total strangers. Do you have a listed phone number? We highly recommend that you avoid this field if you have children and to check periodically that this field is left blank.

- **Office Phone** Avoid entering this information unless you are absolutely sure that you want to share it with total strangers.

- **Mobile Phone** Avoid entering this information unless you are absolutely sure you want to share it with total strangers.

- **Homepage** Enter a Web site URL that you want to share with others. Do not post Web sites that contain personal information about yourself or your family.

About Me Field

The About Me field is an area where you can type information about yourself that does not necessarily apply to any of the other fields. About Me can be used to offer other Skype users insight into your hobbies, interests, what you do for a living, a personal description, or other facts that can be used to inspire conversation. In the case of businesses that use Skype, this field can identify the account as being for a particular use, such as providing help desk or sales support. You can even use it to set limitations on conversation, such as indicating that sex chats are not welcome. The information you provide here is optional but useful in providing information to others who want to chat or call. Avoid placing any personal information in this field.

Private Details

The Private Details section provides an Email field where you can enter an e-mail address. This is not available to view by anyone who uses View Profile, but it allows people who know your e-mail address to search for you in Skype. When you open My Profile for the first time, the Email field will display the e-mail address you provided when you set up your account (assuming that you specified one). If you change Internet providers and get a new e-mail account or decide to set up a free e-mail account on Google, MSN, or Yahoo! for use with Skype, you can change the value of the Email field at any time or enter multiple e-mail addresses. You can even delete the e-mail address in this field if you do not want to provide any e-mail address that people can use to search for you. Skype does not advertise the e-mail addresses, so have little fear of these being misused or added to a spam list.

Details That Only Your Contacts Will See

This section also provides a way to reveal more about yourself to others by including a picture of yourself or an avatar, as it is called, that you would like to represent you. Using this section, you can specify a picture that can only be viewed by users that you have authorized to see your online status. Clicking the **Change...** button will cause a dialog box to appear that allows you to modify the picture. Here you can select another picture from a list, and that picture is displayed when people view your profile information. If there is no picture in the list that you like, you can click the **Get New Pictures** button to open your Web browser and load the http://personal.skype.com Web site, where other pictures are available to download. If you already have a picture, such as a photo of yourself that is small and that you would like to use, click the **Browse...** button to open a dialog box use it to find the picture file. A copy will be placed in the Documents and Settings*local computer username*\\My Documents\\My Skype Pictures folder. You might have to resize a picture you select so that it appears correctly. Once you have selected the picture on your hard disk that you would like to use, click **Open** to load the picture into your profile. If you decide not to use the picture later, you can click the **Reset to Default** button to remove the picture from your profile and use the basic icon that was initially there.

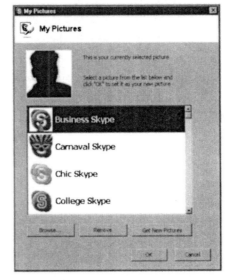

Configuring Sound Alerts

Sound alerts are audible indicators of an event that has occurred. A sound can be played in Skype to indicate that you are calling someone, someone is calling you, or other events. As we will see in this section, these sounds can be turned off or changed at any time.

The various sound alerts in Skype are controlled using the Options dialog box. You can open Skype's Options by clicking the **Tools** menu and then clicking the **Options** menu item. Once the menu is opened, clicking the **Sounds** icon in the left side of the dialog box will display a screen similar to that shown in the following picture.

Buttons

The Sounds screen in Skype's Options contains a listing of all the events that you can associate with sounds. Beside each of the events are three controls that you can use to listen to and change the various sound files associated with those events.

As shown by the ⬤ icon, this button is used to play the sound file associated with a particular event. When you click this control, the sound will play through whatever sound device you configured your computer to use for sound playback.

As shown by the 🔺 icon, this button is used to select a new sound for an event. If you do not like the default sound associated with an event, you can click this button and load a new file.

When you click the 🔺 button, Skype opens the My Sounds dialog box, which is shown in the following figure. The top part of the dialog box displays the event that the sound is associated with. Below this is a listing of various sounds that have previously been used or reviewed. When you click any of the entries in this list, the sound file will play. If you would like to use this new sound for the event, you can click **OK** to associate it with the event, or click **Cancel** to keep the current sound.

The **Browse...** button on the bottom of the dialog box is used to open another dialog box titled Choose Your Sound, which you can navigate your hard drive to select existing sound files on your computer. Once you select a file in the Choose Your Sound dialog box and click **OK**, the file is loaded into the My Sounds list of sounds. In Windows, this file is also copied to the Documents and Settings*local computer username*\\My Documents\\My Skype Content folder.

Because you may load a file into My Sounds and later decide you do not want to use it, you can use the Remove button to delete a file from your listing. The file is also deleted from the Documents and Settings*local computer username*\\My Documents\\My Skype Content folder on your hard drive. On the chance that you might want to use the file again in the future, you should copy the file from this folder to another location before clicking the **Remove** button and then clicking **Yes** on the confirmation message box that appears.

Get New Sounds is another button on the My Sounds dialog box; click **Get New Sounds** and it will open your Web browser and take you to the Skype store. On this Web site, you can acquire new sound files to use with your Skype program.

The button restores the default sound. If you change your mind about the sound file you associated with a particular event, you can click the button and Skype will associate the event with the original sound file that was used when you first installed Skype.

Play Sounds for ...

There are nine different events that sounds can be associated with in Skype. Each of these events has a check box beside it, which can be unchecked to mute the sound. If you do not want any sounds associated with events, you can click the **Mute All Sounds** button to uncheck all the check boxes. To effectively decide which of these events should be muted, however, you need to know under what circumstances the sound will play.

Connecting Call

The **connecting call** check box is used to indicate whether a sound is played when you first begin a call and Skype is attempting to connect to the other party. To compare this to a conventional phone, this is the phase of the call when you are dialing the number. As Skype connects to the other party, additional sounds may be played.

Ringtone

When someone calls you, the **ringtone** sound is played as an audible alert that someone is trying to contact you.

Dial Tone

Once a connection is made in Skype, there is a period of time during which you will need to wait for the other party to answer the call. During this time, the **dial tone** sound is played.

Busy Signal

If the person is unavailable, perhaps talking with someone else using Skype, the **busy signal** sound is played. This lets you know that the person is using Skype but unavailable at the moment.

Call on Hold

If you place a **call on hold** in Skype, the sound file associated with this event will play. When a call is placed on hold in Skype, the connection between you and the other person still exists so that you do not need to call the person, or vice versa. Skype simply pauses the call so that the other party cannot hear, just as with the Hold feature in a regular telephone call.

Resuming Call

The **resuming call** sound is played when you take a person off hold in Skype so that the call is resumed and you can now hear one another again.

Hang Up

The **hang up** sound is played when a call is terminated. When you click the red **cancel call** button during a call, the connection with the other person is ended, and this sound is played.

Incoming Chat

When someone requests a chat with you, the **incoming chat** sound is played to indicate the request. This allows you to know when someone wants to chat with you, without relying on the visual alerts or popup chat window that is also available in Skype.

Contact Online

When the **contact online** check box is checked, a sound is played when someone in your Contacts list starts Skype and goes online. By default this sound is turned off, but it can be turned on at any time. However, because you might have a number of contacts going on and offline while you are using Skype, this sound can become annoying if you have numerous contacts in your Contacts list.

Sound Devices

Because Skype is used to transmit and receive voice over IP, it follows that configuring sound devices is an important part of using Skype. Without proper configuration, you might not be able to hear or talk with others. There are configuration options in the Sound Devices screen of the Options dialog box, but you can also make most of the changes for these devices through your operating system.

Skype Sound Device Options

You can set Skype's sound devices through the Options dialog box, which is accessed by clicking the **Tools** menu and then clicking the **Options** menu item. As shown in the following figure, the left side of the dialog box is used to navigate between the various option areas. Clicking **Sound Devices** displays settings for configuring the devices to use with Skype or using the default ones configured for the operating system.

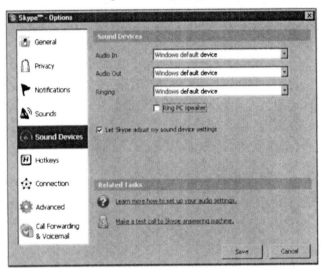

The Sound Devices section provides three drop-down lists that store the same values. Each list contains the names of sound devices installed on your computer and the option to use the default sound device that you set up previously on the operating system. To use the device that was configured earlier through the operating system, select the **Windows default device** option; otherwise, select the name of a specific device you want to use. The three drop-down lists control the following types of sound devices:

■ **Audio In** controls the microphone or other device that you will use when speaking or recording sound in Skype.

- **Audio Out** controls the sound card or other device you will use for playing sound over speakers or a headset.

- **Ringing** controls the device that will be used to play a ring or other sound when a call comes in through Skype.

Below these drop-down lists is a check box to **Ring PC speaker**. When this check box is checked, it provides the alternative to have the ring sound of an incoming call played through the internal speaker of your computer. This could be handy to have selected if you have a headset connected to your audio card most of the time, if your speakers happen to be muted or if the volume is turned down.

The final option on this screen is to **Let Skype adjust my sound device settings**. If you want Skype to control the settings of sound devices, check this check box. If you experience problems afterward and/or would like to control your own sound device settings through the operating system, uncheck this box.

Understanding the Basics...
Let Skype Adjust My Sound Device Settings

Most users should be able to set this check box and let Skype adjust the sound device settings. If you experience low volume on either your speakers or microphone, try deselecting this option.

If You Have Two Sound Devices

As we discuss in Chapter 8, if you add a Skype telephone adapter, Skype telephone gateway, or USB phone, you will see these devices show up as additional sound devices. If you want to switch between the cordless phone attached to a Skype gateway and your sound card to do a video call, for example, you would switch between the two audio devices in the Skype's Sound Devices tab. Some Skype gateways, such as the VoSky Internet Phone Wizard, automatically switch to the correct sound device when you pick up the telephone to make or answer a Skype call.

Understanding the Basics... Changing Sound Devices

If you have multiple sound devices, such as a sound card and a device like the VoSky IPW, you would switch between the two using the Sound Devices option boxes. If you want to make a video call at your computer and want to use your sound card, for example, you can switch it from the Actiontec Internet Phone Wizard to your sound card.

Making a Test Call to Ensure Your Settings Are Correct

After you have made any changes to the sound devices on your system, you should make a test call to ensure that everything is working correctly. Skype provides an automated user called Skype Test Call (or echo123) that you can call any time. Refer to Chapter 3, "Making a Test Call," for more information.

Connection Parameters

To chat and call other people using Skype, you need to have an Internet connection. Many people simply install Skype on a computer with an existing Internet connection and set up their account, but others find they get errors connecting to the Internet and need to perform additional steps. This is especially the case in businesses where a proxy or firewall is used. Home users will rarely if ever have to worry about these settings. For more on proxy servers and firewalls, please read Chapter 13.

Understanding the Basics...
Connection Parameters for Home Users

Home users should not have to worry about the Connection Parameters setting. If you have some type of custom configuration, you will know when to apply these advanced settings.

Skype Connection Settings

Internet Options allow you to configure proxy server settings for programs connecting to the Internet, but these options are available only on Windows machines. Because Skype can be run on other operating systems, Skype also has configuration settings that can be used to control connections that use proxy servers such as many large companies have. Skype's Connection options can be set by using the Options dialog box, which is accessed by clicking the **Tools** menu and then clicking the **Options** menu item. As shown in the following picture, clicking **Connections** displays the proxy settings. Refer to Chapter 13 for more on this topic.

The top section on the Connection screen is for your local computer, on which Skype is being used. It allows you to control the ports that Skype uses for incoming connections from people who are calling or want to chat. The first field is **Use port ... for incoming connections**. In this field, you can enter the port number that will be used to listen for incoming connections to your computer. Below this is a check box that provides additional ports that Skype can use to function if a local firewall is blocking the port you specified. When this check box is selected, ports 80 and 443 can also be used to listen for incoming connections, if the port you specified fails to work for some reason. Because port 80 is generally used for HTTP and 443 is commonly used for HTTPS, if you experience problems with software that relies on ports 80 and/or 443, make sure that this check box is unchecked. More on this option when using firewalls or complex networks is covered in Chapter 13.

Understanding the Basics...
Connection Settings for Home Users

Home users should not have to adjust this setting, but making it 443 and choosing to use both port 80 and 443 are recommended, as indicated below.

The second section on the Connection screen is where you enter information that Skype will use to connect to a proxy server. Home users will rarely if ever need to worry about this setting. The drop-down list provides three options:

- Automatic Proxy Detection

- HTTPS

- SOCKS5

As we discussed earlier in this chapter, Automatic Proxy Detection is used to automatically find and set the IP address and port of a proxy server that is located on your internal network. The configuration information that is provided by the proxy server is used to configure your machine, thereby eliminating the need for you to manually enter any settings. Because no additional input is needed once you select this option, the other fields in this section are disabled when Automatic Proxy Detection is selected.

The other two options in the drop-down list require manual configuration. When either HTTPS or SOCKS5 is selected, you must identify which server is the network's proxy server and the port it uses. The Host field is used to enter the proxy server's name or IP address; the Port field identifies the port that the proxy server listens to for making connections. For connections using HTTPS, the default port number is 443, whereas SOCKS5 usually uses 1080 as the default port.

The second option in the drop-down list is HTTPS, which is a secure version of the Hypertext Transfer Protocol. Proxy servers that use HTTPS provide additional security because authentication is required and data can be encrypted. When data is passed between your machine and the proxy server, HTTPS allows it to be encrypted using the Secure Sockets Layer (SSL) or Transport Layer Security (TLS), which prevents others from eavesdropping on any data sent between the two machines.

The third option in the drop-down list is SOCKS5, a version 5 of the SOCKS protocol, which is an abbreviation of the word *sockets*. Proxy servers use SOCKS to control access to servers beyond the barrier a firewall or proxy server provides. With SOCKS, an extra layer of security is added because the SOCKS proxy server requires authentication before serving clients and passing any requests on to servers on the Internet or outside the network.

When checked, the **Enable proxy authentication** check box, below the drop-down list and its corresponding fields, enables the Username and Password fields below it. Proxy authentication is used to determine who is using a particular program so that they can be authenticated and have the necessary credentials to use a program or access resources through the proxy server. If proxy authentication has to be set up on the server, the username and password that you provide identify you as the person using Skype so that you can be authenticated on the server. If additional privileges have been provided for your user account on the proxy server (such as the necessary access needed to use Skype through the proxy server), providing the username and password may be necessary to enable Skype to function properly.

Once you have made the changes you want to the Connections options, you can then save them by clicking the **Save** button. No changes are applied until you have saved them. If you are unsure about the changes you made and you want to disregard them, simply click the **Cancel** button. More on the use of firewalls and proxy servers are discussed in Chapter 13.

Skype's Advanced Options Dialog Box

Advanced options in Skype are set using the Options dialog box. In Skype, click the **Tools** menu and then click the **Options** menu item to launch a dialog box. The left side of the dialog box has a number of option areas that can be selected, bringing up individual tabs or options in the dialog. Clicking the one labeled **Advanced** will show the advanced settings that are available to you.

We discussed some of the Advanced options in Chapter 3, and we review and expand on some of these features in this chapter. It is important that you note that any settings you change will not be set until you save them. The Save button on the bottom of the dialog box saves the settings and closes Options. The Cancel button simply closes the dialog box without saving any of your changes.

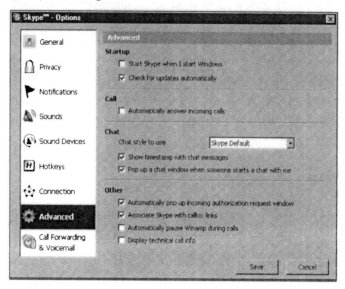

Startup Options

The Startup section of the Advanced options allows you to control how Skype starts and the actions it will take on startup. When the **Start Skype when I start Windows** check box is checked, Skype starts when Windows starts up. If this box is unchecked, you need to start Skype by either clicking the desktop icon created at installation or from the Windows Start menu. There is a lot more to this issue than can be covered in the available space, so it is better left out altogether.

If the **Check for updates automatically** check box is checked, Skype will also connect over the Internet and determine whether a newer version of the software is available, thereby saving you the need to periodically check Skype's Web site to see if you are using an old version and whether a significant update has been released. You could also check for updates manually by clicking the **Help** menu in Skype and then choosing the **Check for Update** menu item. You are then taken to Skype's website where you are informed of the latest version and given an opportunity to download it directly. Occasionally upgrades are forced upon the user at login time regardless of this setting, and there is no choice but to upgrade if you wish to continue using Skype.

Call Option

The Call section of the Advanced options has only a single feature that can be set. When the **Automatically answer incoming calls** check box is checked, the application will answer any incoming phone calls it receives, without intervention from you. If this option is unchecked, you will need to listen for the sound of a telephone ringing and visually monitor the icon in your computer's system tray, which will flash and temporarily show a message saying that someone is attempting to call you. When a call comes in and automatic answering is not enabled, you will need to go the **Call List** tab in Skype and select whether to answer or reject the call. We do not recommend setting this to auto-answer unless you are absolutely certain this is the right setting for you, since you will not always be at your computer.

Chat Options

The Chat section of the Advanced options allows you to control the appearance and functionality of the interface used for chatting with others and determines what will happen when someone initiates a chat with you. The **Chat style to use** drop-down list configures Skype to use one of two designs for the way text messages are formatted in a chat session. We covered samples of each style in Chapter 3:

- Skype default
- IRC-like style

The Skype Default chat style displays the person's name in a rounded box. The **Show timestamp with chat messages** check box configures whether Skype includes the time that a message was received with each message. When this option is checked, the time of a received message appears beside that message in the chat and is added to the chat history. This allows you to monitor when each message was received and maintain a record of how long you chatted with a particular person. We recommend that you leave this setting enabled.

Understanding the Basics... Chat History

A *chat history* documents all the messages that have been sent and received between you and a particular person. In short, it is a record of everything that was said during a Skype chat. Chat histories can be particularly useful if you want to review a previous chat you have had with someone or need the information for a complaint against someone who has been abusive.

In Skype, chat histories are not stored on a network server; if stored at all, they're stored on your local computer. Whether they are stored on your computer depends on the Privacy settings you have set. You can configure these settings by clicking the **Tools** menu in Skype, clicking the **Options** menu item, and then clicking **Privacy**. Because the chat histories are converted as HTML files, they can be viewed with any Web browser. When chat histories are archived on a Windows computer, they are in the Documents and Settings*local username*\Application Data\Skype*skype username*\IMHistory folder.

The **Popup a chat window when someone starts a chat with me** check box in the Chat section of the Advanced options is used to configure what happens when someone initiates a chat with you. It controls whether Skype automatically opens a chat window or whether you must manually open one when someone requests to chat. If this option is checked, the chat interface will open as soon as you receive a chat message from someone. If it is unchecked, you need to visually monitor the icon in the system tray for messages saying that someone wants to chat. We recommend leaving this setting enabled. When you minimize an open chat session, it will not pop up automatically when the other party sends a new chat message.

Other Settings

As discussed in Chapter 3, there are four additional advanced settings under the heading **Other**:

- Automatically pop up the incoming authorization request window
- Associate Skype with *callto:* links
- Auto-pause Winamp during calls
- Display technical call info

What follows is more in-depth discussion of two of these **Other** settings, namely:

- Associate Skype with *callto:* links
- Display technical call info.

Associate Skype with *callto:* Links

When the **Associate Skype with callto: links** check box is checked, other programs on your computer, such as Web browsers, will open Skype when a particular type of hyperlink on a Web page is clicked. When a user clicks a *callto:* hyperlink, Skype will automatically open and call the person or number associated with that link.

If you have used the Internet, you are probably familiar with clicking text or images to load another Web page into your browser or open your e-mail program to send e-mail to a specific person. These hyperlinks are created in Hypertext Markup Language (HTML) using a text editor or Web page-editing software. Without going too far into detail on HTML, if you have never seen the HTML code of a Web page, basic code could appear as follows:

```
<HTML>
<HEAD>
</HEAD>
<BODY>
Text in my Web page
</BODY>
</HTML>
```

Generally speaking, the information you write between the *<body>* and *</body>* tags is what is displayed in your Web page. If you wrote the code shown in the previous example into a text editor like Windows Notepad, saved the file with an .htm or .html extension, and then opened it in your Web browser, you would see a simple Web page with the words *Text in my Web page* appearing on it.

To create a textual *callto:* link, enter HTML code similar to the following into the body of a Web page:

```
<a href="callto://skypename-or-number/">text to display in link</a>
```

In this code, *skypename-or-number* is the name you created for yourself in Skype or an actual phone number; *text to display in link* is your name or other information you would like to appear to the user in the hyperlink. If you clicked this link and had the **Associate Skype with callto: links** check box option checked, Skype would open and automatically call the name or number specified in the link.

In addition to the textual links that allow people to call you in Skype, you can also use images in a hyperlink for Skype calls. By visiting the Skype Web site at http://share.skype.com/tools_for_sharing/tools_for_sharing/skype_me_buttons/, you can acquire images for use on your Web page that are specifically designed for this purpose and find additional information on creating *callto:* hyperlinks using images.

Whether you use a textual or graphical hyperlink, when **Associate Skype with callto: links** is checked, Skype automatically opens when someone clicks the *callto:* hyperlink. As shown in the following figure, when you create an HTML document with a *callto:* link, users accessing this Web page will see a graphic or text that they can click. Once the *callto:* link is clicked, Skype opens and begins to call the Skype name or number specified in the link. Using *callto:* links is one of the simplest ways of accommodating visitors to your Web site, enabling them to contact you quickly and easily.

Using the Display Technical Call Info Option

When the **Display technical call info** check box is selected, technical information about a Skype call is provided during an active call. When this check box is selected and you move your mouse pointer over the avatar or picture of the contact or contacts you are talking to, a small box appears with information about that call. This information provides data about not only your sound setup (input and output devices used for the call) but also packets sent and lost during transmission and whether the call is being relayed. Such information can be useful in determining whether a problem exists with your setup or equipment. This technical information is updated every few seconds during the call, so long as you hover your pointer over the contacts avatar. The **Display technical call info** feature for troubleshooting is also covered in Chapter 13.

Input/Output

The technical call information displays data on the sound device or devices Skype uses for calls:

- **Input** Displays the device that's been set up for audio input, such as a sound card with a microphone jack or other equipment that accepts voice input when you're speaking.

- **Output** Displays information on what device has been configured in Skype for audio output, such as a sound card with speakers or other equipment. This is the same information that you provided when you configured Skype's Sound options, so if a device other than the one you wanted to use appears here, you should check your Sound options.

Understanding the Basics... Input/Output

The average user does not need to worry about this option, but for troubleshooting it can be used to show you what your input and output sound device is set to if you have multiple sound devices.

Call Status

Call Status identifies the current stage or progress of a call. A numerical value is provided in the technical call information, indicating whether Skype is in the process of connecting, receiving a busy signal, ringing, and so forth. Rather than simply providing a number to reflect the status of a call, words that describe the status are also displayed below the avatar of the person you're calling. For example, when the call is connecting, the Call Status displays 1 and then changes to 3 when it is ringing. To see what the Call Status number translates to in user-friendly terminology, simply look at the text appearing below the avatar of the person you're calling. The information provided in the Call Status entry allows you to view the progression of the call while viewing other technical call information.

Understanding the Basics... Call Status

The average user does not need to worry about this option, but for troubleshooting it can be used to show you the place you are in the call in case you experience problems.

Codec

Codec is short for *encoder/decoder* and is used for processing sound and/or video to data. When you speak into a headset using Skype, the signal of your voice is converted by the codec to a digital format so that packets of data can then be sent over the Internet. At the receiving end, these packets are reconstructed and the signal of your voice can then be played over the receiver's speakers or headset.

Understanding the Basics... Codec

The average user does not need to worry about this option, since it does not change.

Packet Loss and Other Issues

Because Skype allows calls to be made using Voice over IP, calls are made by transferring chunks of data called *packets* over the Internet. These packets are transmitted from your computer over the Internet and reconstructed on the receiving computer. Because some packets may be lost or take more time than others to reach the receiving computer, Skype also provides a number of entries in the technical call information that deal with packet loss and other network issues that can cause disruptions in the sound quality of a call.

Jitter

The Jitter entry is used to display variations in the time it takes for packets to arrive. This can be the result of heavy network congestion, changes that occurred when the packets were routed, or other issues related to the transfer of packets between your machine and the computer receiving them. When the jitter is too great, sound quality can be adversely affected, which is the reason that data is buffered in a storage area called a *jitter buffer*. The jitter buffer stores the packets, creating a delay that allows them to be sent to the voice processor at even intervals.

Understanding the Basics... Jitter

The average user does not need to worry about this option, but for troubleshooting it can be used to show information about your network traffic. In general, the more jitter you have, the more the quality of your voice call can be reduced. This information is more for the network administrator to troubleshoot or improve network routing.

Packet Loss/Send Packet Loss/Recv Packet Loss

Several entries in the technical call information are used to display the monitoring of packets that were lost during transmission. **Packet loss** provides an overall display of lost packets, showing a percentage and an actual number of lost packets in brackets. The technical call information further breaks it down to show **Send packet loss**, which displays the number of packets that were lost after being sent from your machine, and **Recv packet loss**, which shows the number that were lost during transmission to your computer. Some packet loss is expected during transmission of data, and a low number of lost packets (such as 5 percent) shouldn't greatly affect the sound quality of calls. However, a large number of lost packets indicates that either you or the person you're talking to should check their network connection, network card, or other devices that are used to transmit data over the Internet.

Understanding the Basics... Packet Loss

The average user does not need to worry about this option, but for troubleshooting it can be used to show how much traffic is being dropped. In general, the larger the network, the larger the packet loss, which can reduce your voice call quality. This information is more for the network administrator to troubleshoot or improve network routing.

SessionIn and SessionOut

Similarly, the SessionIn and SessionOut entries provide information on packets that were sent using the User Datagram Protocol (UDP). UDP is a connectionless protocol and is part of the TCP/IP protocol suite. TCP/IP provides error correction and will attempt to resend a packet that is lost or corrupted; UDP provides very little in the way of error correction. This protocol is often used for sending messages or other information because it is quick and has little overhead. In the case of voice messages, so much data is being sent and processed at quick intervals, it makes little sense to have delays caused by waiting for packets of data to be resent. The SessionIn entry shows the number of UDP packets that were received by your computer, whereas SessionOut shows the number of UDP packets that were sent during a call (assuming a pure P2P UDP session in both directions).

Understanding the Basics... SessionIn and SessionOut

This is one of the two items that the average user will need to know about. If you see the words:

- Good remote: Bad
- Relayed 'TCP'

your call and/or file transfers are being relayed, which will significantly reduce your call quality and file transfer times. Either you or your other contact do not have a P2P-friendly device or are behind a restrictive firewall.

Relays

The Relays entry is used to indicate the number of times data is relayed through supernodes or relay hosts, as in the case where one or both parties are behind a firewall. In such a case, a user might find another Skype user unreachable but might be able to relay data through another Skype node that is reachable. The data is sent to this relay host, which then passes it on to either another relay host or the party that is being called. Rather than connecting directly to one another, a connection is made through a third party or parties that pass packets of data between the two computers. Even though these packets of data are being passed through the third party, they remain encrypted and secure.

Understanding the Basics... Relays

The average user does not need to worry about this option.

UDP Status

The **UDP status** line indicates the status of the connection between you (the local machine) and the person you're calling (the remote machine). The entries in the technical call data provide information on whether one or both people in the call have a good P2P connection and may indicate a problem with Skype's setup or hardware used for making the Internet connection. There are two entries on the UDP status line:

- **Local**, which refers to your connection
- **Remote**, which refers to the connection of the person you're calling.

Each of these entries can have a value of Good or Bad, making it very simple to analyze whether you, the other person, or both of you have a good or bad connection.

Understanding the Basics... UDP Status Local

This is one of the two items that the average user will need to know about. If you see the words:

- **Local:Good Remote: Good** Tells you that both users have a good P2P connection.
- **Local:Bad Remote: Good** Tells you that your connection is not P2P friendly.
- **Local:Good Remote: Bad** Tells you that you have a good P2P connection and your remote is not P2P friendly.

■ **Local:Bad Remote: Bad** Tells you that both sides are not P2P
friendly.

If home users get Bad, their DSL/cable router is most likely not P2P
friendly; run Nat Check.

If businesses behind a firewall get Bad, the network and/or firewall is
not allowing P2P connections. Run Nat Check to verify and troubleshoot. See
Chapter 13 for more information.

CPU Usage

The CPU Usage entry informs you of the amount of processing the CPU of your computer is doing to perform the call. This entry is in a percentage and will usually vary
throughout the call as processing requirements change.

Understanding the Basics... CPU Usage

The average user does not need to worry about this option.

Call Forwarding and Voice Mail

Forwarding Calls

Skype allows you to forward incoming Skype calls to the following choices:

■ One or more Skype contacts

■ One or more landline telephone

■ One or more cell phones

■ Any combination of these options

To forward calls to a telephone number, you will need to subscribe to SkypeOut for
this to work, but you can forward calls to other Skype contacts for free. Because SkypeOut
enables you to dial anywhere, you could configure Skype to forward a call to either your
landline or your mobile phone. This allows you to receive any important Skype calls even
though you are not at your original computer. SkypeOut is discussed later in this chapter.

Configuring the settings for call forwarding is done by clicking the **Tools** menu in Skype and then clicking the **Options** menu item. A dialog box is displayed that provides various options that can be set for Skype. By clicking the **Call Forwarding & Voice-mail** icon in Skype options, you can access the **Call Forwarding Settings** section.

By clicking the **Forward calls when I'm not on Skype** check box, you can then enter a phone number or Skype contact in the drop-down list. Once numbers or contacts are entered here, you can use the drop-down list to select any previous phone numbers or contacts you entered. If you would like to forward a call to more than one number or contact, you can click the **Advanced settings** link to the right, which will produce two additional drop-down lists. In doing so, you will be able to enter phone numbers or contacts in each of these lists so that a call is forwarded to up to three different choices at the same time.

Leave Skype Open or Close Skype When Forwarding Calls

You have another option when using Call Forwarding: whether you will leave the Skype application open or closed when you forward calls. If you leave Skype open, when a Skype call is received it will ring at your computer first for four rings, stop ringing, and then forward the incoming call to your Call Forwarding list. If you close Skype, your status will be updated and your contacts will see the 🔲 icon in their contact lists, indicating that you are forwarding your Skype calls.

- **If the Skype application is Open** Call Forwarding will ring the computer four times before forwarding.

- **If the user is logged out of the Skype Application.** Call Forwarding changes your status to the 🖼 icon and calls are forwarded immediately.

Understanding the Basics... Forwarding Calls

For Call Forwarding to work, you need to decide whether you are forwarding calls to an ordinary phone number (landline or mobile phone) or to another Skype user. To forward calls to a conventional phone number, you must have a sufficient balance of SkypeOut credits. These credits are needed because the call is being sent from the Internet to the traditional phone network. Without SkypeOut credits, you will not be able to forward calls to a landline or mobile phone and will only be able to forward them to another Skype name.

Voice Mail

The voice-mail service in Skype is similar to what you might have on your regular phone line. When someone attempts to contact you when you are not online with Skype or otherwise are unavailable, you can set up an outgoing message that allows you to explain that you are not available. The caller then has the option of leaving up to a 10-minute message for you, which you can review the next time you log into Skype.

Although this is a nice feature in Skype, it is not free. It must be purchased on a subscription basis of three months or a year. However, voice mail is free when it is bundled with SkypeIn, if you purchase this option. SkypeIn is discussed later in this chapter.

When voice mail is set up, if a Skype user is unavailable, a voice-mail message can still be left for him or her. The voice mail remains on the user's computer until he or she decides to review or delete it. If you already have an answering machine connected to or built into your home telephone, you might want to read Chapters 8 and 9, which discuss how to connect Skype to your existing telephone and use the same phone for both landline and Skype calls before you purchase or configure Skype voice mail.

Setting Up Voice Mail

Because voice mail is an additional feature, you need to subscribe to it before you will see it available in Skype. To purchase voice mail, click the **Tools** menu in Skype and then click **Go to My Account Page**, and your Internet browser will open and load a Web page on

Skype's site, where you will be required to enter your Skype username and password. Once you have done so, clicking the **Sign Me In** button will open another Web page containing your account information. On this page, click the **Buy Skype Voicemail** link to open a page where you can begin setting up voice mail.

The process begins by clicking a link to subscribe to voice mail for three months or 12 months. Once you click the link related to how many months you would like Skype, another Web page will open a message informing you that that e-mail has been sent to you with a confirmation number. This number must be entered on the Web page to confirm your purchase, and you need to click the **Submit Confirmation Number** link. As we saw when we set up SkypeIn and SkypeOut, after clicking this link another page will appear asking you to specify how you would like to pay for the service and whether you would like to use existing billing information or provide a new billing address. Once payment information has been entered, a new page with the details of your purchase will appear. At any time during this operation, you can cancel out of the purchase.

Using Voice Mail

When you receive a voice mail, the Windows Task Bar Skype icon will rotate through the three ▣ ◬ ✖ icons indicating an event exists. This sequence indicates an event and missed call and/or voice mail. Voice mails can be played on Skype's Call List tab. By clicking the ▣ icon resembling an audiocassette tape, you can view a list of any existing voice mails on your system. The drop-down list beside this icon allows you to view a list of voice mails for all the Skype usernames or select specific usernames to filter the listing to only one user.

If there are no voice mails, no entries will be listed on the Call List tab. Any existing or new voice mails will remain in the list until you delete them by clicking the trash-can 🗑 icon beside the entry you want to remove. Regardless of whether you have no messages or some that have been played, a message will appear at the top of the tab stating "No New Voicemails." Any new voice mails will be indicated at the top of the tab, stating the number of new voice mails you have, with each new voice-mail entry appearing in a bold font. If you want to play a particular voice mail, you only need to click the Play ⊙ icon to play that particular voice mail.

Voices Carry... Saving Voice Mail

Once a voice mail is played, it remains on your computer, since you might want to play it again at a future time. If you are using Skype on a Windows machine, these messages are saved as .DAT files in the Documents and Settings*local username*\Application Data\Skype*skype username*\voicemail folder. If you are using Skype on a computer running Macintosh OS X, these messages are saved in the Library | Application Support | Skype | skype username | Voicemail folder.

Once you have a subscription to voice mail, you can control who can leave voice mail via the Privacy settings in the Options dialog box. Click the **Tools** menu in Skype and then click the **Options** menu item, and the **Options** dialog box appears. Click the **Privacy** icon, and the settings appear that allow you to control who can contact you and adjust the settings to your needs.

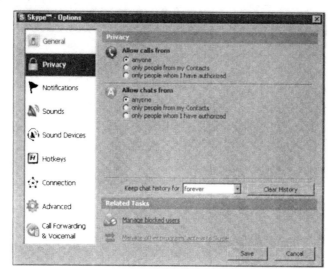

Advanced Architecture

Skype's architecture is made up of a variety of components that together provide the features that allow text, audio, and video conferencing between two or more people. Skype uses a *peer-to-peer* (P2P) architecture, whereby everyone using the Skype software acts as both a client who requests resources and a server that responds to those requests and provides resources. Because resources are not located on a single machine or a small group of machines acting as network servers, this type of network is also referred to as *decentralized*. It should be pointed out that, since Skype is a *closed/proprietary* application, portions of the following discussion are based on assumptions and conjecture.

Decentralized Peer-to-Peer Networks

We discuss peer-to-peer networks in greater detail later in this chapter, but for now it is important to remember that in a P2P architecture, every member of the network is both a client and a server. In a traditional network, each computer on the network will log on and use resources from a single machine or group of machines that authenticate the users and provide specific resources. For example, if you were to send e-mail, you would need to log onto the network and then gain access to an e-mail server (which could require another username and password) so that your e-mail can be transferred to the appropriate person. If either of these servers failed, you would be unable to send or receive an e-mail message.

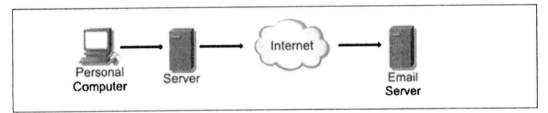

When you have a decentralized P2P network, it does not rely on costly servers to provide resources. Each computer in the network is used to provide resources, meaning that if one becomes unavailable, the ability to access files or send messages to others in the network is unaffected. If one computer goes down, there are always others that can be accessed, and the network remains stable.

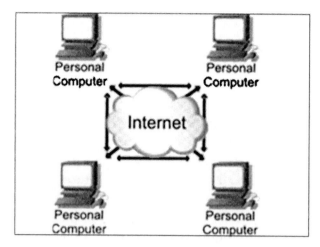

An added benefit of this architecture is that it is highly scalable, with little or no cost. In a traditional network, increasing the size or resource capabilities requires adding new servers and possibly additional cabling and/or other components to the network infrastructure. In P2P networks, each new computer that joins the network lends its processing power, bandwidth, and storage space so that the resources of the network can grow proportionally to the network's size.

Components of Skype's Architecture

Using a distributed P2P architecture, Skype is made up of a variety of components. These interact to allow users to perform a variety of functions, inclusive to those that allow users to communicate with one another. After looking at the elements involved in this architecture, we will examine the way they work together in the P2P network.

Client Software or Nodes

We have spent considerable time discussing the interface we are using in this book, which is required if you want to communicate with others and send files in Skype. The software you use to connect to Skype allows your computer to function as a *node*, which is a machine that participates in the Skype network. Without this interface, you would be unable to log onto the Skype network or perform any of the functions associated with this communication system.

Login Server

Although the Skype architecture is that of a distributed P2P network, this does not mean that there are absolutely no centralized servers. The login server authenticates users which allows them to log into the network, and is one of the few centralized servers you will encounter when you use Skype. The server stores usernames and password information and provides authentication when people attempt to log into Skype. Because a login process is required before you can use Skype, the login server also provides the method of identifying the users who are online or offline.

The other primary role of the login server is ensuring that usernames created for accounts are unique within the Skype namespace. Skype usernames must be unique because they identify the account that belongs to a specific person and they are used when you decide to send a message or place a call to someone. Because the usernames are stored on centralized servers, the server can determine whether a particular username is available or not when you initially set up a Skype account.

Once users log into Skype using their usernames and passwords, they are also issued an electronic credential. This credential is digitally signed by Skype and used to prove that users are who they say they are. When a communication is sent between two computers in Skype, one computer will present the credential to the other as a form of identification, thereby validating the user as authentic. This method of authentication provides continued verification of a user's legitimacy without needing to contact the login server after you log into Skype.

In addition to these services, centralized servers are also used to provide other communication services. Centralized servers store contact lists, which contain information that is used to connect to people in your Skype Contacts list. This information enables Skype to connect to other Skype users and to call people who are using landlines and mobile phones. As we will see later in this chapter, a SkypeOut server enables you to call phone numbers on conventional phone lines, whereas SkypeIn servers allow people using conventional phones to call you on Skype. SkypeIn and SkypeOut servers bridge the traditional phone system and the Internet, allowing Skype users to call people on either system. Using these centralized servers, Skype provides the necessary services for communicating with others on or beyond the Internet.

Global Index

The Global Index is a distributed directory that contains information about Skype users, allowing clients to find information about other people using Skype and communicate with them by sending messages and placing calls. When a call is made through Skype, the clients interact with one another to ensure that the Global Index is up to date.

When you set up an account with Skype, you provide information related to yourself that will be available to others, including a unique username that will identify you in Skype. This information is added to the Global Index, which propagates across the Skype network to keep track of users, regardless of whether they are online or offline.

Another piece of information that is added to the Global Index is your current IP address and port number when you log into the network. The IP address is a unique number that identifies your computer on the Internet and is associated with the unique username you use in Skype. When someone searches for a particular person or attempts to send a message to a user, the Global Index is used to resolve the user's Skype name to the proper IP address he or she is using. This resolution ensures that a message is sent to the computer that the user is currently using.

Encryption

The electronic credential passed to a client at login is an important part of communication between two nodes in Skype and the way encrypted communication is set up. When two nodes attempt communication with one another, the digitally signed credentials are exchanged and they agree on a 256-bit encryption key to use during the session. This process occurs before any messages are exchanged between the two parties.

The communication between these users is then sent over Skype's session layer, which is encrypted using the Advanced Encryption Standard (AES), also known as Rijndael. This 256-bit encryption, also used by the U.S. government to encrypt sensitive data, uses 1.1×10^{77} possible keys, making it almost impossible for outside parties who are not participating in the communication to decrypt it.

The encryption in Skype not only provides security for all forms of communication, it also allows for file transfers. This encryption can make transferring files between Skype users slower than other methods, but it ensures that other outside parties cannot view sensitive materials during the transfer. For more information and details on how Skype security and encryption works, read Skype's security white paper by Tom Berson of Anagram Laboratories, a well-known cryptographer, that outlines how Skype uses encryption. You can find this paper at www.skype.com/security/.

Supernodes

The login server is used to ensure that usernames are unique, and it stores information on usernames and passwords, but much of the information about online and offline users is maintained by supernodes. *Supernodes* are clients that provide additional services to the network. They act as hubs for other clients, store Global Index information, and provide the means of connecting clients.

Skype clients make network connections to supernodes and update the Global Index with their information. These connections allow the Global Index to remain accurate and provide the basis for clients' ability to have their communications routed to the proper person. When you search for a particular user, information stored and propagated by the supernodes is queried. Because of the supernode's role in the network, this makes it one of the most important elements of Skype's infrastructure and architecture.

Supernodes do not run any additional software, except of course the Skype software that is used by every node on the Skype network. Any Skype client can become a supernode as long as it has an Internet IP address; sufficient CPU, memory, and bandwidth; and is not behind a firewall or Network Address Translation (NAT) gateway that prevents unsolicited inbound network connections. Because any node meeting these criteria could become a supernode, it follows that Skype does not maintain supernodes (except in the ways Skype provides support to any other node).

Advanced Peer-to-Peer Technology

Skype is the result of development by Niklas Zennstrom and Janus Friis, who had earlier success with file-sharing software named Kazaa. Because the same people who developed Skype in 2003 also developed Kazaa, it should come as no surprise that they built on their success and utilized a peer-to-peer architecture. Rather than relying on central servers located on the Internet to provide a majority of services and resources, P2P technology allows the individual computers participating in the Skype network to act as both clients and servers. These individual nodes provide similar services to one another and therefore are peers to one another. Because there are so many peers making up the infrastructure of the network, if one peer fails, the total network of peers is unaffected and can continue to function normally.

File Sharing and P2P

P2P networks are relatively new to computer networks, but they did not develop overnight. P2P has evolved over the last few years, mostly due to the controversy of P2P file-sharing applications such as Kazaa and Napster, which allowed users to share files on their computers with other people, allowing them to search for music, video files, images, software, and documents and download them from other people's computers. The sharing of these files raised an old argument that had been around since people began taping music from the radio and taping movies from TV—that of copyrighted material and the loss of royalties. Because copyrighted material was being shared without permission between people on these networks, those who produced the original work and owned the copyright could not make any money from the distribution of these materials. This not only forced an evolution in how P2P communication operated; it also lent notoriety to the technology itself.

The first generation of file-sharing software like Napster did not have a pure P2P architecture; it used a centralized file list on servers that could be searched to find files to download. This centralized list of files proved to be a lynchpin of Napster's design. In legal battles between Napster and the music-recording industry, U.S. courts decided that whoever controlled such central file lists with copyright material on them was also responsible for copyright infringement. This forced Napster to shut down for a time and restructure; it also led to new P2P development that did not involve information being stored on a central server or group of servers.

When Friis and Zennstrom developed Kazaa, they avoided the issues related to Napster's temporary demise and used a design of nodes and supernodes. Nodes are normal clients that have the software installed and participate in the functions of the P2P network. As we discussed earlier in this chapter, a client may also participate as a supernode and provide additional services to other clients. Because this architecture worked so well in previous P2P software, it became the foundation on which Skype was built to allow communication between clients.

Skype's P2P Architecture

To understand how Skype's architecture works, it is best to look at it in action. By reviewing the events that occur when you use Skype, you will better understand the structure of its P2P network and how all the various elements work together.

After Skype has been installed and configured, the first step in using the software is to log into Skype via a login server. No other central servers are used in this architecture. As we mentioned earlier in this chapter, the login server is the only component in Skype's architecture that does not run on a participant's machine, and it is used to store the usernames and passwords of all Skype accounts. When you use the client software to log in to Skype, your username and password are compared to information stored on this server, authenticating the information to ensure that you are the valid user for a particular account.

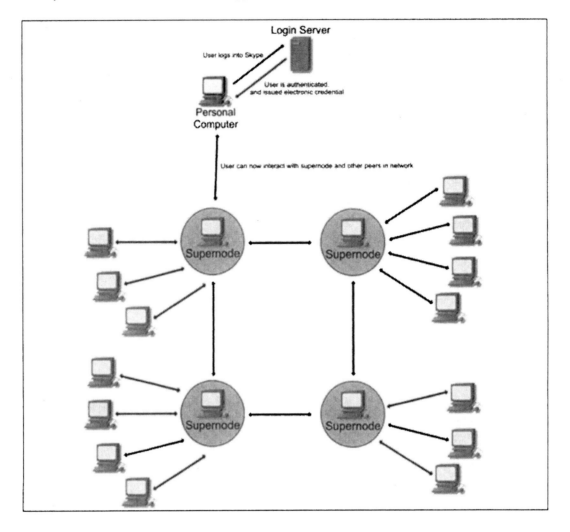

Once you are successfully logged into Skype, the login server performs a number of other functions. It advertises that you are now online and/or your status and identifies supernodes that your Skype client will use to maintain connections to the network. The login server also provides the user with an electronic credential that identifies the user on the network and authenticates him or her as being valid. This credential allows authentication between nodes of the network without needing to repeatedly contact the login server. It is also used during the process of setting up encrypted communication between clients that exchange communications with one another.

It is at this point that interaction with the login server ends and the role of the supernode takes over. As we discussed earlier in this chapter, supernodes act as hubs by handling contact lists containing information on users of the network and routing calls to their proper destination. This is done through the Global Index, which is a distributed directory that is spread across the clients acting as supernodes on the Internet and that have the ability to support tens of millions of users who are simultaneously using Skype. When a search for a user is performed, the Global Index is referenced, allowing any user who has logged in within the last 72 hours to always be found.

When you decide to chat with someone or set up an audio call, several steps occur between the two clients before the session is established. The electronic credentials that Skype received when you logged in are exchanged to authenticate each party. Once this is done, the two clients then agree on a 256-bit encryption key, which is used to encrypt any further communications between the two. After agreeing on the encryption key to use, the chat or call begins and communications are then transmitted in an encrypted format over Skype's session layer.

Skype's Premium Services

As we have discussed throughout this book, Skype-to-Skype calls are free, but Skype also has some premium services, namely SkypeOut, SkypeIn, and voice mail. This section covers these services to help you understand what they provide.

SkypeOut

After you use Skype for any length of time, it becomes clear rather quickly that you are limited to making Skype voice calls to others who are using Skype software on your computer only. With its basic services, Skype does not provide the functionality to make voice calls to regular phone numbers associated with landlines and mobile phones. That is where SkypeOut comes into play. SkypeOut is an additional feature that you must pay for that allows connectivity with any phone on the public switched telephone network (PSTN). It works just like a calling card by providing you credits that will be used up as you make SkypeOut calls.

You can sign up for this additional service through the Skype software by clicking the **Tools** menu, then clicking **Go to My Account Page**. Once you do so, your Internet browser will open and load a Web page on Skype's Web site where you will be required to enter your Skype username and password. When you provide this information and click the **Sign Me In** button, another Web page will load, containing your account information. Because your account will already have been set up, no additional information is required, but a valid e-mail address is necessary to complete the subscription. All you have to do at this point is click the link to buy SkypeOut credits, select the amount of credit you want to purchase, and provide your payment information. Payment options are in Euros, US Dollars, the Japanese Yen, and the British Pound, and the credits you purchase are good until you use them up or 180 days after the last time you made a call using SkypeOut. Additional credits can be purchased using the same procedure.

One of the benefits of using SkypeOut over a regular phone line is when you call long distance. When calling from a normal phone, the distance between where you and the area you are calling determines the long distance rate. However, since you are calling from a computer over the Internet, such a rating scheme would not really apply. For this reason, SkypeOut does not consider where you are calling from, only where you are calling to. SkypeOut uses factors including the volume of calls to and from the country you are calling and access charges related to the call (such as when calling cell phones) and provides a global rate that allows you to call a wide variety of countries at the same rate per minute.

Using SkypeOut

Once you have purchased SkypeOut credits, you are then able to use Skype to call a telephone anywhere in the world. If you have already installed Skype on your computer, no additional installation is required. SkypeOut calls are made using the Dial tab of the Skype user interface.

The Dial tab provides a graphic interface of a telephone keypad, which you can click with your mouse to dial a specific number. As an alternative method, phone numbers can also be entered into the address field that is always in view in the main Skype window by typing the number using your keyboard. In dialing the number, however, you must begin with the + symbol and country code before entering the full phone number (which includes the area code or city code). For example, to call a number for information in the 905 area code in Canada, you would enter **+19055551212**. The country code is the international dialing number that precedes the actual phone number and is used to indicate the country in which the phone number is located. If you are unsure of the country code for the number you are calling, don't worry. Skype provides an easy-to-use method of looking that up; further information is provided later in this chapter.

The + symbol must be used at the beginning of a phone number you want to call using Skype, which may lend some confusion as to how the keypad interface on the Dial tab is used to enter this symbol. If you click and hold down your left mouse button on the 0 (zero) button for a few seconds, the + symbol will be entered into the address field. You may also substitute **00** or **011** for the + symbol.

If you need to dial an extension after a phone number has been dialed, you can use the Dial tab during the call to enter extensions. Because the interface resembles the keypad of a conventional phone, you would click the numbers just as you would press the keys on your phone's keypad to enter the extension.

Phone numbers can also be entered using your keyboard. Using the address field box below the Services button, you can type in the number you are calling and then press the **Enter** button on your keyboard to initiate the call. It is not possible to enter a **pause** into the dial string. If you prefer using your mouse, you could also begin your call using the red and green call buttons at the bottom of the screen. Once you are ready to make your call, click the large green phone 📞 button, which opens another tab for that call session. To cancel or hang up on the call, click the large red phone 📞 button at the bottom of the tab.

Understanding the Basics... Using Emergency Numbers

SkypeOut is a great tool for making long distance calls, but it is important to realize that it is not a full replacement for a normal phone line. SkypeOut does not have the ability to make calls to emergency numbers that allow you to make fast connections to police, fire departments, and ambulance. Emergency numbers that Skype is unable to call include:

- **911**, used in such places as Anquilla, Aruba, Antigua and Barbuda, Bahamas, Barbados, Canada, Cayman Islands, the Dominican Republic, the United States, and the United Kingdom
- **919**, used in Bahamas
- **511**, used in Barbados
- **711**, used in the Dominican Republic
- **112**, the international emergency number used in Europe
- **999**, used in such places as Antigua and Barbuda, Dominica, Hong Kong, Trinidad and Tobago, and the United Kingdom

What this means is that in life-threatening situations where you need police, fire department, or ambulance assistance, you still need to use a conventional phone or cell phone to call for help. Before deciding to replace your normal phone with Skype, you should carefully consider this issue.

SkypeOut Dialing Wizard

Because there are so many country codes used for international dialing, you can use the SkypeOut Dialing wizard that is available on Skype's Web site at www.skype.com/products/skypeout/rates/dialing.html. This Web page begins with a drop-down list that asks which currency you would like to use for determining SkypeOut rates, offering two options:

- Euros
- U.S. dollars

After providing additional information, the Dialing Wizard uses your choice of currency to determine the rate per minute of your call. It is, however, not necessary to choose a currency for SkypeOut rates to determine the country code to use.

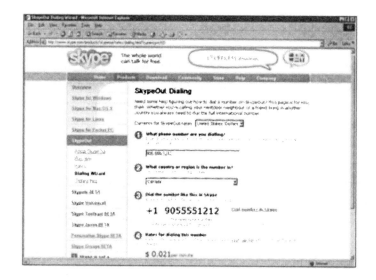

The first step in determining the country code begins by entering the phone number you want to dial in the **What phone number are you dialing?** field. When entering this number, you need to include the city code or area code, and optionally the number you are calling. The webpage updates dynamically with each keystroke and warns the user when the number is incorrect.

The second step in the wizard is specifying the country that you are calling in the **What country or region is the number in?** drop-down list. This list is broken into two sections, with the 10 most commonly called countries displayed first and then all countries displayed below that group. Also, by keying the appropriate first letter, the country you are after can be quickly located.

Once the phone number and country have been provided in this Web page, a number automatically appears in the section for Step 3. You can then manually enter this number into the **Dial** tab of Skype, or click the link called **Dial number in Skype**, which opens Skype and begins dialing the number indicated in Step 3.

International Dialing Codes

The following URLs provides information on country and area/city codes that can be used for making calls in Skype. In using these numbers, however, do not forget that the number you enter in Skype must begin with the **+** symbol. Also, it is important to remember that as new countries emerge, change, or cease to exist and area or city codes are added or changed, you might need to refer to the SkypeOut Dialing wizard from time to time.

- www.countrycallingcodes.com/
- www.timeanddate.com/worldclock/dialing.html
- www.fonefinder.net/

SkypeIn

SkypeOut allows you to call conventional phone numbers associated with landlines and mobile phones; SkypeIn allows the people with these regular phones to call you on your computer. SkypeIn provides the means of obtaining a phone number in a particular area that people can use to call you on Skype. Although it appears to others that they are dialing a regular phone number, the call actually comes to you via Skype over the Internet.

One of the major benefits of SkypeIn is that you can get up to 10 different phone numbers in different areas of the world. When someone in a different country dials a number associated with his area, it is usually the same as if they are calling a local number. Even though they are calling you from a different country, they avoid paying any long distance fees to talk to you. This can be of great significance for businesses that have clients located throughout the world or for individuals who have friends and family that they often communicate with in other countries. You must have one of the following versions of Skype installed to use SkypeIn:

- Skype for Windows version 1.1.0.61 or later

- Skype for Linux version 0.94.0.1 or later

- Skype for Mac OS X version 0.15.0.4 or later

Setting Up SkypeIn

Signing up for the SkypeIn service and obtaining a phone number is a similar process to what we covered earlier with SkypeOut. When you click the **Tools** menu in Skype and then click **Go to My Account Page**, your Internet browser will open and load a Web page on Skype's Web site where you will be required to enter your Skype username and password. After you provide this information and click the **Sign Me In** button, another Web page will load containing your account information. On this page, click the **Buy SkypeIn number** link to open a page that will begin the process of setting up your new phone number.

The first step is choosing the country you would like your phone number to be in. On the Web page, you will see links for the various countries available. At the time of this writing, there are nine options:

- Denmark

- Estonia

- Finland

- France

- Hong Kong S.A.R., China

- Poland

- Sweden

- United Kingdom

- United States

After clicking the name of the country you would like your phone number in, a new page will appear containing additional options. The first option to choose is the area code or city code you would like your phone number. As we mentioned earlier in this chapter, the area/city code identifies the location of where that phone number exists. The drop-down list provides a variety of area/city codes to choose from. To find a code in a city or area that suits your needs, you might want to refer to the Web sites cited earlier for more information on country codes and area codes.

Once you select the area/city code you want to use, you will see a number of suggested phone numbers that are available in that area. If there is a particular series of numbers you want (such as those that spell a word), you can enter the series of numbers into the field in Step 2. This will initiate a search of all available phone numbers that use this series and display the results. When you find a number you would like to use, click that number to claim it for your own. Before doing so, however, it is important that you choose the number you really want, since a number cannot be exchanged for another one after it is purchased.

To complete the setup of your SkypeIn number, you must then select a subscription option of either three or 12 months and click the **Buy selected number** link. Clicking this link will take you to another Web page displaying a message that informs you that e-mail has been sent to you with a confirmation number. This number must be entered on the Web page to confirm your purchase, and you will need to click the **Submit Confirmation Number** link.

After you click this link, another page will appear asking you to specify how you would like to pay for the service and whether you would like to use existing billing information or provide a new billing address. Once payment information has been entered, a new page with the details of your purchase will appear. At any time during this operation, you can cancel out of the purchase.

Tweaking the Technology... Versions

Because new versions of software generally provide new features and set-tings, you should ensure that you are using the latest version of Skype. SkypeIn does not work with every version of Skype, so you could experience problems with its function if you have not upgraded to the latest version. To ensure that SkypeIn will work properly, you need to be using the latest ver-sions, which at the time of this writing are Version 1.4.0.78 (for Windows), Version 1.3.0.14 (for Mac), Version 1.2.0.17 (for Linux), or Version 1.1.0.6 (for Pocket PC).

Using SkypeIn

Once you have a SkypeIn number, you are ready to begin using it. You can share it with your friends, colleagues, and customers. The Skype number is good for the length of your subscription, and the number will be reserved for you 90 days after your subscription runs out. This provides you with time to renew SkypeIn without having to change your number once the subscription expires.

As with calls from one Skype user to another, called *Skype-to-Skype calls*, you must be logged onto Skype to receive a call with SkypeIn, unless you have call-forwarded to a land-line or cell phone number. When a SkypeIn call is received, you will hear the sound of a telephone ringing and see the Skype icon flashing in your system tray and you can answer or reject the call.

The information about a particular user calling you could consist of varying informa-tion on the Call List tab. When a call is received using SkypeIn, the name and/or phone number related to the incoming call may be displayed, and the word *SkypeIn* will appear in brackets beside it. However, if the person calling you is calling from a location that does not support Caller ID, his or her name might not appear. Aside from this, it will appear identical and use the same command structure as when a Skype call is received.

Forwarding to and from SkypeIn Numbers

Because your SkypeIn number has same the appearance and functionality to callers as a normal phone number, you might be able to forward calls from your landline or mobile phone to it. When a call is received by your normal phone number, it is forwarded to your Skype number, where you could answer the call and talk using Skype. Whether you can do this depends on whether you have that feature available on your landline or mobile phone. To find how to forward the calls, you need to consult your phone company or cell phone provider. The user should be aware of additional charges that may be applicable to calls that are call-forwarded to a SkypeIn number.

As we discussed earlier in this chapter in the section on SkypeOut, you can also forward calls from Skype to another phone number. If you have both SkypeOut and SkypeIn, a call to your SkypeIn number can be forwarded to your landline or mobile phone. Even if your computer is turned off, these calls can be sent to contacts or the phone number(s) you specify in Call Forwarding. Calls that are forwarded in this way are charged at the applicable SkypeOut rate.

Another option under Privacy will appear once you sign up for SkypeIn to control who may call you from SkypeIn. The following picture shows you the additional settings that appear:

The settings in the **Allow SkypeIn calls from** section determine not only who can call you using SkypeIn but also who may leave voice mail. You have three options that you can choose from:

- **Anyone** Any person can call you using SkypeIn.

- **Known numbers** Only calls from people who transmit their Caller ID information can call you using SkypeIn.

- **My Contacts** People you have entered a SkypeOut number for in your Contacts list can call you using SkypeIn.

Other Advanced Topics

Here we look at a few more advanced features: editing the Skype language file, tips and tricks, and command-line options.

Editing the Skype Language File

Language files are used in Skype to manage the text that appears on screens throughout the program. With the exception of the About box (which contains legal information) that is displayed through the Help menu, all the menus, hints, captions, and other text in Skype can be modified through the use of Skype language files. Because the Skype program was written in English, language barriers can make it difficult for those who speak or read another language. To allow information to be displayed in other languages, Skype allows you to create and load language files into the program so that items appearing in Skype can appear in any other language.

Language files are simple text files that are saved with the .lang extension. Because they are text files, they can be edited using any text-editing program. As shown in the following figure, the left side of each line shows the item that can be edited, whereas an equals sign (=) links it to the actual text that is displayed. By modifying the text on the right side of the equals sign, you can change the text in Skype to anything you want.

```
mylanguagefile.lang  Notepad
File  Edit  Format  Help
$TOOLBAR_HINT_GETUSERINFO=View Profile
$TOOLBAR_HINT_ADDFRIEND=Add User to Contact List
$TOOLBAR_HINT_BLOCKUSER=Block User
$TOOLBAR_HINT_CALLHISTORY=View Call List
$TOOLBAR_HINT_MUTE=Mute Microphone
$TOOLBAR_HINT_HOLD=Hold Call
$TOOLBAR_HINT_BUSY=Busy Signal
$TOOLBAR_HINT_AEC=Echo Cancellation
$TOOLBAR_HINT_AGC=Automatic Gain Control
$CALLHISTORYBUTTON_HINT_ALL=All Calls
$CALLHISTORYBUTTON_HINT_MISSED=Missed Calls
$CALLHISTORYBUTTON_HINT_INCOMING=Incoming Calls
$CALLHISTORYBUTTON_HINT_OUTGOING=Outgoing Calls
$STATUSMENU_CAPTION_ONLINE=Online
$STATUSMENU_CAPTION_OFFLINE=Offline
$STATUSMENU_CAPTION_AWAY=Away
$STATUSMENU_CAPTION_DND=Do Not Disturb
$STATUSMENU_CAPTION_NA=Not Available
$STATUSMENU_CAPTION_INVISIBLE=Invisible
$CLOSETABMENU_CAPTION_CLOSECALL=End Call and Close Tab
```

An even easier way of editing the language file is to use the editing tool that is included in Skype. This tool can be opened by clicking the **Tools** menu and then clicking the **Edit Skype Language File...** menu item. Once this is done, the **Skype UI Text Editor** shown in the following figure appears. As shown in this figure, the Comment column shows the items available to be translated, and the Original column shows the text that was currently used when you opened the language file with this tool. The Current column, which appears to the right, is where you can translate the current text to another language. The text in this column displays what is currently used and can be edited to any words or phrases you choose.

Tweaking the Technology... Editing Language Files

Although the original intended use of language files was so that English text could be translated to another language, it can also be used to personalize Skype. This way, the language in Skype becomes more akin to what you are used to. You can modify the menus, hints, and other text in Skype to use a regional dialect, slang terms, or humorous sayings to make your experience with Skype more enjoyable.

In using the language files, you might also think that they can be used to translate text in chats with people who speak languages other than your own. However, this is not the case. The language files only translate or modify text used in the Skype program, not text that appears in chats with other Skype users.

In modifying the various entries in a language file, you could be somewhat confused by the names of items in the Comment column. When you review them, however, you will see a common theme to their naming scheme. Items in this column include the names of various features or elements in Skype and have several words that help to define what the text relates to:

- **Menu** Items with this word in their names refer to text that appears in the menus and menu items in Skype.

- **Caption** The items with this word in their names refer to titles or captions of the dialog boxes in Skype.

- **Hint** Items with this word relate to tool tips or hints that appear when you hover your mouse pointer over a particular item.

To immediately see what a particular entry that you modify relates to or the effects of your modification, you can use the Apply button at the top of the editing tool. When **Apply** is clicked, changes made in the language file instantly appear in the Skype program. This allows you to make and review changes on the fly, without closing the editor.

In addition to this button, two other buttons appear on the Skype UI Text Editor: Save As… and Load. The **Save As…** button opens a dialog box that allows you to name your .lang file and save it to a location of your choosing. Once you have saved various language files, you can then load them by clicking the **Load** button. Once this button is clicked, an Open dialog box appears, allowing you to navigate your hard drive to select the language files you have saved or acquired from other Skype users.

Other Tips and Tricks

In addition to the settings we have covered so far, a number of tips and tricks can be used to enhance your experience with Skype. Some of these are areas where configuration can make Skype more suited to your tastes, improve personal privacy, or augment your use of its features. These tips and tricks include:

- Personalizing Skype
- Privacy issues with information displayed in Skype
- Dragging and dropping people (figuratively speaking) into chat rooms
- System commands used in chats
- Authorization of new contacts

In using Skype and talking with other users, you might find additional suggestions and techniques to improve your use of this software.

Chat Tips and Tricks

In addition to making calls, which we have covered for most of this chapter, a major component of Skype is its functionality for instant messaging or chats. In the sections that follow, we discuss some tips and tricks for chatting with one or more people in Skype and commands you can use to make chatting with others easier and more effective.

Drag and Drop in Chat

You can add other people to a chat by clicking the **Add** button in the Chat window, but people in your Contacts list can also be "dragged and dropped" into an existing chat. The Contacts tab of Skype provides a listing of people you have added to your list. If you have an existing chat with someone and would like to add others from your contact list to the chat, click the name of the person you want to add, hold down the left mouse button, and move your pointer over the chat window. When you release the left mouse button, the name of the person from your contact list will have been added to the chat window.

Using System Commands in a Chat

System commands allow you to perform functions without clicking buttons and menu items in the program. In some instances, these commands are the only method of performing a certain function. During a chat, enter these commands in the text field you use to type your message. Once you enter the command, information related to the command having been processed may appear somewhere in the program's interface or chat area. The system commands available in a Skype chat are:

- **/add *skypename*** Adds the Skype user you specified by name to the chat—for example, */add jennifer* would add the user named jennifer to the chat.

- **/help** Displays a listing of all system commands in the chat area, appearing as though you would type them as a message.

- **/topic *newtopic*** Sets or changes the topic of the chat. For example, */topic Skype Tips* would change the topic to Skype Tips. A message will appear in the chat area that you have changed the topic to the new topic name, and the topic name will also appear at the top of the chat window.

- **/me *action*** Used to specify an action you are performing that others would not be able to see. This command adds a bubble (in Skype default) or writes an italic line (in IRC-like chat) containing the full name you provided in your profile, followed by the action you typed. For example, if a user named Michael entered **/me jumps up and down,** a bubble or italic line of text would appear with the words *Michael jumps up and down.*

- **/history** Displays the chat history, which you can review and search. Chat histories are stored in the Documents and Settings*local username*\\Application Data\\Skype*skype username*\\IMHistory folder on computers running Microsoft Windows.

- **/find text** Searches the text of the chat for a certain word or phrase. Once found, the word or phrase appears highlighted in the chat window.

- **/fa** Repeats the last search performed with the */find* command and is used to find the next instance of the word or phrase you are searching for.

- **/** is the same as */fa.*

- **/alertsoff** Turns off the alerts that indicate a new message is posted to the chat, so you know which chats you need to respond to when working in another window. Alerts cause the current chat window to pop up or the Windows taskbar entry for this chat to blink.

- **/alertson** Restores the default setting for new message alerts in Skype, allowing the current chat window to pop up or the Windows taskbar entry for this chat to blink.

- **/alertson text** Causes you to be alerted only when a new text message is posted to the chat. When this occurs, the current chat window pops up or the Windows taskbar entry for this chat blinks.

- **/leave** Exits you from the chat.

Command-Line Options

In addition to the Startup options we discussed earlier in this chapter, there are other methods of configuring what happens when Skype starts. When Skype is used on a machine using a Windows operating system, several command-line switches can be added to a shortcut or when starting Skype using the *Run* command. These switches can improve the speed at which Skype starts and what happens after Skype has loaded.

To illustrate the way a switch is used, let's look at the properties of a Skype shortcut. By right-clicking the desktop icon for Skype and selecting **Properties** from the menu that appears, you will see a dialog box. The Target text box shows the path to Skype's location on the hard drive. This path configures the shortcut as to which program is launched when the shortcut is double-clicked. Additional commands can be typed after this text, modifying how the program starts.

Four switches can be used with the command line to start Skype:

- **/nosplash** Instructs Skype not to display a splash screen when Skype starts.

- **/minimized** Starts Skype in a reduced state, so it is minimized to the system tray at startup.

- **/callto:*name-or-number*** Instructs Skype to call a name or number that you specify after the */callto:* switch. This can be any Skype name or SkypeOut number that you specify. SkypeOut is discussed in detail earlier in this chapter.

- **/shutdown** Closes the Skype program.

Authorization

More of a feature than architecture is how Skype handles user authorization. We discussed in Chapter 3 how users will do a search for you or add you to their contacts from your invitation or your Skype names advertised in e-mail or on a Web site. We also discussed in Chapter 3 the Blocked User feature. When a person searches or adds you to their contact list, you are sent an authorization request. Once you accept this request and authorize a contact, it can never be revoked. The only option you have is to block the user if they begin harassing you. Authorization only allows the other contacts to see your online status. To control this further, you must use your Privacy settings to change who may chat or call you:

- Anyone

- Only people from my contacts

- Only people whom I have authorized

For people who do not want to be bothered by skam (Skype spam), you can set your Privacy option to **Only people from my contacts**. This will prevent anyone who is not in your contact list from contacting you directly through Skype without you adding them first. The user would first have to send you an IM from another client, send you e-mail or telephone you to give you their Skype username and add them to your contact list. For people who need the public to contact them, as I do with our www.SkypeTips.com site, this option is too restrictive. However, I could set my Privacy option to **Only people whom I have authorized** so that people must first ask for authorization before contacting me with questions.

I have adjusted these settings in an effort to find a happy balance, but find that if I simply remove contacts that are no longer active, and block those that require it, I am good to go, as I need to be able to accept unsolicited calls in support of my Web site. I now set my Privacy setting to **Anyone** so that I may respond to questions without having to authorize every caller. If you want more control over users that you authorized and now want to de-authorize, your only real option is to remove them from your Contacts list and add them to your Blocked Users list, and they will have to find another way to contact you to be removed from your Blocked Users list.

Chapter 7

Software Add-ons for Skype

Solutions in this chapter:

- Expanding Skype's Capabilities
- Voice Mail
- Recording Skype Calls
- Integrating with Outlook
- SMS Text Messaging
- Forwarding Your Skype Calls
- SkypeCasting
- Skype Web Toolbars
- Other Plug-ins

Expanding Skype's Capabilities

One of the powers of Skype is the ability it gives you to create add-on products to expand Skype's capabilities and add more features. This is accomplished through the application programming interfaces (APIs) that are discussed in Chapter 14 and the clever ideas of developers worldwide. A perfect example of these add-ons is found on Skype's Personalize Skype Web page at www.skype.com/products/personalise.

Developers have joined with Skype to market and sell additional sounds and avatars for you to use with Skype. So if you have some ideas for selling Skype add-ons, have developed a new software solution, or have an idea to sell voice content such as news or weather, visit Skype's partner program Web site for more information at www.skype.com/partners/.

If you know of more products that are not covered in this chapter, send us an e-mail through out Web site at www.SkypeTips.com so we can add it to the list. Vendors, if you want us to rate your product, contact us through the site and send us an evaluation version of your product so that we can rate your product for our readers.

Voice Mail

Adding voice mail to Skype is one of the more popular features and requests. Since many of us leave our computers on all the time or want to get messages when we are not at the computer, voice mail of some sort is a good idea so that people can leave messages for us anytime.

Skype's own voice mail was covered in Chapter 6, so we will not cover it here; rather, we will discuss other voice-mail options that are available for Skype.

Your Own Answering Machine

We obviously cannot talk in any depth about voice mail without discussing the fact that many of us already have existing standalone hardware answering machines or answering machines built into our cordless telephone base—or possibly we pay for an answering machine service through our telephone provider. I use an answering machine that is included with my cordless telephone base for both my Vonage and Skype voice mail. If you purchase SkypeIn, you get a free voicemail account, or you can purchase voice mail separately from Skype. Chapter 9 discusses using Skype away from the computer and touches on voice-mail use.

No matter what solution you have to capture messages, I think you will find that you'll end up with a combination of voice-mail options. For example, I have Vonage e-mail me my Vonage voice mails so I don't have to check Vonage for voice mail. I also get voice mail from users who call me or just want to leave me a message on Skype, and I use my home answering unit for both Skype and Vonage; I can check it from home or from anywhere in the world for free using Skype. But on many occasions, a more robust voice-mail solution is needed, and that is what we discuss in the following section—software options for voice mail that integrates with Skype.

Pamela

Pamela, one of the premier voice-mail products for Skype, is loaded with features, especially the Pro version, which includes podcasting features. So if you are looking for a full-featured software answering machine solution with lots of features, Pamela is one to consider. You will see Pamela again in the "SkypeCasting" section because it can handle multiple areas.

Key Points

- **User level** Targeted at intermediate and advanced users
- **Platforms** Runs on Microsoft Windows only
- **Cost** Free for Pamela Basic, US$7.50 for Pamela Standard, and US$17.50 for Pamela Professional

You can download Pamela from www.pamela-systems.de/.

Features of Pamela Basic

- Automatic answering of Skype chat messages
- Answering set dependent on Skype status (e.g., to answer only when Skype status is Away)
- Automatic answering of Skype calls
- Maximum recording time: 10 minutes
- Balloon notifications of Skype connection status
- Call back directly from Pamela
- Compatible with any sound card and USB phone
- Compatible with Windows 2000, Windows XP, and Windows Server 2003
- Easy recording of your greeting messages directly from within Pamela
- More then 30 languages included
- Send chat messages directly from Pamela

- Pamela can change Skype status automatically during a call (status type can be chosen)

- Record all audio files in native MP3 format (separate installation of codecs required)

- Recording and playback device can be selected by the user (and optionally synchronized automatically with Skype)

- User can select sampling rate and bit rate of audio recordings

Features of Pamela Standard

- Maximum recording time: 4 hours

- Automatic chat message confirmation of recordings (with indication of the duration and editable)

- Automatic chat message notification of call transfer to Pamela (editable)

- Detailed balloon notifications of contact status changes

- "I'm in a call" chat message sent with automatic hangup of new caller for undisturbed conversations

- Optical identification of new vs. played recordings

- Optional voice greeting mode with recording disabled

- Return of call to Skype during recording

- Pamela/Skype API Console (view only)

Features of Pamela Professional

- Maximum recording time: Unlimited

- Pamela/Skype API Console (view and entry)

- Two-way call recording (automatically or manually) and full support for conference call recording

- E-mail forwarding of voice messages (automatic or manually)

- Full automatic podcasting support with XML file generation and optional automatic FTP upload (MP3 codecs required)

- Personalization of answering settings per contact (greeting and chat messages)

- Time scheduling function for activation and deactivation of Pamela
- SkypeAPI logging option

The following screen shows Pamela's basic operation:

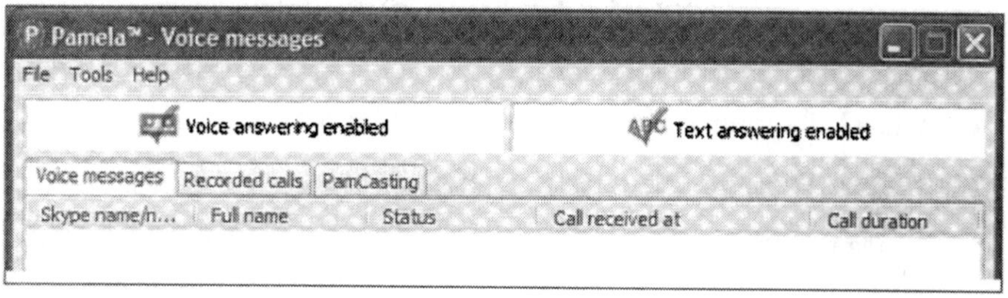

The following screen shows the status of the users:

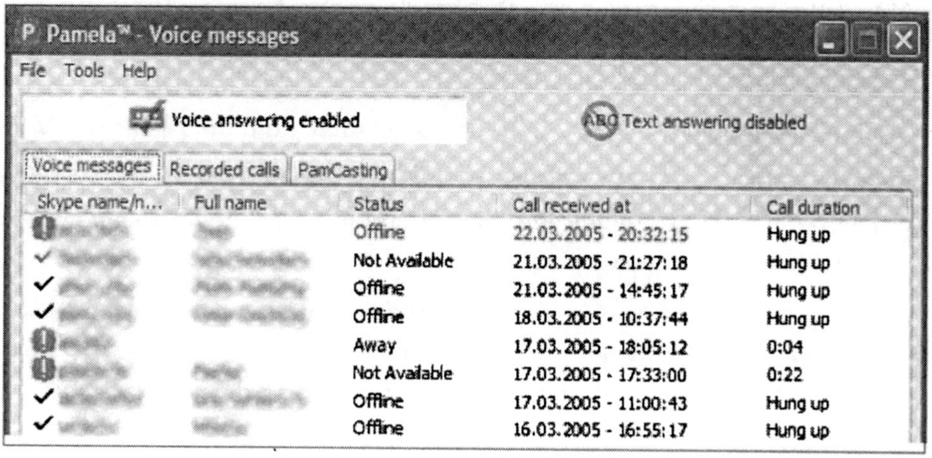

Pamela's General settings, showing a Skype-like interface:

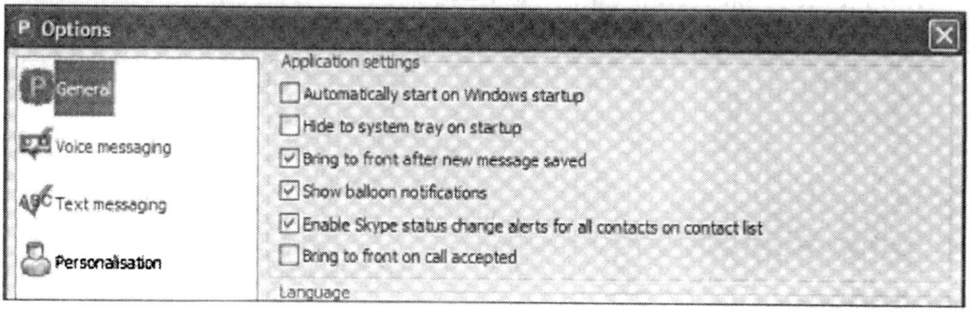

Answering Machine by YapperNut (AMY)

AMY is a good option for an answering machine add-in for Skype if you do not use
SkypeIn or the Skype voice-mail option. This solution integrates with a telephone gateway

device called the YapperBox that allows you to use your home cordless phones anywhere in your house with Skype and *not* have to sit at your computer. The YapperBox is covered in Chapter 9.

Key Points

- **User level** Targeted at intermediate and advanced users
- **Platforms** Runs on Microsoft Windows XP only
- **Cost** AMY is free

You can download AMY from www.yappernut.com/us/en/ybFeatures.htm.

Features of AMY

- **Personalize your voice-mail greeting** Record your own greeting, copy one from a friend, rip it from a CD, or download some from the YapperNut Web site.

- **Customize voice-mail settings for various Skype modes** AMY gives you the flexibility to pick up (or not) during various Skype modes. You can also tell AMY how long to wait before answering.

- **Set AMY to auto-answer during certain hours** Does that pesky relative from overseas always wake you up in the middle of the night? AMY is smart enough to auto-answer during the night, or whenever else you want it to.

- **Forward voice mail to your buddies** Let the gossiping begin. Pass on your voice mail with a few simple clicks.

- **Seamlessly integrates with YapperBox** AMY works as a stand-alone software addition to Skype, but it is designed from the ground up to work seamlessly with YapperBox. Guess who makes both AMY and YapperBox? YapperNut!

The following screen shows how to display messages and schedule a delayed message:

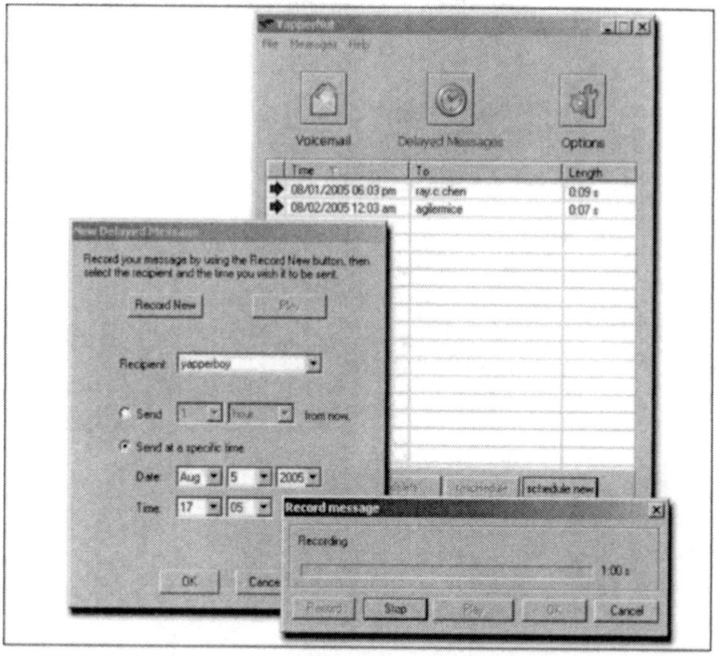

Some of AMY's answering machine settings are shown in the next screen.

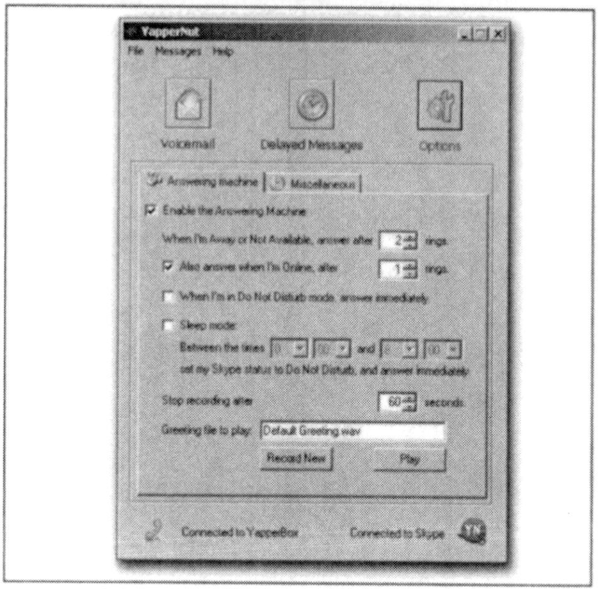

Here's how to play your voice-mail messages:

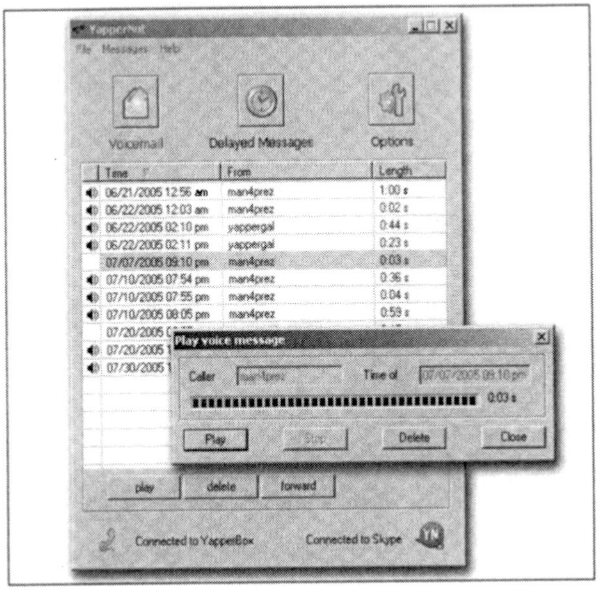

SAM

Skype Answering Machine (SAM) is a good option for an answering machine add-in for Skype if you do not use SkypeIn or the Skype voice-mail option and want a basic answering machine solution.

Key Points

- **User level** Targeted at intermediate and advanced users
- **Platforms** Runs on Windows only
- **Cost** Free with ads and only basic SAM features; US$5.00 for an ad-free version with all features and functions

You can download SAM from www.freewebs.com/skypeansweringmachine/.

Features of SAM

- Uses a dedicated software audio device (included) for compatibility with all sound cards and USB phone devices
- Supports 24 languages for user interface
- User-configurable text and voice greeting messages

- User-configurable global answering mode: Enable or Disable

- User-configurable answering On or Off for Skype's Online mode

- User-configurable delay before answering incoming calls

- User-configurable voice message recording duration anywhere between 0 and 10 hours!

- Option for a separate set of configurations for non-buddy callers

- Notification of operational status using changing icons in the system tray

- Recorded voice message information: caller name, ID and Skype Online status, time of call, duration, indication if the message is new or has been heard

- User can "Force Answering of Call" by SAM while incoming call is ringing

- User can "Take Control over Call" from SAM while voice greeting is played and while recording the caller's voice message

- "Play All New Messages" with the press of one button when you return to computer

- Control of speaker volume (mute) of speakers while incoming call is answered

- Run multiple instances of SAM under different Windows users

The following screens show SAM's basic operation:

Advanced Options Dialog Window

When you purchase SAM, you will have access to the following features:

- Enter the Advanced Options dialog window to select how you want SAM to handle callers that are not on your buddy list.

- Manage the Saved Messages folder by controlling its location and maximum folder size.

- For better privacy, mute the master volume while SAM answers calls so that people in your surroundings will not hear the message left on SAM.

- You can also select one of many languages as SAM's user interface.

Recording Skype Calls

Recording a Skype call has many applications. If you are preparing for a speech or presentation, for example, you might talk with a friend to practice your speech. I am often on the radio doing interviews on my video call legislation efforts, so I use SkypeOut to allow me to record my Skype calls and podcast them to my Web site. I can record the Skype call and then replay and edit it and listen to how it sounds before posting it on the Web. If your company has approved the use of Skype, you might use Skype just like a regular conference call device and record it so that others can listen to the conference call at a later time. There are many reasons to record your Skype calls, and the following solutions will help you do just that.

Hot Recorder

Hot Recorder is a basic Skype call-recording tool that also records GoogleTalk.

Key Points

- **User level** Targeted at intermediate and advanced users
- **Platforms** Runs on Microsoft Windows only
- **Cost** Hot Recorder Basic is free; Hot Recorder Premium is priced at US$14.95

You can download Hot Recorder from www.hotrecorder.com.

Features of Hot Recorder Basic

- The Basic version is supported by advertisements (*no* popups)
- This version will allow you to enjoy all the advantages of Hot Recorder for free (record, add Emotisounds, play, file, share your conversations held over the Web, and use the voice mail for GoogleTalk and Skype)
- No spyware, no malware, no adware—guaranteed
- Proprietary format for audio calls

Features of Hot Recorder Premium

- The Premium version is 100-percent advertisement free
- Gives you the possibility to use and try the version of the audio converter for Hot Recorder
- Enjoy all the advantages of Hot Recorder (record, add Emotisounds, play, file, share your conversations held over the Web, and use the voice mail for GoogleTalk and Skype)

SkyLook

SkyLook is another basic recording tool for Skype calls that integrates with Outlook to store and manage your recorded calls.

Key Points

- **User level** Targeted at intermediate and advanced users
- **Platforms** Runs on Microsoft Windows only with Outlook 2000, 2003, and XP
- **Cost** Free for a 14-day evaluation period; US$14.95 for Hot Recorder Premium

You can download SkyLook from www.skylook.biz/.

Features of SkyLook

- Record Skype VoIP calls (both inbound and outbound) directly into Outlook items as MP3 attachments
- Automatically archive your Skype IM chats into Outlook
- Record Skype IM Chats straight into Outlook as mailbox items
- Manage your Skype VoIP calls and Skype IM chats
- Organizes all your Skype calls and Skype text chats together with e-mail and appointments
- Organize all communication items the way you organize e-mails
- See all communications with a particular contact in one place
- Rich integration with Outlook
- See your Skype contacts come online in real time inside Outlook
- See who is online in the SkyLook toolbar

PowerGramo

PowerGramo is a recording solution for Skype that allows you to record and replay any call. Also, the latest version of PowerGramo has dual-track capability, meaning that it will record the two sides of a call to different files so that they can be edited and adjusted independently. This is a nice feature, since the side with the recorder is usually louder than the other side of the call; dual-track would allow you to equalize the recording before posting it to the Web or letting others listen to it.

Key Points

- **User level** Targeted at intermediate and advanced users
- **Platforms** Runs on Microsoft Windows only
- **Cost** Free with no tech support and without the ability to disable the "recording the call" message; US$19.95 for a version with unlimited tech support

You can download PowerGramo from www.powergramo.com.

Features of PowerGramo

- Record whatever calls you have
- Option to alert other users they are being recorded
- Keep your calls in a safe place
- Share your calls with friends
- Get started in less than 3 minutes!
- Totally free for download

PowerGramo is equipped with a nice basic interface with Skype integration:

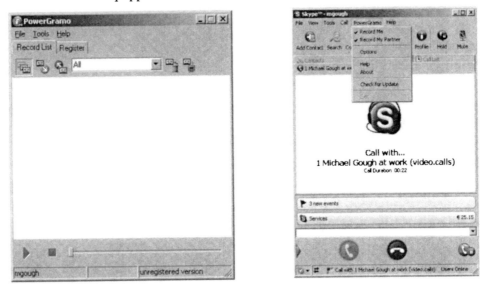

The free version sends the users an IM that indicates the call is being recorded. This option may be controlled in the fully licensed version.

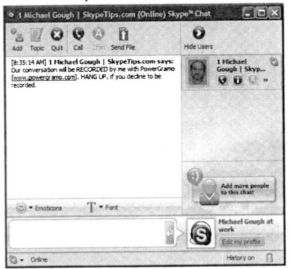

Integrating with Outlook

For Microsoft Outlook users, the ability to integrate Skype with all our personal information is an attractive feature. Since e-mail is so popular, being able to see which users are online and call them directly from Outlook as you compose e-mail is a nice feature. Businesses tend to use Microsoft Office and Outlook exclusively, so this integration feature is very appealing to Outlook users who also use Skype. Why send an e-mail when you can see a user is online with Skype and you can have a quick call with them for free instead?

Skype for Outlook

If you are wondering where Skype got its Skype Toolbar for Outlook, it came from Peter Kalmström, a well-known developer for Outlook plug-ins who has developed many Outlook and Microsoft add-on solutions. I was one of the beta testers for Skype for Outlook, as it was called before Skype decided to use Peter's solution. See more information at www.kalmstrom.nu/.

The following screen shows you the Outlook Toolbar for Skype:

Look2Skype

Look2Skype is another add-on that gives you Skype integration with Microsoft Outlook.

Key Points

- **User level** Targeted at intermediate and advanced users
- **Platforms** Runs on Microsoft Windows only with Outlook 2000, 2003, or XP
- **Cost** Free for a 30-day evaluation period; UK£14.99 for a version with one–nine licenses

You can download Look2Skype from www.look2skype.com/index.htm.

Features of Look2Skype

- **Automatically import Skype contacts in Outlook** Before you get started, you'll need to transfer all your Skype contacts into Outlook. Using the Import feature, Look2Skype will automatically create contact entries for each of your Skype contacts, containing Skype names and any other details your contacts used in creating their accounts.

- **Define Skype name for contacts** If you want to manually set up Skype names for your existing contacts, Look2Skype automatically adds a Skype Name field to each contact. Once you have defined the Skype Name, you can start to make direct Skype calls with your contacts from both your contact list and your inbox.

- **Instant access via Skype to your contacts from your Outlook address book** Once you've installed Skype, Look2Skype gives you to instant access to Skype features such as Skype IP Telephony, SkypeOut (calls from Skype to landlines), and Skype Instant Messaging.

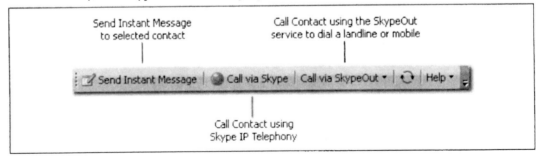

- **Simplified SkypeOut, defaulted local dialing** SkypeOut gives you the prospect of cheap calls to landlines; but you need to add international dialing codes to all your existing phone numbers. Look2Skype enhances this feature by allowing you set a default local country code, which Look2Skype will use on all numbers that don't have an existing international dialing code.

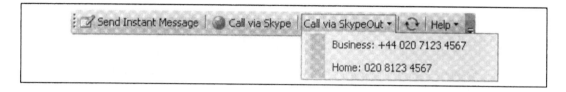

- **Simplify communications—reply to e-mails via Skype** Look2Skype also allows you to respond to e-mails using Skype Instant Messaging and voice calls. If the sender of your e-mail has been set up in your contact list with both his e-mail address and his Skype name, you can quickly go from a slow e-mail conversation to a real-time voice or IM conversation.

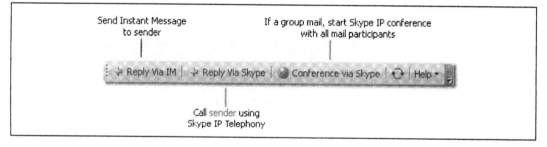

SkyLook

SkyLook is another Skype Outlook integration that offers the ability to record calls and manage them directly in Outlook.

Key Points

- **User level** Targeted at intermediate and advanced users

- **Platforms** Runs on Microsoft Windows only with Outlook 2000, 2003, or XP

- **Cost** Pricing for SkyLook is free for a 14-day evaluation period, US$24.95 for an academic user, US$49.95 for a home user, and US$99.95 for a business user

You can download SkyLook from www.skylook.biz/.

Features of SkyLook

- Record Skype VoIP calls (both inbound and outbound) directly into Outlook items as MP3 attachments

- Automatically archive your Skype IM chats into Outlook

- Record Skype IM chats straight into Outlook as mailbox items

- Manage your Skype VoIP calls and Skype IM chats

- Organizes all your Skype calls and Skype text chats together with e-mail and appointments

- Organize all communication items the way you organize e-mails

- See all communications with a particular contact in one place

- Rich integration with Outlook

- See your Skype contacts come online in real time inside Outlook

- See who is online in the SkyLook toolbar

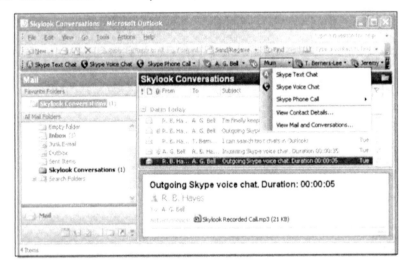

SMS Text Messaging

SMS text messaging provides an interesting way to integrate the cell phone network and the IM world, including Skype. This is popular among AOL, MSN, and Yahoo Instant Messenger users who have integrated their solutions with cell and Pocket PCs. Now Skype has an option to do the same.

Connectotel SMS to Skype

Connectotel SMS to Skype is a service that allows you to send a text message from a cell phone to a Skype user. Only the sender of an SMS message, in this case the cell user, pays for message delivery. Connectotel delivers these messages to Skype users for free and the service is in full production now.

Key Points

- **User level** Targeted at intermediate and advanced users
- **Platforms** Runs on Microsoft Windows only
- **Cost** Free

Simple instructions are available from www.conntectotel.com/sms/skype.html.

Features of SMS to Skype

SMS to Skype is a free service from Connectotel that allows GSM mobile phone users to send Skype instant messages to any Skype user. SMS to Skype is based on M-Mail, Connectotel's free SMS-to-e-mail service, established in 1999.

Connectotel Skype to SMS

Connectotel Skype to SMS is a service that allows you to send a chat message from Skype to a cell phone. Currently, the service is not available because the beta period is over, but expect it to become a pay-per-use service soon.

Key Points

- **User level** Targeted at intermediate and advanced users
- **Platforms** Runs on Microsoft Windows only
- **Cost** Pay-per-use when available

You can download Skype to SMS from www.connectotel.com/sms/skypetosms.html.

Features of Connectotel Skype to SMS

The Connectotel M-Mail service allows you to send SMS to e-mail from any GSM mobile phone. For information about M-Mail and its additional features, such as reply path, signature, aliases, memo, and SMSstore, please see the M-Mail FAQ.

Forwarding Your Skype Calls

This highly requested feature for Skype allows Skype users to forward any incoming calls to their cell phone, another Skype user, or another landline telephone number. Be sure to read Chapter 8, which discusses Skype gateway solutions that have or will have call-forwarding ability with more features than Skype currently provides with its Call Forwarding option that was discussed in Chapter 6. The following call-forwarding software solutions are currently available.

iSkoot

iSkoot is the first call-forwarding solution and offers more than the Skype Call Forwarding option.

Key Points

- **User level** Targeted at intermediate and advanced users
- **Platforms** Runs on Microsoft Windows only
- **Cost** US$9.95 per year

You can download iSkoot from www.iskoot.com.

Features of iSkoot

- Automatically forwards calls from your PC to your phone, including your cell phone
- Calls your buddy's PC from your phone
- Switches a call from your PC to your phone without disconnecting

SkypeCasting

SkypeCasting is a new term that has been coined to refer to the act of doing an interview using a Skype call and podcasting it as an MP3 file on an RSS feed or to a Web site as an audio file. So if you have the desire to post Skype calls to a Web site or RSS feed, that's what this section is all about. We have provided several links to articles that discuss how to SkypeCast for your reference.

You can also use the recording solutions mentioned earlier, such as Pamela and PowerGramo, to record your Skype calls and interviews.

Skype Casting for Windows

Here's a brief list of articles written about SkypeCasting for Windows:

- An article on SkypeCasting written by Stuart Henshall and Bill Campbell of *Skype Journal*: www.henshall.com/docs/Skype%20Recording% 20WinXp%2012202004.pdf

- Another Skype Journal article on SkypeCasting: www.skypejournal.com/blog/archives/2004/12/skype_podcast_r.php

- An article discussing SkypeCasting on a Mac: www.insanelygreatapps.com/2005/03/skype_nicecast_.html

- An article discussing SkypeCasting for Linux: www.henshall.com/docs/Skype%20Recording%20WinXp%2012202004.pdf

Virtual Audio Cable

Virtual Audio Cable (VAC) is a Windows multimedia driver that allows you to transfer audio (wave) streams from one application to another. It creates a pair of wave-in/out devices for each virtual cable. Any application can send audio stream to the Out device, and any other application can receive this stream from the In device. All transfers are made *digitally*, providing *no* sound quality loss. VAC is a "wave version" of the MIDI loopback cable such as MultiMid or Hubi's Loopback drivers. Think of it this way: You can change your speakers or output device to feed into another program like a microphone. For example, you could play a previously recorded Skype call for someone else in a future Skype call.

Key Points

- **User level** Targeted at intermediate and advanced users
- **Platforms** Runs on Microsoft Windows only
- **Cost** Free for Pamela Basic

You can download VAC from http://spider.nrcde.ru/music/software/eng/vac.html.

Features of VAC

- Up to 256 cables
- 1.100 milliseconds per interrupt
- Almost no sound latency, with maximal interrupt frequency
- Almost any PCM sound formats (sample rate, size, and number of channels); number of bits per sample is limited to 32, and number of channels is limited to 65,535
- Unlimited number of clients connected to each port
- Sound mixing (with saturation) between output port clients
- DirectSound output support under Windows 98/ME
- Synchronous mode transfer support to achieve maximal reliability
- Control Panel application to dynamically configure cables
- Audio Repeater application that transfers from any wave-in to any wave-out port

Pamela

Pamela shows up again for SkypeCasting because it is a full-featured product for this application as well. One of Pamela's features is the ability to record and post the recording to an FTP site, so it's a perfect tool for the SkypeCaster.

Key Points

- **User level** Intermediate and advanced
- **Platforms** Runs on Microsoft Windows only
- **Cost** Free for Pamela Basic, US$7.50 for Pamela Standard, and US$17.50 for Pamela Professional

You can download Pamela from www.pamela-systems.de/.

Features of Pamela Basic

- Automatic answering of Skype chat messages
- Answering set dependent on Skype status (e.g., to answer only when Skype status is Away)
- Automatic answering of Skype calls
- Maximum recording time: 10 minutes
- Balloon notifications of Skype connection status
- Call back directly from Pamela
- Compatible with any sound card and USB phone
- Compatible with Windows 2000, Windows XP, and Windows Server 2003
- Easy recording of your greeting messages directly from within Pamela
- More then 30 languages included
- Send chat messages directly from Pamela
- Pamela can change Skype status automatically during a call (status type can be chosen)
- Record all audio files in native MP3 format (separate installation of codecs required)

- Recording and playback device can be selected by the user (and optionally synchronized automatically with Skype)
- User can select sampling rate and bit rate of audio recordings

Features of Pamela Standard

- Maximum recording time: 4 hours
- Automatic chat message confirmation of recordings (with indication of the duration and editable)
- Automatic chat message notification of call transfer to Pamela (editable)
- Detailed balloon notifications of contact status changes
- "I'm in a call" chat message sent with automatic hangup of new caller for undisturbed conversations
- Optical identification of new vs. played recordings
- Optional voice greeting mode with recording disabled
- Return of call to Skype during recording
- Pamela/Skype API Console (view only)

Features of Pamela Professional

- Maximum recording time: Unlimited
- Pamela/Skype API Console (view and entry)
- Two-way call recording (automatically or manually) and full support for conference call recording
- E-mail forwarding of voice messages (automatic or manually)
- Full automatic podcasting support with XML file generation and optional automatic FTP upload (MP3 codecs required)
- Personalization of answering settings per contact (greeting and chat messages)
- Time scheduling function for activation and de-activation of Pamela
- SkypeAPI logging option

The following screen shows the PamCasting options:

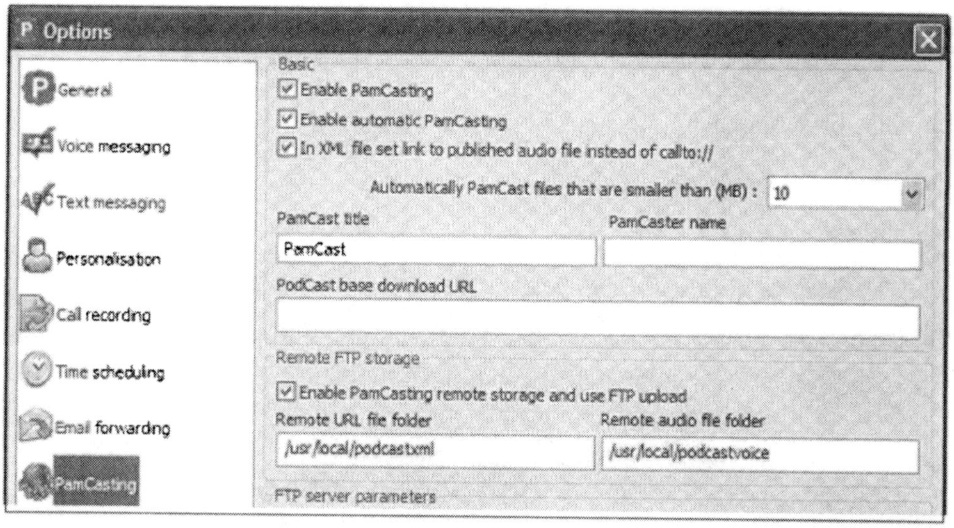

The following screen shows the automatic posting of the PamCast:

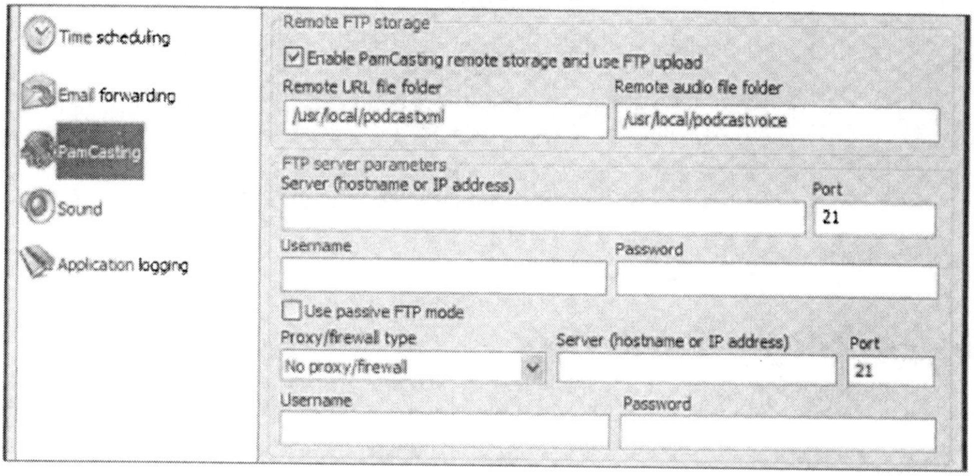

Nicecast for the Mac

Here is an add-on that allows Nicecast to record Skype calls for things like podcasts.

Key Points

- **User level** Targeted at intermediate and advanced users
- **Platforms** Apple
- **Cost** US$40.00

You can download Nicecast from www.rogueamoeba.com/nicecast/.

Features of Nicecast

- Forget one-click purchasing
- Broadcast live events
- iTunes, anywhere
- Professional quality, amateur prices
- Adjustable quality settings, listener statistics, listing in the Stream Tracker, audio effects to enhance sound quality, and much more

Skype Web Toolbars

Skype has a browser plug-in for both Microsoft Internet Explorer and Mozilla Firefox that enables you to change your status, call any of your contacts, and call people using SkypeOut directly from your Web browser.

Key Points

- **User level** Targeted at basic, intermediate, and advanced users
- **Platforms** Microsoft Internet Explorer and Mozilla Firefox
- **Cost** Free

You can download the Skype Web Toolbar at: http://www.skype.com/products/skypewebtoolbar/.

Here is a picture of the Microsoft Internet Explorer Toolbar.

You can set options and the language you want to use.

Both Web Toolbars have the same options to call a SkypeOut number.

Here is a picture of the Microsoft Internet Explorer Toolbar.

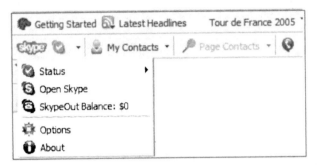

Other Plug-ins

This section discusses other Skype add-ons to do various things—muting other music players, plug-ins for Mozilla Web browsers, and interfaces for Windows Media to other miscellaneous tools.

MuteForSkype Music Player Plug-in

MuteForSkype is an add-on that allows you to mute several music players when you make or receive a Skype call. It even "unmutes" the music when you are done.

Key Points

- **User level** Targeted at basic, intermediate, and advanced users
- **Platforms** Runs on Microsoft Windows only
- **Cost** Free

You can download MuteForSkype from http://blog.vyvojar.cz/michal/articles/3494.aspx.

Features of MuteForSkype

MuteForSkype works for the following music players:

- WinAmp
- Microsoft Media Player
- Sonique

You must install Microsoft .NET Framework 1.1 or later on your computer. You can download it from Microsoft at www.microsoft.com/downloads/details.aspx? FaimlyId=262D25E3-F589-4842-8157-034D1E7CF3A3&displaylang=en.

MiTunes Music Player Plug-in

MiTunes is an add-on that allows control of your music applications directly in Skype, so when a call comes in iTunes is muted.

Key Points

- **User level** Targeted at basic, intermediate, and advanced users
- **Platforms** Runs on Microsoft Windows only
- **Cost** Free

You can download MiTunes from www.skypeteer.com/index.pho?q=node/4.

Features of MiTunes

MiTunes for Skype works for the following music players:

- iTunes

SkypeIt! Mozilla Mail and Thunderbird E-Mail Plug-in

SkypeIt! is an add-on for Mozilla and Thunderbird Mail that integrates your Skype users.

Key Points

- **User level** Targeted at basic, intermediate, and advanced users
- **Platforms** Runs on Microsoft Windows and Linux
- **Cost** Free

You can download SkypeIt! from www.s3ven.freesurf.fr/index.php?1=EN&menuid=2g.

Features of SkypeIt!

- SkypeIt! is the first extension that allows you to call your contacts from Thunderbird and Mozilla Mail and both Windows and Linux!
- Its use is very simple. When a contact is selected in the address book with the right mouse button, the SkypeIt! menu shows all the phone numbers you can dial. If the contact uses Skype, you'll be able to call him for free by clicking **Skype call** if you have entered his Skype ID in his Nickname info.

Skype Interfaces

mcePhone for Skype

mcePhone for Skype adds the most common functions of Skype and makes them available in your Microsoft Windows XP Media Center 2005 and accessible using your remote control. So if you want a different interface and are running Windows XP Media Center 2005, give it a try. This is perfect example of what can be done using the Skype API. For more on the Skype API, read Chapter 14.

Key Points

- **User level** Targeted at intermediate to advanced users
- **Platforms** Runs on Windows XP Media Center 2005 only
- **Cost** Free

You can download mcePhone for Skype at www.cbuenger.com/mcephone/.

Features of mcePhone

- Call any Skype user
- Call any "normal" telephone number (SkypeOut required)
- Accept incoming calls
- Listen to Skype voice mails
- Show all call lists from Skype (incoming, outgoing, and missed calls)

- Mute or pause any playing video, TV show, or music in your Media Center on an incoming call

- Show information about missed calls and new voice mails on Media Center startup

- Seamless integration into Windows XP Media Center with two skins to choose from

- Can be controlled by remote control—no mouse or keyboard required

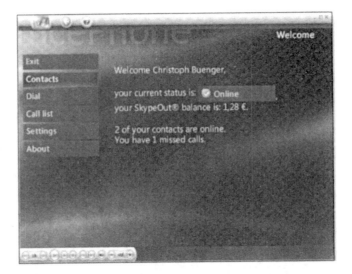

Skype Forwarder

Skype Forwarder is another add-on for computers running Windows XP Media Center 2005 that gives you answering machine and call transfer capabilities.

Key Points

- **User level** Targeted at intermediate to advanced users
- **Platforms** Runs on Windows XP Media Center 2005 only
- **Cost** Free for a demo version; US$19.95 for full version

You can download Skype Forwarder from www.twilightutilities.com/SkypeForwarder.html.

Features of Skype Forwarder

- Intelligently detects most voice modem types
- Complete telephone answering machine (TAM)
- Complete Skype Answering Machine (SAM)
- Transfers incoming telephone calls to Skype buddies
- Transfers incoming Skype calls to phone

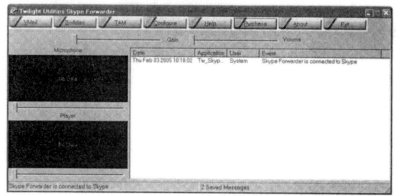

Free Tools from Skypeteer

Key Points

- **User level** Targeted at intermediate to advanced users
- **Platforms** Windows
- **Cost** Free

You can download the tools from www.skypeteer.com/index.php?q=product.

Skypeteer Keep It Simple Status Indicator (KISSI) Plug-in

If you post somewhere, include an image tag to the location of the file, like this:

 This is my status indication.

Skypeteer World Clock Plug-in

This version of Skypeteer has only one purpose—to show the local time of the user you are talking or chatting to in Skype. Because Skype has no real time zone information available, this product uses information from the Skype profile, like country and city. It's is not fully bulletproof, but it is a solution that works pretty well.

Skypeteer IE Extension Plug-in

With this extension you can send contacts a Skype IM with the correct information by right-clicking in a Web page.

Skypeteer Call Calculator

With this add-on you can calculate cost savings when you use Skype. You don't need to log into the Skype portal to see all recent calls.

Free Tools from s3ven

S3ven's freeware includes some more utilities and tools that can be used for Skype.

Key Points

- **User level** Targeted at intermediate to advanced users
- **Platforms** Windows
- **Cost** Free

You can download the tools from www.s3ven.freesurf.fr/index.php?l=EN&menuid=2&PHPSESSID=e1045d8a8a500ee1bdf2edc929ef0e52

Outlook Skype Plug-in

- This program adds a new toolbar to Outlook, so when you click a contact, the bar will show all the contact's phone numbers and will allow you to call him or send him an instant message with Skype
- Works on Outlook 2000 to 2003

Skype Tools Plug-in

Add ringtones and some other features to Skype.

Skyp2Out Plug-in

Export your Skype contacts to Outlook and choose what you want to export.

Skype Backup Tool Plug-in

Back up your Skype information and configuration to file and FTP servers.

Chapter 8

Hardware Add-ons for Skype

Solutions in this chapter:

- Headsets. Microphones, and Speakers
- Telephone Gateways
- Telephone Adapters
- USB Phones
- Speaker Phones
- Other Hardware

How to Use This Chapter

This chapter is designed to help you understand the many hardware options available for Skype. Many of these devices might not be available in your country, so the intention is to show you various types of devices and their basic features so that you can understand what these devices could do for you, and then you can set out and find one or more that are available in your part of the world. We have provided some basic information to help you understand the characteristics of these devices—user level, supported operating systems, approximate cost, where to get more information, and a basic feature list. Most if not all of these devices currently support only Microsoft Windows operating systems, but several vendors have told us they are planning versions for Apple in the future, and one vendor has told us they are looking at a Linux version as well.

Many of the inquiries we have received over the past year have related to whether a particular device is easy to install, what it costs, and whether there is a version for the Mac or Linux. So we have compiled these items to give you a quick idea about each product. The "User Level" category is designed to tell you the level of difficulty involved for the user; Basic is for any home user who is not a Skype guru, Intermediate is for users who are more literate with Skype and might need some additional configuration, and Advanced is for the truly technically proficient. By no means is this a complete list; new products are coming out almost weekly. If you know of more devices that you have had a good experience with or if you are a vendor and want us to test, evaluate, and rate your products on www.SkypeTips.com, as we have done for many of these products, send us an e-mail, or of course, Skype Me!

Headsets, Microphones, and Speakers

You can use just about any headset, microphone, or speakers with Skype. There are several headsets and microphones that are Skype certified and available at your favorite computer store or Web shop. The more expensive headsets generally provide better sound quality and are usually more comfortable. Skype uses software-based sound-processing technology that allows even the most basic microphones to provide acceptable results. I have my Logitech noise-canceling microphone mounted to my FlexStand with my computer speakers and it works fine when I am at the computer or performing a video call. You can see a picture of my setup at www.VideoCallTips.com. You can read more about the topic at http://video-call.internetvisitation.org/web_pages/ratings_misc.html.

If you want to have a more private conversation and avoid background noise, a headset is the best solution. This is an area that is completely of personal choice and experience. Or you can opt for one of the many options we discuss in this chapter.

Bluetooth Headsets

As we will discuss in Chapter 12, Bluetooth is another headset option you might consider. Though I am not a fan of Bluetooth due to warbling, range, and battery-life issues with many of these headsets, I am aware of many people who are quite satisfied with the Bluetooth headsets they use with their cell phones. As we discuss in Chapter 12, there are several solutions that can be made to work with Skype on your computer, but very few Bluetooth headsets are specifically designed for your computer. Be sure to test Bluetooth headsets thoroughly and make sure you understand Bluetooth's distance limitations—roughly 30 feet (10 meters). Obstructions in the line-of-sight will lower the effective range dramatically. So if you wander very far from your desk, sound quality issues and dropped calls will result.

Plantronics CS-50 USB Bluetooth Headset

Key Points

- **User level** Targeted at basic, intermediate, and advanced users
- **Platforms** Microsoft Windows only
- **Cost** US $299

You can get more information at www.plantronics.com/north_america/en_US/products/cat640035/cat5480033/prod5300004.

Features of the CS-50

- Instant USB connectivity for easy compatibility and quick setup for softphones

- The only complete wireless VoIP solution—take conversations up to 200 feet with no headset cables

- The first wireless with remote-ring detection and call answer/end at the touch of a button, thanks to Plantronics' PerSonoCall™ software

- Superior sound quality for clear, private, and completely secure calls, including noise-canceling microphone and TIA810a compliance for echo elimination

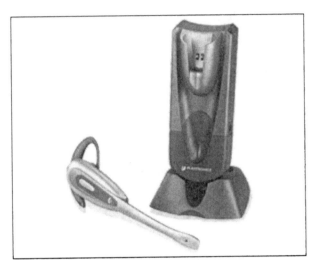

Photo as featured on www.plantronics.com

Telephone Gateways

A telephone gateway allows you to make Skype calls *or* calls from your existing telephone service using the same telephone that you use now. The following picture shows a typical telephone gateway configuration.

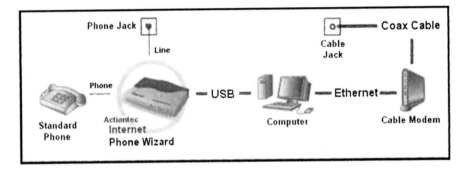

Diagram courtesy of Actiontec.com

The following picture is the back of a typical device to show you the three ports of a gateway. Some gateways have a fourth port to connect a fax machine.

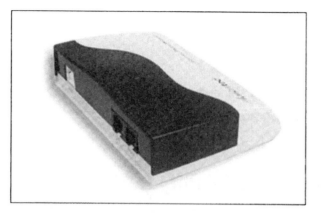

Photo as featured on Actiontec.com

The basic idea of a telephone gateway, or *Skype gateway* as we will now refer to them, is that they allow you to connect your existing telephone, corded or cordless base station (which may also include answering machine capabilities). You are then free to use the cordless handset anywhere in the house to make or receive both Skype calls and regular telephone calls. In Chapter 9 we cover how to install one of these units to allow you to make Skype calls away from your computer. The following section details some of the providers of these devices and their features. We will leave it up to you to decide which unit to purchase based on features, availability in your country, and cost.

Understanding the Basics... Telephone Gateways

A Skype gateway is the best device to purchase to free yourself from using the computer to make Skype calls and be able to use your existing cordless telephone.

VoSky (Actiontec) Internet Phone Wizard

Actiontec recently renamed its Skype product line to VoSky to better focus the Skype products. The VoSky Internet Phone Wizard (IPW) is probably one of the most popular Skype gateways available. It provides an excellent software driver and is as easy to use as any gateway, though easy to use is what all Skype gateways should be. One key feature that many gateways do not have is the ability to place a Skype call on hold when a landline call is received (and vice versa), and to switch between the two calls. Several gateways allow only one call at a time, which causes callers on the other line to receive busy signal.

Key Points

- **User level** Targeted at basic, intermediate, and advanced users
- **Platforms** Microsoft Windows only
- **Cost** US $69.95, UK £39.95

You can get more information at www.vosky.com/index.htm.

Features of the Internet Phone Wizard

- Easy to install and use
- Patented I-Phone Switch for switching between Internet and regular phone modes
- Call waiting between Skype and landline calls
- Echo-cancellation technology
- Speed-dial integration with Skype
- No external power required
- Phone rings on incoming Skype or regular calls

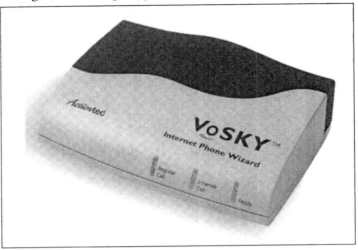

Photo as featured on Actiontec.com

VoSky (Actiontec) Call Center

The VoSky Call Center is the latest Skype gateway from VoSky that does everything the IPW does and more. If you want to be able to call home on your cell phone, for example, and make a Skype call to Austria via Skype or SkypeOut, you can do all that with the VoSky Call Center. If your Skype contact is offline, the device will call you back and let you know when he or she is online. It also has Call Forwarding and a software answering machine. Below is a picture of the VoSky Call Center configuration.

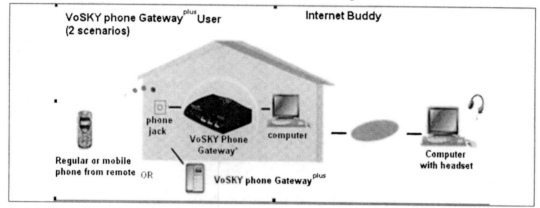

Diagram courtesy of Actiontec.

Key Points

- **Potential users** Home, small businesses, medium-sized businesses, and corporations

- **User level** Targeted at basic, intermediate, and advanced users

- **Platforms** Microsoft Windows only

- **Cost** Varies depending on the country

You can get more information at www.vosky.com/index.htm.

Features of the VoSky Call Center

- Outgoing call forwarding (Internet calls to ordinary phones)

- Incoming call forwarding (ordinary phone calls to Internet calls)

- Call notification when Skype contact is online

- Computer answering machine software included

- Connects directly to your home phone so you can make and receive Skype and regular calls from your phone

- Patented I-Phone switch for switching your phone between Skype and ordinary phone modes

- Call waiting

- Caller ID for Internet calls

- Patented I-Phone switch for switching your phone between Skype and ordinary phone modes

- Supports Skype speed-dial and SkypeOut service

- Voice menu

- No external power required

- Echo-cancellation technology

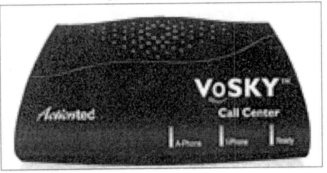

Photo as featured on Actiontec.com

YapperNut YapperBox

This is a feature-rich Skype gateway that includes a software answering machine, and it performs well.

Key Points

- **User level** Targeted at basic, intermediate, and advanced users

- **Platforms** Microsoft Windows only

- **Cost** US $49.95

You can get more information at www.yappernut.com/us/en/yapperBox.htm.

Features of the YapperBox

- Amy software answering machine software

- Morning call – wake up call

- Separate audio for Skype calls

- Pass-through line allows regular telephone to ring if the computer is off

- Call switching

- USB powered

Note: The phone is not included with the YapperBox. The cell phone photo (left) is featured on Panasonic.com. The Yapperbox photo is featured on Yappernut.com.

RapidBox

The RapidBox is another Skype gateway that offers all the basic functions you would need.

Key Points

- **User level** Targeted at basic, intermediate, and advanced users

- **Platforms** Microsoft Windows only

- **Cost** US $49.95

You can get more information at http://rapidvoip.com/products.html.

Features of the RapidBox

- Send/receive both VoIP calls and PSTN regular calls

- PC-to-PC, PC-to-phone, phone-to-phone operation

- Built-in driver; no additional driver is needed

- USB1.1 Plug-and-Play, no sound card needed

- Complies with H.323, MGCP, and SIP

- Echo cancellation, noise reduction

- Full-duplex communication

- Auto Calling Router (ACR) function

- No external power required

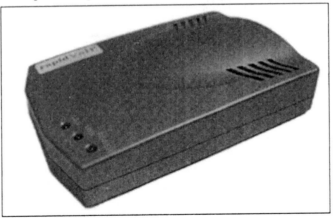

Photo as featured on http://rapidvoip.com

SkyBox

The SkyBox is another Skype gateway that offers all the basic functions you would need.

Key Points

- **User level** Targeted at basic, intermediate, and advanced users

- **Platforms** Microsoft Windows only

- **Cost** US $44.90

You can get more information at www.mplat.com/eng/productdetail.asp?post=22.

Features of the SkyBox

- Make/receive both VoIP calls and PSTN regular calls

- Incoming calls ring loudly

- PC-to-PC, PC-to-phone, phone-to-phone operation

- Driver built-in; no additional driver or plug-in software required

- Plug-and-Play, USB1.1 compatible, no external power/sound card required

- Echo cancellation, noise reduction

- Full-duplex communication with crystal-clear speech

- ACR function

- Complies with H.323, MGCP, and SIP

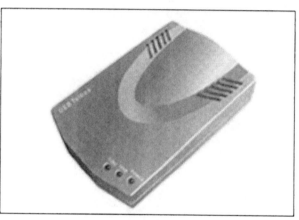

Photo as featured on www.mplat.com

iPMate

iPMate is another Skype gateway maker that has several models to choose from and includes a PCI Card version that installs inside the computer.

Key Points

- **User level** Targeted at basic, intermediate, and advanced users

- **Platforms** Microsoft Windows only

- **Cost** Depends on the country

You can get more information at www.skype.net.cn.

Features of iPMate Devices

- Allows you to forward the Skype phone call into PSTN

- Allows you to forward the PSTN phone call to Skype phones

- Skype follow me: W90 can forward Skype phone calls to mobile phones; allows you to receive Skype phone calls anywhere, anytime

- Skype to any (local) phone: W90 can forward Skype phone calls to any phone

- Allows you to call any phone or mobile phone anywhere in the world at the local phone fee rate if W90 is used in pairs

- Allows you to call any phone or mobile phone anywhere in the world via SkypeOut at the local phone fee plus the SkypeOut fee

- DSP and echo cancellation

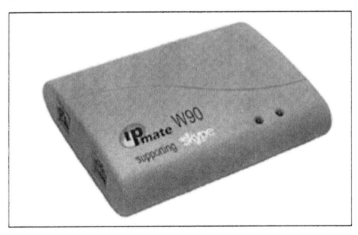

Photo as featured on www.skype.net.cn

Telephone Adapters

Telephone adapters connect your computer to only one phone and do not integrate with any local telephone service. These adapters are for people who know they do not need to integrate a local telephone service but want the flexibility of using a cordless phone, for example. These adapters could be used in small to large businesses to allow a cordless phone to be placed on a desk. The following picture shows how a telephone adapter connects.

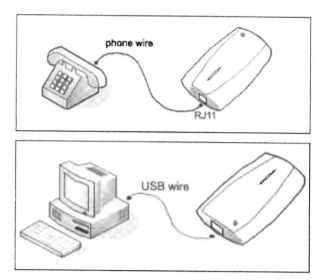

PhoneConnector Phone Adapter

Key Points

- **User level** Targeted at basic, intermediate, and advanced users
- **Platforms** Microsoft Windows only
- **Cost** US $34.95

You can get more information at www.phoneconnector.com/products.aspx.

Features of the PhoneConnector

- Eliminates the need for a headset or microphone/speaker combination
- Adds mobility using a cordless phone
- A hardware-based answering machine may be added to provide voicemail to any VoIP client
- Three-way calling with Skype
- Supports multiple VoIP clients: Skype, Xten, MSN, PCPhone, Yahoo, and others

Photos as featured on www.phoneconnector.com

PCPhoneLine VTA1000

The PCPhoneLine VTA1000 is a basic Skype adapter that provides the ability to connect a telephone to your computer.

Key Points

- **User level** Targeted at basic, intermediate, and advanced users
- **Platforms** Microsoft Windows only
- **Cost** US $59.00

You can get more information at www.pcphoneline.com.

Features of the VTA1000

- Eliminates the need for a headset or microphone/speaker combination
- Adds mobility using a cordless phone
- A hardware-based answering machine may be added to provide voicemail to any VoIP client
- Supports many of the VoIP clients from AOL, MSN, Skype, Yahoo, and others
- Works with H.323 and SIP-compliant VoIP networks

Photo as featured on www.pcphoneline.com

USB Phones

There are many varieties of USB phones, from wired to cordless, and from basic to fully Skype-enabled. There are many sizes and options, so be sure to consider the features you desire before selecting a specific unit.

DualPhone

The DualPhone was the first to appear, and is still the most popular USB cordless and fully Skype-enabled phone. It also acts as a Skype gateway, allowing you to connect your landline to the same base station. We are not aware of any better alternatives that also include the connection of a landline (more on this topic in Chapter 9).

Key Points

- **User level** Targeted at basic, intermediate, and advanced users
- **Platforms** Microsoft Windows only
- **Cost** US $139.99, €134.95 for a base unit; US $79.99, €67.50 for additional extensions

You can get more information at www.dualphone.net.

Features of the DualPhone

- Call free of charge worldwide via Skype to other Skype users; all other calls are charged

- Two-in-one cordless telephone—Internet telephone and standard telephone in one

- Plug and dial, easy to install, easy to use

- International and long distance calls at low rates with SkypeOut (requires purchase of SkypeOut credit online)

- Extra telephone line free of charge—simultaneous ordinary telephone and Internet calls

- Ability to participate in Skype conference calls

- Secure and encrypted communication

- Multiple handset capacity—up to four units

- Caller ID (CLIP)

- Call forwarding, Call waiting

- Future-proof: The software of the handset and base station can be updated via the USB interface

- Dialing via PSTN (requires a telephone subscription with a telecommunications operator)

- Dialing via Internet: Skype to other Skype users

- Dialing via SkypeOut to standard telephone numbers

- Distinctive ringing between standard telephone and Internet calls

- Range: Indoor up to 50 meters/outdoor up to 300 meters

- Talk time/standby time: Up to 6.5 hours/up to 100 hours

- 16KHz audio sampling

- Telephone book: 160 entries

- Redial: 30 entries

- Call log: 30 entries

- Key lock

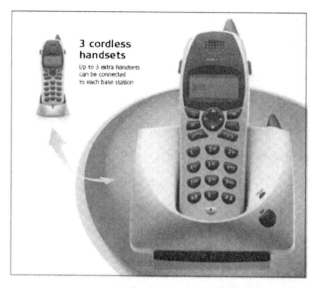

Photo as featured on www.dualphone.net

Linksys CIT200

Linksys has entered the Skype telephone market with this cordless telephone. This device does not connect to your local telephone service, so if you still have a landline it will not eliminate the need for an extra phone, and it will still be attractive to businesses that desire a cordless Skype phone. For a very detailed review of the product, visit the following Web site: http://blog.tmcnet.com/blog/tom-keating/skype/linksys-cit200-skype-phone-review.asp.

Key Points

- **User level** Targeted at basic, intermediate, and advanced users
- **Platforms** Microsoft Windows only
- **Cost** US $129.99

You can get more information at www1.linksys.com/international/product.asp?coid=52&ipid=821.

Features of the CIT200

- Complete cordless Internet phone solution for Skype
- Connects Skype to Skype

- Connects Skype to regular phone lines (with SkypeOut service)

- Accepts calls from the regular phone network to Skype (with SkypeIn service)

- Plug and dial—easy to install and easy to use

- Expandable—a single base station supports up to four handsets

- Intercom support allows talk between multiple handsets

- Built-in speakerphone in handset

- Graphical color LCD display with status indicators

- Superior sound quality

- Voice encryption for maximum security

- Standby time 120 hours, talk time 10 hours

- Base station with USB connection to your PC

Photos as featured on www1.linksys.com

Siemens M34 USB Gigaset Adapter

This device allows you to add a supported Siemens Gigaset cordless telephone to your computer. The supported Siemens Gigaset cordless telephone must be purchased separately if you do not already own one. You can read a review at the following Web site: http://digital-lifestyles.info/display_page.asp?section=platforms&id=1910.

Key Points

- **User level** Basic, intermediate, and advanced

- **Platforms** Microsoft Windows only

- **Cost** US $129.00, plus a compatible Siemens cordless phone

You can get more information at http://gigaset.siemens.com/shc/ 0,1935,hq_en_0_69566_rArNrNrNrN,00.html.

Features of the Siemens M34

- USB data adapter for PCs: Cordless data transmission with ISDN telephone line

- Enables Internet calls via Gigaset S44 and Gigaset C34 cordless handsets

  - Gigaset SX445isdn

  - Gigaset SX440isdn

  - Gigaset SL440, S645, S445, S440, C345 and C340

  - Gigaset CX345isdn

  - Gigaset CX340isdn

- Transmission of Messenger Services to/from Gigaset cordless handsets: News ticker, SMS, etc.

- Internet applications via Gigaset cordless handset: Internet radio anywhere at home

- Compatible with Microsoft Windows 98SE, ME, 2000, XP

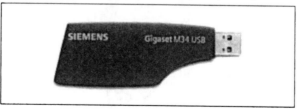

Photo as featured on http://gigaset.siemens.com

VoSky USB Phone

The VoSky USB phone is a basic USB wired phone that can be added to your laptop bag or to your desk. Skype calls can then be made using a device that has the look and feel of a familiar telephone handset.

Key Points

- **User level** Targeted at basic, intermediate, and advanced users
- **Platforms** Microsoft Windows only
- **Cost** Varies depending on the country

You can get more information at www.vosky.com/index.htm.

Features of the VoSky USB Phone

- Easy to install and use
- Speed-dial integration with Skype
- Full-duplex audio with adjustable volume control
- Call waiting and hold features
- Conference calling
- LED displays call status
- Microphone mute to protect your privacy

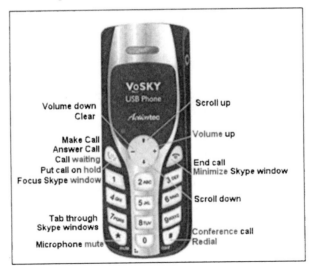

Photo as featured on http://www.vosky.com

SimplyPhone

The SimplyPhone is a basic USB wired phone that can be added to your laptop bag or to your desk. Skype calls can then be made using a device that has the look and feel of a familiar telephone handset.

Key Points

- **User level** Targeted at basic, intermediate, and advanced users
- **Platforms** Microsoft Windows only
- **Cost** €54.50

You can get more information at www.simplyphone.lu.

Features of the SimplyPhone

- Fully Skype certified
- Comes in blue, green, red, or silver
- Comes with country colors and country logo of Germany, France, or the United Kingdom
- Standard phone keypad and LCD display
- Phone rings for incoming calls; select your ring tone
- PC-to-PC and PC-to-phone
- No sound card or external power required
- USB1.1 compatible
- Echo cancellation and noise reduction
- Caller ID functionality

Photos as featured on www.simplyphone.lu

US Robotics USR9600 and USR809600

Key Points

- **User level** Targeted at basic, intermediate, and advanced users
- **Platforms** Microsoft Windows only
- **Cost** Depends on the country

You can get more information at www.usr.com/talk/details.asp.

Features of the USR 9600

- Compatible with Skype
- Auto-interface with Skype accounts
- Excellent voice quality
- Full-duplex operation
- Full-featured LED screen
- Caller ID

Photo as featured on www.usr.com

IPEVO

IPEVO makes two models of USB phone, namely the Free-1 and the Touch-1. Both are available in white or black, and in two-packs. These USB phones have attractive features.

Key Points

- **User level** Targeted at basic, intermediate, and advanced users
- **Platforms** Microsoft Windows only
- **Cost** US $15.99 for the Touch-1 and US $29.99 for the Free-1

You can get more information at www.ipevo.com.

Features of the IPEVO Free-1

- Superior sound quality (16KHz sampling rate)
- User-programmable buttons enhance customization
- Smart and stylish design, small form factor and lightweight
- Ten selectable ring tones (including silent)
- USB Plug-and-Play technology
- PC sound card not required
- Independent use of phone and sound card allows for Skype calls while listening to music on PC
- LED indicates USB connection state plus off-hook condition

- Acoustically isolated speaker and microphone to eliminate echo
- Built-in volume control and mute button

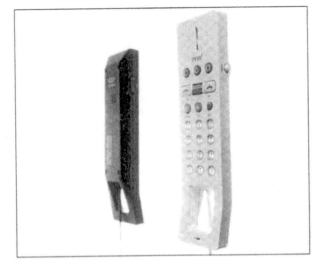

Photos as featured on www.ipevo.com

Features of the IPEVO Free-1

- Fully integrated with Skype
- Flashing LED indicates incoming calls
- Assign up to 100 speed dials to contacts
- Four selectable ring tones
- Easy to install USB Plug-and-Play technology (driver required to integrate with Skype)
- PC sound card not required
- Press the **Show Skype** button and Skype window will pop up
- Independent use of phone and sound card allows for Skype calls while listening to music on PC
- Superior sound quality

Photos as featured on www.ipevo.com

PCPhoneLine VPT1000

The PCPhoneLine VPT1000 is your basic USB corded phone.

Key Points

- **User level** Targeted at basic, intermediate, and advanced users
- **Platforms** Microsoft Windows only
- **Cost** US $49.00

You can get more information at www.pcphoneline.com.

Features of the VPT1000 Device

- Regular telephone call experience with comfort noise generation (CNG)
- Volume control button on phone set
- On-hook/off-hook buttons
- Standard DTMF-style keypad
- H.323/SIP Control Protocol Support
- All types of dialup and broadband Internet connects supported
- Automatic NAT firewall detection and traversal

- DHCP compliant

- DTMF detection/generation and out-of-band signaling (H.323)

- Full-duplex voice compression

- High-performance echo management

- Voice activity detection to save bandwidth by delivering voice, not silence

- Advanced dynamic jitter management

- Gateway ANI authentication support

- Automatic gatekeeper and registrar server registration

- Automatic route to hotline on off-hook

- Call volume control setting

- NetMeeting/Windows Messenger compatible

Photo as featured on www.pcphoneline.com.

CyberPhone K

The CyberPhone K is a good USB desk phone. CyberPhone makes several other devices as well. Visit the product Web site for more details: www.skype.voipvoice.com.

Key Points

- **User level** Targeted at basic, intermediate, and advanced users

- **Platforms** Microsoft Windows only

- **Cost** UK£39.99

You can get more information at www.skype.voipvoice.com.

Features of the CyberPhone Devices

- Solid-state hook switch

- Hook switch button in handset

- CCITT dial pad

- Volume up/down key

- LED for connection/status

- Directory key

- Dial key

- Redial key

- Latching mute key with LED

- USB cable, 2000mm

- Ringer

- Color side panels

Photo as featured on www.skype.voipvoice.com

Speaker Phones

Both home-office and business users like speaker phones because they can be placed on the desk or used in a conference room to provide convenient hands-free operation. They can effectives replace the requirement for a headset, a microphone/speaker combination, or a handheld USB phone.

VoSky Chatterbox

The VoSky Chatterbox is a basic speakerphone that meets the need for conference calls and hands-free operation with Skype.

Key Points

- **User level** Targeted at basic, intermediate, and advanced users
- **Platforms** Microsoft Windows only
- **Cost** Varies by country

You can get more information at www.VoSky.com.

Features of the VoSky Chatterbox

- Verified by and certified for Skype
- Replaces a headset or microphone/speaker combination
- Small, lightweight device goes anywhere you go
- Full-duplex speakerphone with adjustable volume and mute control
- DSP-enhanced sound quality

Photo as featured on www.VoSky.com

CyberSpeaker

The CyberSpeaker, from CyberPhone, provides speaker phone capabilities to Skype.

Key Points

- **User level** Targeted at basic, intermediate, and advanced users

- **Platforms** Microsoft Windows only

- **Cost** UK£36.99

You can get more information at www.skype.voipvoice.com.

Features of the CyberSpeaker

- The CyberSpeaker allows users to make conference calls over the Internet; it can be placed in the middle of a table while colleagues, friends, and family gather round to chat

- A futuristic design of USB handset with a large built-in speaker phone for all conferencing requirements

- The unit is plugged into a USB port and will be recognized by Windows as a USB device

- The product has a magnetic hook switch and LED indicators to show connection and when it's in use

- The CyberSpeaker features enhanced DSP echo cancellation and ASTI™, a proprietary algorithm for injecting artificial side tone, making the product as close to a traditional speaker phone as possible

Photo as featured on www.skype.voipvoice.com

IO Gear USB Speaker Phone

The IO Gear USB Speaker Phone is another small speaker phone unit.

Key Points

- **User level** Targeted at basic, intermediate, and advanced users
- **Platforms** Microsoft Windows only
- **Cost** Varies by country

You can get more information at www.iogear.com/main.php?loc=product&Item=GPH100U.

Features of the IO Gear USB Speaker Phone

- Full-duplex speaker phone with 110dB peak volume
- Use with IM software (AOL, MSN, Yahoo, etc.)
- Use with VoIP software (Skype, Vonage, Webex, etc.)
- Speaker: 2w peak, 40mm, 4ohm, 500Hz to 5KHz
- 8KHz input sampling rate
- USB audio
- 2.5mm headset jack
- Dimensions: 3.2 x 2.2 x 0.8 inches (8.1 x 5.5 x 2.0 cm)
- Weight: 1.5 ounces (42 grams)
- DSP voice processor
- 40mm Mylar speaker and Electret Condenser, omnidirectional microphones

Photo as featured on www.iogear.com

Desktop VoIP Phone with Speaker Phone

This VoIP phone is a full-featured desk phone that works with Skype.

Key Points

- **User level** Targeted at basic, intermediate, and advanced users
- **Platforms** Microsoft Windows only
- **Cost** UK£49.99

You can get more information at www.gadgets.co.uk/voip-phone-skype-desktop.html.

Features Desktop VoIP Phone with Speaker Phone

- Desktop phone with backlit LCD
- Commercial-grade, high-quality speaker phone, ideal for conference calls
- USB1.1 and 2.0 compatible, no need for a sound card
- Phone ring for incoming calls, ring style and volume selectable
- Complies with H.323, MGCP, and SIP
- Skype-ready through Skypelink bundled software
- Echo cancellation, noise reduction
- Full-duplex communication
- Caller ID function of VoIP calls, 199 incoming calls and 199 dialed numbers

Photo as featured on www.gadgets.co.uk

Other Hardware

Here we look at a device that is just a little different.

MPlat Flash Phone Portable USB Phone

The FlashPhone F1K for Skype is a USB audio device plus Flash drive. You can download and install Skype in the Flash drive, make and receive Skype calls with FlashPhone, save your Chat history, and transfer files with the Flash from the drive. The FlashPhone F1K focuses on the mobile user. Drop in any Internet café, keep your important files and chat record, plug in and talk, unplug and leave. This is the perfect stocking stuffer for your favorite Skyper.

Key Points

- **User level** Targeted at basic, intermediate, and advanced users
- **Platforms** Microsoft Windows only
- **Cost** US $46.90

You can get more information at www.mplat.com/eng/productdetail.asp?post=27.

Features MPlat F1K Flash Phone

- Compliant with USB1.1, 2.0 full-speed operation

- Compliant with USB audio device class specification v1.0

- Embedded USB audio device; doesn't require a sound card

- Embedded high-performance 16-bit audio DAC with earphone phone buffer

- Compatible with Win2000/Win XP without additional driver

- Power by USB port without additional power

- Volume up, volume down, and playback mute support

- Echo cancellation, loss noise reduction

- Full-duplex communication

- Embedded 5V to 3.3V regulator for single external 5V operation

- 48K/44.1KHz sampling rate for both playback and recording

- 32-bit DSP modifies and enhances the audio signal

- Includes microphone and speaker

- USB plug and talk, unplug and leave

- 128MB Flash storage capacity to store your files (roughly 90MB after Skype is loaded)

Photo as featured on www.mplat.com

Chapter 9

Getting the Most out of Skype

Solutions in this chapter:

- Using Skype without Sitting at Your Computer

- Using Skype with Your Local and Long Distance Phone Service

- Making Video Calls with Skype

Using Skype without Sitting at Your Computer

We have discussed many things that you can do with Skype. Now it is time to discuss how Skype can be used just as you use a regular telephone today. In Chapter 8 we talked about devices such as telephone gateways, telephone adapters, and Skype-enabled phones. In this chapter we discuss how to use these solutions to free yourself, your family, or your employees from sitting in front of a computer while receiving and making Skype calls.

Let's make it clear: In this chapter we are only talking about Skype voice calls. If you want to make file transfers or chat, you still need to do those tasks the traditional way, sitting at your computer. To make and receive Skype voice calls, on the other hand, you do not need to be sitting at your computer. However, you must have your computer turned on at all times; but you will be free from having to sit at it while you make and receive Skype calls. If you take our recommendations to use a personal firewall software and a DSL/cable router device, you are safe from harm in leaving your computer on all the time. To reduce power consumption, just turn off your monitor.

A Word about REN

REN, which stands for *ringer-equivalent number*, is a measurement of how much ringing power certain telephone equipment takes. RENs are used in the United States to determine how many telephones you can connect to the same telephone line or device such as an adapter or gateway and still get them ringing properly (a typical telephone line can drive about a three to five REN load).

This is important because we are often asked how many telephones can be hooked up to a Skype gateway or Skype adapter. The answer is one, maybe two per port, and that is it! Anything more than one telephone per port will overload the device and cause quality issues and potentially damage the unit. So make it common practice to connect only one telephone to any device we discuss. If you have any questions, check with the manufacturer for specifications on the device to see if more than one telephone can be connected using a splitter or if it can be used to backhaul your home from the device. If you don't know what *backhaul* means, then you don't want to do it.

For the Home User (Windows Only)

Before we begin, the only currently available devices are for Windows-based computers. There are no Apple/Mac or Linux versions yet, but we expect there will be in the months to come. So for Apple/Mac and Linux users, reading this chapter is still a good idea because it will apply to you when a device or devices become available.

Let's start by making some assumptions about what the majority of people have for telephones in their homes today. There are basically three configurations people tell us they have spread out throughout their homes:

- One cordless telephone base with an answering machine and multiple extensions

- One cordless telephone base with extensions and some older wired telephones

- One or two separate cordless telephones and older wired telephones

There are three types of devices that you will be able to use in your home that work with your existing telephone setup or that will replace your existing telephone setup. We covered these in Chapter 8, "Gateways, Adapters, and Skype-Enabled Phones."

If you are like us and other "Skypers," you have been using Skype for awhile and love it and are reading this book to figure out how to simplify your multiple telephones and integrate Skype. Or you are reading this book and wondering how to update your existing setup to be able to take full advantage of Skype.

Existing Cordless Telephone with Answering Machine

Let's look at how to make Skype work "simply" with the optimal telephone setup. It will be up to you to figure out how to integrate everything you have into this optimal setup if you go outside what we are about to recommend.

So our first assumptions are:

- You just recently purchased a new cordless base unit with a built-in answering machine and three to four extensions and have retired all the wired telephones in your home.

- You still have your local and long distance telephone service.

Remember, this section is devoted to discussing how to start using Skype away from your computer; the next section discusses how to potentially reduce your telephone costs. The first goal is to get agreement from everyone in your home that using Skype is truly easy and that Skype can be used anywhere in your home, just like a normal telephone, with your existing telephone.

We are not recommending one type of device over another; our example is simply the most common configuration we have been told through e-mail and Web site inquiries that exists out in the real world or is the easiest for users to convert to.

The first step is to relocate your cordless base unit with or without an answering machine next to your computer. So start here and rearrange your telephones.

The second step is to purchase a Skype telephone gateway like the ones we discussed in Chapter 8. I use the VoSky (Actiontec) Internet Phone Wizard in the example and diagrams because it is what I use, but I also like the YapperBox and there are others, so don't take what I use as an endorsement, since everyone has their own preferences. But if you are looking at purchasing a gateway, review the features, costs, availability, and compatibility in your country and get what you feel is best for your needs. Before we begin, the only currently available devices are for Windows-based computers. There are no Apple/Mac or Linux versions yet, but we expect these to begin appearing in the next few months. So for Apple/Mac and Linux users, reading this chapter is still useful because it will apply to you when such devices become available. A gateway has three connections—one or two for telephones, one for the local telephone service or landline, and a USB jack for connecting it to your computer. An adapter has only one telephone connector and one USB connector for your computer. There is one major reason to use a gateway over an adapter: *A Skype telephone gateway allows your existing local/long distance service and Skype to share the same cordless base-station/handsets that you use today.*

If you want Skype to remain separate from your local telephone service and you don't mind potentially having two telephones on your desk, then a telephone adapter may suffice for you, but bear in mind that a gateway is only marginally more expensive than an adapter, a gateway likely uses newer technology, and does everything an adapter can and more. So my recommendation is to purchase a gateway. The final decision, as always, is yours.

Understanding the Basics... Telephone Gateway or Adapter

Unless you are positive you only need a telephone adapter, purchase a Skype telephone gateway like those available from VoSky or YapperNut.

I will assume you have the typical 2.4GHz or 5.8GHz cordless phone unit. If you have an older 900MHz cordless phone, it is time to upgrade. Do not forget the *teenager factor!* If you have one or more teenagers in your home, I suggest you consider getting two cordless base units—one for the teens to hookup to their computer and the other for main home use. Or you might decide to integrate the Skype gateway for the kids and leave the local telephone service for the adults, and then use one of the kids' extensions when you want to talk with your Skype contacts or make inexpensive long distance calls.

By now we hope we have you thinking about how to set up your home phones and use Skype, so let's now see how. We have already told you to relocate your cordless telephone base near your computer—actually within six feet, or two meters, because the USB cable for the telephone gateway is that long. You could purchase a USB extension cable if necessary to extend the reach.

Connecting the gateway is fairly straightforward. First read the instructions to see how to install the software that you need on your computer *before* connecting the gateway to your computer. Once you install the software that comes with your gateway, connect the gateway to your computer. After it is connected and Windows finds the new hardware, you are ready to take the next step. The following picture shows a typical DSL user's configuration of a telephone gateway.

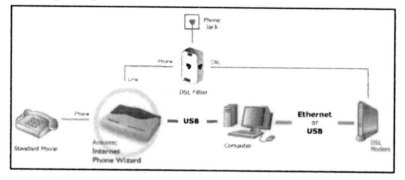

The following picture shows a typical cable modem user's configuration of a telephone gateway:

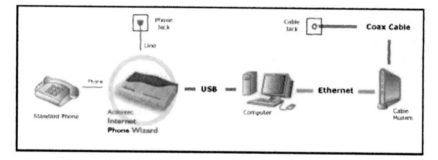

1. After you install the software, plug the USB connector into an available USB slot on your computer.

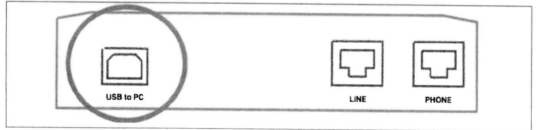

2. Plug your telephone line coming from the wall or DSL filter into the jack labeled *LINE*.

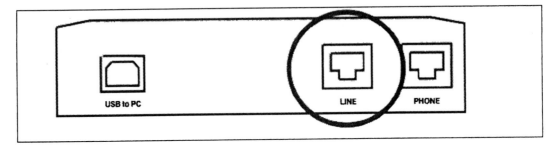

3. Plug your cordless phone base into the *PHONE* jack and you are done.

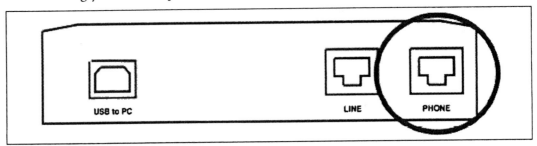

The first test is to pick up the cordless phone that is connected to the gateway and make a few normal landline calls exactly as before. No extra digits are required to make normal local or long distance telephone calls as before. Both incoming landline and incoming Skype calls are also answered exactly as you would expect. The only difference is the ring tone, which will change to allow you to recognize the arrival of incoming Internet (Skype) calls.

So let us proceed to the second test, which will be to have someone you know call you Skype-to-Skype. Your gateway-connected cordless should ring distinctively as mentioned. The gateway senses that this is an Internet call and will switch automatically, so you just answer as normal. Hang up as usual to end the call, and if everything has worked as expected, we will are now ready to set up the phone to make outbound Skype calls very easily.

To tell the gateway you wish to make an Internet call, you need to press some extra buttons. In the case of the VoSky Internet Phone Wizard (IPW), it is two 'pound' keys (##). This will cause the IPW to switch to the Internet call mode. Any Skype or SkypeOut contact that has been assigned a two-digit speed-dial number (00 thru 99) on the PC can then be called simply by pressing the two digits associated with the Contact list entry. SkypeOut calls can also be dialed manually the same way you would using Skype at the computer, except you dial '00' instead of '+' to start the international dial string (e.g. 00 123 456 7890). This is simple enough that anyone in your home should be able to quickly learn how to use the cordless phone to make Skype or SkypeOut calls.

Since most telephones today have memory-dialing capability, you can optionally program your favorite Skype or SkypeOut speed-dial entries directly into the phone. For example, I have recorded **## *pause* 01 in the phone's 01 memory location (and labeled it 'Dad's PC')** to have it automatically launch a Skype-to-Skype speed-dial call my father's PC. Similarly, location 02 is programmed with the SkypeOut number that would be used to dial my parents' home phone (and it is labeled 'Mom and Dad').

To call my parents' PC over the Internet using Skype or their home phone using SkypeOut, all I have to do is pick up my AT&T cordless phone, scroll through the memory-dial list, locate the correct entry visually, and press **Talk**. That's all granny would have to learn once it's all set up!

Most gateways should allow the cordless to be used in a similar fashion. As long as they are Skype-specific even telephone adapters should work out well. But if you are forced to populate a separate phone list on the gateway or adapter, I recommend looking elsewhere, because this should not be required. The device should be able to access and use the pre-existing Skype contact list on the PC.

Replacing Your Existing Telephone System

If you want to know what to replace your older telephone setup with to start over, seriously look at a 5.8GHz telephone that can take as many extensions as you need and has a built-in answering machine. Or take a look at a telephone like the Dualphone that has multiple extensions and does both Skype and regular telephone calls. You might need to purchase an answering machine, too, because the Dualphone or any other Skype-enabled telephones do not come with an answering machine. If you still plan to use local and long distance carriers, you will need an answering machine unless you pay for an answering service through your local telephone company. If you are using a VoIP provider, as I do Vonage, which has voice mail, and Skype, which has voice mail, I still recommend buying a cordless device with an answering machine. By using my cordless phone answering machine for both Skype and my local or VoIP service, I can check my messages for both over the Internet using Skype for free. This setup provides you the flexibility of using any or all combinations of voice mail.

Skype Groups

Skype Groups are a way for a family to purchase SkypeOut credits and apply them to individual users to centrally manage the credits and billing. The group administrator can allocate Skype credit, SkypeIn numbers, and Skype voice mail to all members of the group. For information on Skype Groups, visit Skype's Web site at www.skype.com/products/skypegroups/.

For the Small Business User (Windows Only)

We covered many of the small business possibilities in the "Home User" section; you can apply the same logic to a small business office with only a few telephones. The only exception is that a small business probably needs basic local and long distance service to send faxes because the number is locally recognized. You would not want to inform all your customers or clients of the telephone number change.

You could, however, use Skype the way we used to use the old WATS lines, early MCI calling cards, and other long distance carriers to save money, without having to enter the long access code. By adding Skype to a small business, you could allow access to much cheaper local toll and long distance calling. Think of Skype as a calling card that integrates with your existing equipment.

In the same ways you connect a home system, you could connect an additional cordless phone to a Skype telephone gateway and place an additional cordless phone on each desk for local toll and long distance needs. Keep in mind that the REN or power requirements of many of the multiline office phones might not work with the telephone gateways or adapters we discuss. Check with the manufacturer to see if the telephone system you have is compatible with the device. Keep in mind too that more devices for the small and medium-sized business are coming for applications just like yours.

Another option is to use a USB phone attached to each user's computer and provide SkypeOut credits for long distances calls or a SkypeIn number to help reduce costs. If you have conference calls with remote employees, you could use Skype, SkypeOut, or SkypeIn for these conference calls. SkypeOut now supports *free* 800-number calls, so when you use SkypeOut to call a toll-free number, you are not charged SkypeOut credits. Employees could use their laptops from home or a hotel, use SkypeOut to join a conference call, or use SkypeIn to get hold of someone in the office. If you want something to integrate Skype into your company's PBX, read the "Skype PBX Gateways" section of Chapter 15, "Future Skype-Enabled Devices," to understand what is coming in this space.

Skype Groups

Skype Groups are a way for a business to purchase SkypeOut credits and apply them as a company to individual users to centrally manage the credits and billing. The group administrator can allocate Skype credit, SkypeIn numbers, and Skype voice mail to all members of the group. For information on Skype Groups, visit Skype's Web site at www.skype.com/products/skypegroups/.

For the Medium-Sized and Large Business User (Windows Only)

There is not much difference between the small and medium-sized business as far as Skype goes. You can use devices similar to the ones we discussed in the "Home User" section, to add portability. If you want something to integrate Skype into your company's PBX, read the "Skype PBX Gateways" section of Chapter 15, "Future Skype-Enabled Devices," to understand what is coming in this space. You could also have USB phones issued to employees to make their Skype calls look and feel just like a normal telephone call, as well as being less expensive in terms of local toll or long distance calling.

Consider this example. I worked for a bank with a collections department that called all over the state and often outside the state. These collection department employees could have used Skype with USB phones and SkypeOut to significantly reduce the local toll and long distance costs. Many legitimate telemarketing companies do a large amount of local toll and long distance calling that could benefit from SkypeOut calls as well. If you have a large support organization, you could also use Skype or SkypeIn to reduce costs.

If you have conference calls with remote employees, you could use Skype, SkypeOut, and SkypeIn for these calls. SkypeOut now supports *free* 800-number calls, so when you use SkypeOut to call a toll-free number, you are not charged SkypeOut credits. Employees could use their laptops from home or a hotel, use SkypeOut to join a conference call, or use SkypeIn to get hold of someone in the office.

I do a lot of conference calls, and many companies reimburse employees for a home office telephone every month. With the exception of needing to fax documents, Skype can replace the need for a remote office landline. Also, most of us in the business world have cell phones, so between cell phones and Skype, you might be able to combine the services and save your company communication expenses. The larger the company, the larger the potential telecommunication cost savings using Skype.

If you want to be able to make Skype calls without being at your computer, we cover "Being Mobile with Skype" in Chapter 10. You can also use any of the cordless or wireless options mentioned in Chapter 8. In the medium-sized to large company, the dynamics of the need for telephone service are much more complex, and solutions where Skype may be used might be very tactical in nature—for example, telecommuters only or warehouse workers using WiFi devices. You will have to look at all the factors in deciding what solution to integrate and still be able to support it using your existing Help Desk staff. Take into account larger companies' network complexities, as we discuss in Chapter 13. Also, many larger companies use corporate IP Phone solutions offered by Cisco, Nortel, and others to connect their companies internally over their existing data network, to carry free voice calls within the corporation. All these details have to be evaluated and the pros and cons weighed to determine how best to add a solution like Skype to a medium-sized or large company. Also take a look at Chapter 12, "Business Uses for Skype," for more pertinent information.

Using Skype with Your Local and Long Distance Phone Service

This section is mostly targeted to the home user, but it can also apply to small and medium-sized businesses as well. Many people ask us, "Can Skype replace my existing telephone service?" The answer is, "It depends." We covered some of this subject in a previous chapter, but here is where we give you some ideas for saving money by using Skype with your existing local and long distance telephone carrier or, as in my case, with a VoIP provider like Vonage. The following picture is of my home configuration, with the exception that I also have a fax machine connected in line with my cordless base.

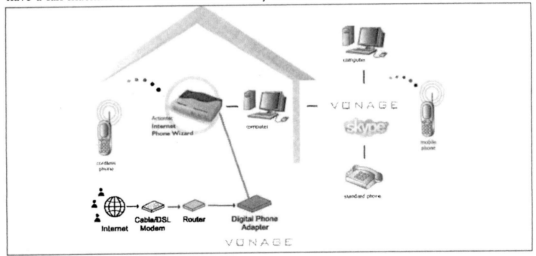

You can read two detailed articles I wrote last year on the cost savings this system provided me on www.SkypeTips.com:

- www.skypetips.internetvisitation.org/articles/Vonage_and_skype.html
- www.skypetips.internetvisitation.org/articles/replacing_local_phone_service_with_Skype.html

The basic idea is that I reduced my telephone bill roughly 60 percent by replacing Ma Bell, as we call it here in the United States, with a combination of Vonage, Skype, SkypeIn, SkypeOut, and, of course, my cell phone, which I use predominantly for business. Even this setup I went to a year ago has allowed me to reduce the minutes of my cell phone plan and save my company money! As we discussed previously, Skype does not have 411 or 911 service, so to use Skype alone will limit some of your capabilities or needs. Not having 911 or the equivalent of an emergency service is also something you need to weigh and that we won't recommend.

I have a cousin who has only Skype and his cell phone at his home and uses cable as his broadband provider. So there are options for you to consider before you go telling your local phone service to take a hike. British Telecom, for example, is so worried about solutions like Skype and other VoIP providers that it recently reduced its long distance rates to match or beat those of Skype.

In the United States, VoIP providers are required to provide e911 service that will allow emergency services to find your address when you call for help. Skype is *not* currently required to provide this service, because it is not a true telephone service provider. However, this could change in time as the growth in this area results in people not getting the emergency services they need, which is what led the United States to pass a law making it a requirement of companies like Vonage, Packet8, AT&T CallVantage, and Time Warner Digital phone to provide direct e911 emergency services..

So once you decide what you need as far as 411 information and 911 emergency services, you can then make a decision as to how to best reduce your regular telephone charges.

I use Vonage for three reasons: one, for the e911 service; two, for inbound and outbound faxes; and three, to have a second or third phone line. Now I use the cheaper monthly plan of US$15 per month for 500 minutes, since that is all I need because I have my cell phone, Skype, SkypeOut, and SkypeIn. Other VoIP providers like Time Warner charge US$39.95 for unlimited local and long distance service and have only one plan—all or nothing. Vonage, for example is US$20 per month less and limited to 500 minutes. I have not spent US$50 in long distance charges in almost two years with Skype and SkypeOut, so by adding Vonage and SkypeOut I saved significantly over my local telephone provider and the VoIP offering from my cable provider.

I was recently in Canada on business and had a conversation with a man who had purchased four cell phones with the minimal service of 500 minutes per phone and a family plan for himself, his wife, and their two children, both of whom live in different cities in Canada than he and his wife. He pays roughly $200 Canadian per month for all four phones and unlimited calls between the phones only. This is basically the cheapest plan that he found in Canada for his situation. The added benefit was the family plan for his family and his children, who are away at college, could call each other anytime for free, and he says it paid for itself in six months.

Could Skype replace this setup and save money? Well, yes, at first glance, when you see the $200 per month figure. But the reality is that most of us already have cell phones, so we have already accepted the monthly cost of $30 or so. So now the added cost of the unlimited family plan is only adding $20 per user. This would be hard to replace with Skype or Vonage because we are so mobile these days, but this plan does require that all family members have the exact same cell carrier and the same cell plan, which in this case Dad pays for.

Most of us need to call more than family—in fact, I call friends and colleagues more than I call my family. Besides, I talk with my father mostly on Skype because he has been completely converted, as have his two brothers and their children. We are all Skypers and talk more with Skype than we did before Skype—so hey, I helped the family communicate more. Since there is little chance that everyone you know uses the same cell service and has the option to join these family plans, using Skype can save money if you hook it up so that even the least tech-savvy user can use it.

There is no doubt you can reduce to the minimum or eliminate your long distance calling plan by adding Skype and SkypeOut and thus save money. You could also potentially save money by replacing your local service with a VoIP provider, as I have with Vonage. My suggestion is to add and integrate Skype with your existing telephone system or replace your older system with a Skype-enabled telephone setup like Dualphone and then turn off or reduce your calling plans as you prove that the new setup is saving you money or that you have truly reduced your reliance on your local and long distance plans.

Understanding the Basics... Add Skype first

We recommend you add Skype to your existing plans and ensure it will save you money before you replace your existing services.

Making Video Calls with Skype

This topic of this section is, without a doubt, the nearest and dearest to my heart as far as Skype goes. We have discussed many aspects of Skype, but one that I find most interesting is the use of Skype to make video calls with your family, friends, and colleagues. We refer to video calls that you make with Skype as *personal video calls*, in contrast with the business solutions that are full-blown videoconferencing solutions that cost more and demand more from network resources.

I use Skype with a couple different add-ons and with MSN Messenger to make great-quality video calls with my six-year-old daughter when I am traveling on business or every other weekend when she is with her mom. I also use Skype to talk with my parents, who live 1,400 miles away in Utah, which includes my daughter participating in video calls with her grandparents and even great-grandparents who now live with my parents.

Video calls are the next big wave that will sweep the Skype community and other IM products as they strive to compete with Skype. Imagine not only being able to talk with your family, friends, and colleagues but also *see* them in real time via video. There are so many applications for video technology that the list is endless. Some examples are:

- Keeping in touch with your children when you travel on business

- Keeping in touch with family

- Keeping in touch with friends

- Business meetings

- Remote education

- Non-custodial parents with their children

- "Empty nesters" when the children go away to college or move away from home

- Communicating with family in elder care facilities

- Hearing-impaired community

Personal Video Calls

We define *personal video calls* as video calls that are between two people only. There are solutions that allow more than two people to participate, but for the home broadband space, we recommend only two users until the speed catches up with the technology and the video technology improves to allow higher-quality video sent in a smaller payload to more people. For now we focus on two-person video calls. If you want to try the multiuser solutions and they work for your needs, by all means let us know what you find and what your application is for video calls.

Currently two video add-on solutions are available for Skype as well as a separate product that you can use with Skype to have a great video call. Here are some important things you need to know before you can do video calls:

- Upload speed of your broadband connection

- Webcam selection

- Screen size or screen resolution

- Lighting

- Bandwidth requirements of the video call solution

- Frame rate vs. image quality

We provide an overview of making video calls, since the subject is a book in itself—which is why shortly after this book is released, I will be releasing another book on everything you need to know to make great video calls with your family, friends, and colleagues. Watch our Web sites, www.SkypeTips.com and www.VideoCallTips.com, for the release of the video call book, *Making Video Calls: Using Skype, MSN Messenger, SightSpeed, iChat AV with Your Webcam Along with Other Solutions to Make Video Calls.*

That book will also cover topics such as cell phone video calls, Pocket PC video calls, specialized hardware to make video calls, and many business videoconferencing solutions—even Web-based conferencing solutions.

Upload Speed

First, video calls require a high-speed broadband Internet connection—the faster, the better. Video is one option that can use up every bite of speed your Internet connection can provide. Most important, the upload speed of the Internet connection is key to making and having good video calls. The minimum upload speed for having a decent video call is 128Kbps, but we recommend your broadband connection have at least:

- 200Kbps upload speed
- 1Mbps Download speed

Of course, if you can get more speed than this for a reasonable cost, by all means, do it! There is a simple rule for video calls: You can never have too much bandwidth. Also keep in mind that both sides of the video call need high-speed connections. Your video call will be only as good as the slowest Internet connection between the users participating in the video call.

Internet Speed Tests

You can go to the following Web sites to run a speed test to find out your Internet speed. Be sure to select a site that will provide you both the upload and download speeds:

- www.dslreports.com/stest
- www.internetfrog.com

Webcam Choice

The first piece of equipment you need to have a video call is a webcam. These are readily available at any computer store, office supply, or any online store. The three big vendors of webcams are Logitech, Creative, and Ezonics, with Logitech the largest, and in my opinion, the best. I use and recommend the high-end Logitech webcams like the Quickcam 4000 and 5000 and Quickcam Pro for notebooks. Two types of webcam sensor make up the bulk of all webcams:

- CCD sensor
- CMOS sensor

The only webcams we recommend you consider are those using CCD sensors. The CCD sensor provides a crisper video and better lighting than the older CMOS sensors. On my www.VideoCallTips.com site you can find the latest updated information about webcams and all the solutions and tips you'll need to start making great-quality video calls.

Understanding the Basics... Webcam Selection

The better the webcam, the better the image quality. When it comes to webcams, you get what you pay for.

Screen Size or Screen Resolution

When you first start to participate in video calls, you will wonder why the video screen tends to default to the size of a credit card. This is because the video codecs used are 320 × 240 resolution by default. You cannot change this setting. Each provider controls the video codec they use and how big the image will be due to the size of video that can be consistently sent over broadband connections without overwhelming the connection.

Many of the solutions have a full-screen option, and you will notice the picture gets grainy or "pixilated" when it's viewed full screen. This is the same concept of taking a small photograph and blowing it up to a full page. You will get a grainier picture from increasing the size. Increasing the size of a video call window does not increase the data you send or receive, only the size of the picture you view.

Full-screen video is the reason the resolution of your screen and monitor will be important when you make video calls. The larger resolution your monitor and video card can support, the more pixilated the full-screen video will become. To minimize this issue, you can set your computer's screen resolution to a lower setting.

- **640 x 480** Optimal for full screen

- **800 x 600** Better in full screen

- **1024 x 768** Good in full screen

- **1280 x 1024** Gets pixilated in full screen

- **1600 x 1280** Will produce a poor image in full screen

Understanding the Basics... Screen Resolution

For the best full screen video call, use the lowest setting your video card and monitor can support and that you are comfortable with.

Lighting

Lighting is important because it can cause a washout if the lighting is too bright or a grainy picture if there is not enough light—or if a light source is behind a user and the camera can see it, there will be a sunspot on your video. Try to illuminate the front of your face for best results.

Understanding the Basics... Lighting for Video Calls

To have a crisp video call, be sure to light the front of your face and turn off all overhead lights and lighting behind you.

Bandwidth Requirements

Each video call application uses a different amount of bandwidth. The amount it uses directly controls the quality or crispness of the video and the frame rate in which the video is sent and received. The general rule of thumb is the more frame rate used, the larger the video data being sent, thus requiring more bandwidth from your broadband connection.

Solutions that use less frame rate versus better image quality will take up less bandwidth. MSN Messenger, for example, has a very crisp picture but a slower frame rate. Many solutions give you the ability to adjust frame rate versus quality to best suit your broadband connection.

Frame Rate versus Image Quality

One of the factors you will notice in selecting a video call solution to use with Skype will be the trade-off between frame rate and image quality. As we just mentioned, the sharper the image, the fewer frames per second or fluid motion you will send and receive. The lower-quality image you send and receive, the faster frame rate or fluid motion you will have. Think of it this way: The better the image, the slower the video movement, and the faster the video movement, the lower the quality of the image. This is all due to the bandwidth limitations of broadband we have at home.

As we see faster broadband connections being offered, we will see better quality and faster frame rates for video calls. For now, you will see a trade-off between image quality and frame rate in the video call solutions, and you have to select what you like best. Regardless, the options for video calls with Skype are pretty good, and the experience you will have will be very good if you have a decent broadband connection.

Video Call Solutions

Here we discuss three applications that work well with Skype. Two of them are direct add-ons that work with Skype; the other is a completely different solution but worth looking at. The three applications are:

- **Spontania Video4IM** Skype plug-in

- **Santa Cruz Networks Festoon** Skype plug-in

- **MSN Messenger** Stand-alone solution for webcam only

NOTE

These video call applications work only with Microsoft Windows. For solutions that work with Windows and Apple, please read my forthcoming book on video calls, mentioned earlier in this chapter.

As we discussed earlier, an important aspect of video calls is the bandwidth required by the application. Will it be choppy over slower DSL or wireless hotspot broadband connections, or is the application designed for these slower connections? The slowest broadband connections you will most likely find are in public hotspots, hotels, or, some cases, your home DSL broadband connection. These applications will work well from home and hotels with good bandwidth and with or without NAT, but you could have issues if you are behind a corporate firewall and need to set a proxy server, as discussed in Chapters 6 and 13.

If you have a slower broadband connection, selecting a video call application that works well over slower connections, as well as over faster connections, will most likely be the best choice for you. Also, the more simple the features, the better for slower connections. Festoon, for example, can handle multiparty video calls. This requires more bandwidth and thus would not be the best choice for video calls in slower broadband situations.

We recommend that you test each application for your environment and decide which one works best for you. We point out some strong points and weaknesses of each of the video call applications to help you make a choice for your video call experience. Or you might decide to use all of them, since different people use different applications. I use three or four different video call applications on a regular basis. As long as they play well together and release the webcam when the application is minimized, you can run multiple plug-ins or applications and be ready for anyone who wants to do a video call with you.

Understanding the Basics...
Webcam Released When Minimized

A good video call application releases the webcam when minimized so that other applications can share the webcam when needed. Avoid video call applications that do not release the webcam when minimized, unless you know it is the only application you will ever use.

Getting Started

The first step is to install the webcam driver and application software and make sure your webcam is working with the webcam application before you begin to test any video call applications. This will help ensure that your webcam is not the issue if you run into problems testing various video call applications. Also be sure to use a supported webcam that the vendor supports. If your webcam is older than three years, be sure to check that the vendor supports your webcam. A general rule of thumb is, if the webcam has Windows XP drivers, it should work fine.

The screen shots that are shown in the following section were all taken during the same time of day to give you some perspective on the differences between the products.

Spontania Video4IM

One of the simpler video call plug-ins is Spontania's Video4IM. This application is still in beta testing but is a simple add-in for Skype that allows you to have good video calls with other Skype users. Let's look at some advantages and disadvantages.

Advantages

- Simple interface
- Both picture-in-picture and side-by-side video screens
- Full-screen capability with or without picture-in-picture
- Low bandwidth use
- Works in most environments
- Works well over a good WiFi connection

Disadvantages

The full screen is not adjustable.

Where to Get Video4IM

After you have verified that your webcam is installed, you will need to download Spontania Video4IM from www.video4im.com.

Once you install Video4IM, Skype will pop up a screen that asks you if it is OK for Spontania4IM.exe to be allowed to use Skype. Select **Allow this program to use Skype**, as shown in the following screen:

When Video4Im starts, you will see the following screen. Here you can test your webcam to make sure everything is working.

If your webcam is installed correctly, all you have to do is select the  icon or the button to start your webcam. You should see yourself on the screen, similar to the way the following picture shows me:

Here is a full-screen picture from Video4IM.

This full-screen picture has the option of picture-in-picture as well in the lower-right corner so the sender can see him or herself.

Focus your webcam and you are now ready to make a video call with another Skype user who has Video4IM. Just close Video4IM and you should see the  icon in the taskbar.

Before you can use Video4IM automatically with a Skype call, you should enable two option settings:

- **Start with any video call** This option allows you to start a video call with any incoming Skype call or invite users who do not have Video4IM installed. If both users have this option selected, the video call will automatically start when the Skype call is answered. If you'd rather be prompted to start a video call, do not select this item.

- **Run with Skype** Video4IM will be launched any time Skype starts.

Understanding the Basics... Video4IM Options

We recommend setting **Run with Skype** as a minimum setting so that Video4IM is always available to you for a video call.

Making a Video Call with Video4IM and Skype

Before you attempt a video call with one of your Skype contacts, you should first be sure you have the Video4IM  icon in your taskbar. When you place a Skype call to one of your contacts who has Video4IM, you will see the following screen appear as Video4IM checks to see that the other contact has Video4IM installed.

After the Skype call is established, if you both have Video4IM installed and Start with any video call selected, Video4IM will start a video call automatically. If your other contact does not have Start with any video call selected, you will be presented with the following screen:

If your contact does not have Video4IM installed, you will see a screen similar to this one:

You can invite your contact to use Video4IM with a chat message that looks like the following:

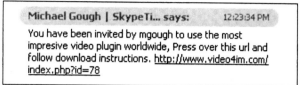

Your contact will then be able to follow the URL in the chat message and download Video4IM to start having Video Calls with you. For more information and details on using Video4IM, please read the forthcoming book, *Making Video Calls*. We will announce the release on www.SkypeTips.com and www.VideoCallTips.com when it is available.

Santa Cruz Networks Festoon (Formerly VSkype)

Santa Cruz Networks makes VidiTel, a full-featured videoconferencing solution targeted mostly to businesses. Festoon, its latest edition, is a Skype video add-on and has many different options than the other two solutions mentioned. This product, like Video4IM, is still in beta testing, and getting all the bugs worked out. This solution is more targeted toward companies that want multiple users and presentation capabilities, but you could also use it for family fun, with its EyeCandy special effects and multiuser capabilities.

Advantages

- Screen size options
- Full-screen capability for both video screens
- Desktop sharing for remote viewing only
- Special fun features; EyeCandy special effects
- Up to 200 users, with eight displayed
- Low bandwidth use

Disadvantages

- Slow connection time; takes 30–60 seconds to connect
- Slow frame rate
- Long delay in sending video
- Interface not intuitive
- Full screen interferes with sender's picture
- Has advertising

Where to Get Festoon

After you have verified that your webcam is installed, you will need to download Festoon from www.festooninc.com.

Once you install Festoon, Skype will pop up a screen that asks you if it is OK for Festoon.exe to be allowed to use Skype. Select **Allow this program to use Skype**, as shown in the following screen:

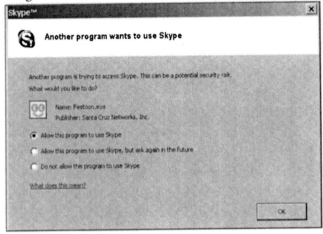

When Festoon launches, you will see the Festoon [icon] icon in the taskbar. You have two ways to launch Festoon for a video call. One is to double-click the [icon] icon in the taskbar or the [icon] icon that is added to Skype. Or you can access Festoon from the **Video** menu that is added to Skype as a result of the Festoon installation. Either way, your computer will launch the invitation screen as shown here:

Here you select a contact you want to have a video call with, and click **Start Call**. The video call will invite the other user to start a call via a chat message or to download Festoon, as the next screen shows:

Once an invitation is accepted, Festoon will start, and you will be in the main program, as the following screen indicates:

Festoon also allows for multiparty calls, as the following screen shows—me and Scooby Doo:

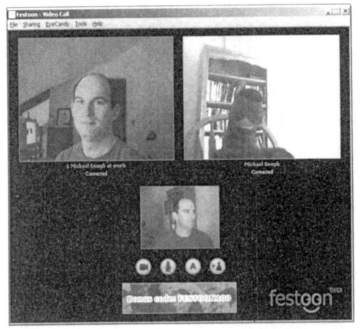

Festoon also enables you to adjust the screens to any size you want by double-clicking any one of the video screens. This will open a new, separate window that you can size and place on your desktop as you want. The following screen shows a full-screen image:

Festoon also has some fun features called EyeCandy that add special effects to the sender's video. The following screen shows the oh-so-wise video Skyper:

For more information and details on using Festoon, please read the forthcoming book, *Making Video Calls*. We will announce the release on www.SkypeTips.com and www.VideoCallTips.com when it is available.

Microsoft MSN Messenger

MSN Messenger offers a good example of how and why you might want to use multiple IM applications. MSN Messenger has a good webcam option and just added full-screen capability with version 7.5. Unfortunately, the audio portion is not as good as Skype and is nowhere near as network-friendly, requiring custom configuration in many cases.

So why not use the best of both? I use MSN Messenger and Skype together when doing video calls with my six-year-old daughter. Of course, this means that both sides that want to perform a video call also have MSN Messenger accounts. So start off by getting MSN Messenger up and running for IM. There is nothing you will need to do to Skype to allow MSN Messenger to work. You are basically using two different applications at the same time to have a video call.

Advantages

- Simple interface
- Top-to-bottom video screens
- Full-screen capability with picture-in-picture
- Low bandwidth use

- Works in most environments

- Works well over a good WiFi connection

- Nice video quality

Disadvantages

- Uses two applications and two accounts

- Slower frame rate than other video call solutions (depends on bandwidth)

- Audio is not a good as Skype's

- Audio does not work under all configurations

- Full screen is not adjustable

- MSN interface has advertising

Where to Get MSN Messenger

After you have verified that your webcam is installed, you will need to download MSN Messenger from http://messenger.msn.com/xp/downloadDefault.aspx.

After you have MSN working on both sides and are able to do IM, you start the video call process by establishing a Skype call with the contact you want to have a video call with. You can do this first or second, it does not matter. Next start a MSN Messenger video call by selecting the 🎥 icon at the top of the MSN Messenger screen.

Here I have captured a video call with MSN Messenger 7.5 to show you the quality compared with that of the other applications:

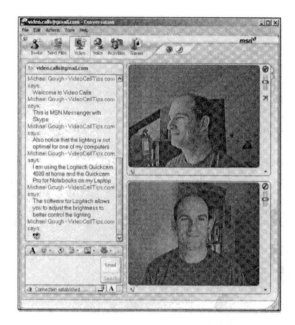

To keep MSN Messenger from providing audio feedback, you must mute the MSN Messenger microphone and speaker on one side of the video call. You can mute both sides if you want, but it is not required. You can mute the MSN Messenger mic by selecting the icon on the top right of the sender's video screen so that the receiving audio is disabled. The icon will then look like. Also select the icon so that the sending audio is also disabled; it will then look like.

Now you can have a good video call using Skype for audio and MSN Messenger for video.

Understanding the Basics... MSN Messenger Audio

Be sure to mute both the speaker and microphone on one side of the MSN Messenger video call to prevent audio feedback between MSN and Skype.

To make MSN Messenger go to full screen, select the icon in the upper-right corner of the receiving video image, and you will see the following screen. Notice that the quality is not as good as it was when the screen was smaller because it pixilated the image as it was enlarged.

For more information and details on using MSN Messenger, please read the forthcoming book, *Making Video Calls*. We will announce the release on www.SkypeTips.com and www.VideoCallTips.com when it is available.

Chapter 10

Being Mobile with Skype

Solutions in this chapter:

- Using Skype with Your Laptop
- Using Skype with Pocket PCs
- Using Skype with Wireless Pocket PCs
- USB Phones for the Mobile Traveler
- Finding WiFi Hotspots

Using Skype with Your Laptop

The most obvious mobile use for Skype is while using your laptop. Many of us have laptops issued to us for work or have our own personal laptops so we can surf the Net while we sit on our porches looking at the trees and sipping a latte.

We discussed in a previous chapter why you would want to set up two accounts, and in Chapter 9 we discussed how to use Skype without sitting at your computer. So you can either use the same primary Skype account for both your laptop and your home computer, or you can use a different account for your laptop. One of the reasons you would want to use multiple accounts is so that people will know where you are and where to leave you a message or contact you. Think of Skype as being just like a cell phone and your home telephone—one of them is for your home and one of them allows you to be mobile.

As I discussed in Chapter 9, if you Skype me at home and I don't answer, you will get my home answering machine. Then if you still wanted to reach me and I was online, you would call my other Skype account. Since Skype automatically changes the status to Away and Not Available, you would know when I am not at home, and when you saw my video.calls Skype contact come online, you would know I am on my laptop and mobile.

One good use of a USB phone, as we discussed in Chapter 8, is to carry it with your laptop to use just as a regular phone. USB phones are inexpensive and compact enough that they will fit nicely in your laptop bag and be available to you when you receive a Skype call. If you want to try it, give me a call when you see me online with video.calls and I can talk with you on my laptop with and without my USB phone.

Understanding the Basics... Use a Headset

Since laptops tend to have mediocre microphones and speakers, be sure to purchase a small headset or USB phone to use with your laptop to improve your Skype call quality.

Available USB Ports

Most laptops have two USB ports. This can pose a problem for those of us who use a small USB mouse and perform video calls using a Webcam that also connects via the USB interface. So if you are going to start using and exploiting Skype, we suggest you get a small USB hub to expand your available USB ports. For example, I have the following items connected to my laptop when I am traveling on the road:

- USB mouse

- Webcam

- Thumb or Flash drive

- USB Phone

- Digital camera

As you can see, the number of gadgets far exceeds a laptop's available USB ports. I travel with a tiny USB hub that gives me four additional ports, for a total of five ports on my laptop, so I don't have to unplug one device to plug in another.

Photo as featured on www.Targus.com

In addition, we suggest you get a couple of USB extension cables to make connections even easier. Some USB devices are too wide to allow another device to plug in next to them, or the USB port is recessed and too short. You will need "Male A to Female A" cables to solve this problem.

Photo as featured on www.belkin.com

Understanding the Basics... USB Cables

Get a couple of short USB dongles or extension cables to make it easier to connect multiple devices to a laptop or USB hub.

Using Skype with Pocket PCs

Lots of people have Pocket PCs that have built-in wireless cards or are combination Pocket PCs/cell phones with built-in WiFi, like the Samsung i730, the Siemens SX66, or the iMate KJam. Any Pocket PC with a 400MHz or faster processor and built-in or add-on wireless can also perform Skype calls. Feel free to give us a call on your Pocket PC device for a quality and sound test and we will add your device to the list we maintain on our Web site.

Pocket PC Cell Phones

Pocket PCs are for people who want Outlook functionality with them at all times, for calendar, contacts, Solitaire, and even e-mail. These devices are also designed for cell phone users who also want Microsoft Windows Mobile functionality. These devices sync well with Microsoft Office and Outlook, and you can listen to music, store files, and of course, make Skype calls over wireless. The list of devices discussed in this section is not complete by any means, but we did get e-mails on or various forums reported on all these units working with Skype. These devices can work with Skype using either built-in WiFi or the cell provider's high-speed cellular network Internet offering.

NOTE

There is an additional cost to use a cell provider's high-speed Internet access. Check the provider's plan and costs to see if it is cost-effective for you. WiFi, on the other hand, is inexpensive or often free and works very well with Skype. Also, if you are going to use one of these devices, I recommend you keep a stock of multiple batteries, since power consumption will be an issue.

Samsung i730

The i730 is probably the leader in the Pocket PC phone space. This device gets rave reviews, and the only drawback I know of is that WiFi does not operate when in cell mode. You must manually switch between Cell and WiFi modes. This is probably due to battery use, since having both running would drain the battery faster. Learn more at www.phonescoop.com/phones/phone.php?p=667.

Features

- Modes: CDMA 850/CDMA 1900

- OS: Windows Mobile for Pocket PCs version: 2003 Second Edition

- Processor: 520MHz Intel Bulverde processor

- Memory: 64MB RAM plus SDIO expansion slot for added memory

- Display: Type: LCD (color TFT/TFD), colors: 65,536 (16-bit), size: 240 x 320 pixels

- Bluetooth: Version 1.1/primary supported profiles: headset, hands free, OBEX

- Headset: 2.5mm

- WiFi: Yes, 802.11b

- Keyboard: Slide-out QWERTY

- Speakerphone

Photos as featured on www.phonescoop.com

Siemens SX66

The Siemens SX66 seems to generate either a love or a hate scenario. Many reviews claim early versions of this device are flawed and lock up frequently. I have two friends who use this phone with Cingular and love it, though they do complain about battery consumption. Learn more at www.phonescoop.com/phones/phone.php?p=569.

Features

- Modes: GSM 850/GSM 900/GSM 1800/GSM 1900

- OS: Windows Mobile for Pocket PCs version: 2003 Second Edition up to 96MB Flash memory

- Processor: 400MHz xScale processor

- Memory: 96MB (built-in, Flash shared memory) plus 128MB SDRAM

- Display: Type: LCD (color TFT/TFD), colors: 65,536 (16-bit), size: 240 x 320 pixels transflective TFT; supports landscape mode

- Bluetooth: Version 1.1/class 2

- Headset: 2.5mm

- WiFi: Yes

- Keyboard: Slide-out QWERTY

Photos as seen on www.phonescoop.com

iMate K-Jam

iMate is the leader in Skype integration for Pocket PC phones, and several of the iMate phones are used by many cellular providers. The Siemens SX66 shown in the previous section is the iMate PDA2K. If you have access to a provider for these devices, take a serious look. You can learn more at www.image.com/DETAILS_KJAM.htm.

Features

- Modes: 850/900/1800/1900MHz, GSM/GPRS/EDGE

- OS: Windows Mobile 5.0 Pocket PC Phone Edition

- Processor: TI OMAP 850, 200MHz

- Memory: 128MB ROM/64MB RAM

- Display: Type: LCD (color TFT/TFD), colors: 65,536 (16-bit), size: 240 x 320 pixels transflective TFT; supports landscape mode

- Bluetooth: Version 1.1/class 2

- Headset: 2.5mm

- WiFi: Yes, 802.11b,g,e

- Keyboard: Slide-out QWERTY

Photo as featured on www.imate.com

Sprint PPC-6700

The Sprint PPC-6700 Pocket PC phone gets very high user ratings for ease of use. As with the iMate, the slide-out keyboard is very popular with reviewers. Learn more at www.spring.com/business/products/phones/ppc6700_allPcsPhones.jsp.

Features

- Modes: CDMA (800/1900MHz) and 1x-EVDO

- OS: Windows Mobile 5.0 Pocket PC Phone Edition Software

- Processor: Intel PXA 270 416MHz Processor

- Memory: 64MB RAM; 128MB Flash ROM

- Display: 240 x 320 Pixel TFT Touch Screen supporting over 65K colors

- Bluetooth: Version 1.2

- Headset: 2.5mm

- WiFi: Yes

- Keyboard: Slide-out QWERTY

- Speakerphone

Photo as featured on www.sprint.com

HP HW6710/6715

HP's latest Pocket PC Phone looks and feels like a RIM Blackberry device with Pocket PC functionality. This device is smaller than a standard Pocket PC device. Learn more at www.bargainpda.com/default.asp?newsID=2624.

Features

- Modes: Quad band 850/900/1800/1900MHz with GSM/GPRS and EDGE

- OS: Windows Mobile 5.0, Phone Edition

- Processor: Intel PXA270 312MHz CPU

- Memory: 128MB Flash ROM

- Display: 3-inch TFT 240 x 240 pixel display

- Bluetooth: Yes

- WiFi: 802.11g

- Keyboard: QWERTY

Photo as featured on www.bargainpda.com

Using Skype with Smartphones

Smartphones are more cell phone than Pocket PC; they do have Windows Mobile software but not all the features of a Pocket PC. If you are looking for a smaller device than a Pocket

PC, a smartphone might be for you. In this section we list a few of the more popular models that are reported to work with Skype. These devices use the cell provider's high-speed cellular network Internet offering to connect with Skype, since smartphones do not have integrated WiFi and a Pocket PC phone can have WiFi. Skype works using the cellular provider's high-speed network. You will have to sign up for the provider's Internet service offering at an additional cost; Internet access plans will vary by provider.

> **NOTE**
>
> There is an additional cost to use a cell provider's high-speed Internet access. Check the provider's plan and costs to see if this is cost effective for you.

AudioVox SMT5600 (Orange SPV C500)

The AudioVox SMT5600 phone is used by Orange and other cellular providers. This phone does not have WiFi but does have a speakerphone, which is key in my opinion. Learn more at www.audiovox.com/webapp/wcs/stores/servlet/ProductDisplay?catalogId= 10001&storeId=10001&productId=13758&langId=-1.

Features

- Modes: Tri Band GSM 850/1800/1900MHz GPRS Class 10
- OS: Microsoft Windows Mobile 2003 Second Edition software for Smartphone
- Processor: TI OMAP 730 ARM family 200MHz
- Memory: 32 MB RAM
- Display: 2.2 inch, 176 x 220 pixels TFT LCD with 64K colors
- Bluetooth: Yes
- Headset: 2.5mm
- WiFi: No
- Speakerphone

Photo as featured on www.infosyncworld.com

Samsung i600

The Samsung i600 is an older-style flip phone that is compact and Skype capable. Find out more at http://product.samsung.com/cgi-bin/nabc/product/b2c_product_detail.jsp?prod_id=SP-i600.

Features

- OS: Microsoft Windows Mobile 2003 Software

- Processor: PXA250 200MHz

- Memory: 32 MB RAM, 32MB ROM

- Display: 2.2 inch, 176 x 220 pixels TFT LCD with 64K colors

- Bluetooth: No

- Headset: 2.5mm

- WiFi: No

- Speakerphone

Photo as featured on http://product.samsung.com

Motorola MPX220

Motorola has announced that it will be integrating WiFi into its phones, and the company makes a good-quality phone. I believe Motorola will have Skype-enabled phones in the near future. Learn more at www.motorola.com/motoinfo/product/details/0,,53,00.html.

Features

- Modes: Quad Band Performance (850/900/1800/1900)

- OS: Windows Mobile for Smartphones 2003 version

- Processor: TI OMAP 1611 200MHz

- Memory: 64MB ROM

- Display: Type: LCD (color TFT/TFD), colors: 262,144 (18-bit), size: 176 x 220 pixels TFT/65,000 colors for wallpaper

- Bluetooth: Yes

- Headset: 2.5mm

- WiFi: No

- Speakerphone

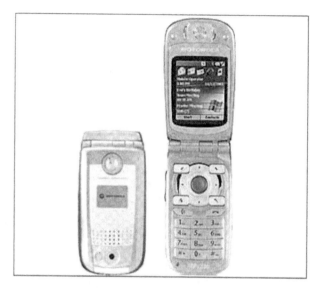

Photos as featured on www.motorola.com

Nokia 6630

Nokia makes some of the first true cellular-based video phones that are capable of two-way video phone calls. Nokia makes good phones with a variety of functions. Many have been tested to work with Skype. Learn more at www.europe.nokia.com/nokia/0,,1072,00.html.

Features

- Modes: UMTS/GSM 900/GSM 1800/GSM 1900

- OS: Symbian OS 8.0a, Series 60 UI

- Memory: 64MB card included, hot swap 10MB shared memory for storage

- Display: TFT, 256K colors, size: 176 x 208 pixels

- Bluetooth: Yes

- Headset: 2.5mm

- WiFi: No

- Speakerphone

Photo as featured on www.europe.nokia.com

Nokia 6680

Nokia makes some of the first true cellular-based video phones that are capable of two-way video phone calls. The 6680 has a built-in camera for video calls. Learn more at www.europe.nokia.com/nokia/0,,1072,00.html.

Features

- Modes: UMTS/GSM 900/GSM 1800/GSM 1900

- OS: Symbian OS 8.0a, Series 60 UI

- Memory: 64MB card included, hot swap 10MB shared memory for storage

- Display: TFT, 256K colors, size 176 x 208 pixels

- Bluetooth: Yes

- Headset: 2.5mm

- WiFi: No

- Speakerphone

Photo as featured on www.europe.nokia.com

Using Skype with Wireless Pocket PCs

These devices do not have cell phone capabilities. With typical WiFi 802.11b and 802.11g, you can connect with any computer, laptop, or Pocket PC that can run Skype. We don't recommend 802.11a, since it does not run on a Pocket PC, but if you have it on your laptop, 802.11a will work fine as long as you can connect. Most public hotspots are 802.11b or 802.11g. Skype will work well in any WiFi location with a signal strength of 50 percent or stronger. Your local Starbucks, WiFi hotspot, airport, home, and business that has wireless running will work well for Skype.

We are asked all the time what devices work well with Skype on a Pocket PC. The minimum requirements are:

- Windows Mobile 2003 for Pocket PC

- 400MHz processor

- WiFi-enabled

You can read the article we did last year in testing Pocket PC units with Skype at www.skypetips.internetvisitation.org/articles/pocketPC.html.

The following is a list of older Pocket PCs about which we had feedback that they worked with Skype. It is not a complete list; new units are coming out all the time, but this is a place to start if you have an older unit. Keep in mind that many of the Pocket PCs that have wireless do *not* have a Bluetooth headset profile. Be sure to look up the manufacturer's specifications and/or look on the Skype forums for people who have successfully tested Bluetooth headset profiles with a specific Pocket PC if you want to use a Bluetooth headset.

Pocket PC Devices Capable of Skype Calls

Device	Processor	Wireless 802.11b	Bluetooth
HP iPaq 4700	624MHz XScale	X	X
HP iPaq 4705	624MHz XScale	X	X
HP iPaq hx2000	624MHz XScale	X	X
HP iPaq hx2410	520MHz XScale	X	X
HP iPaq 4150/4350	400MHz XScale	X	X
HP iPaq H5550	400MHz XScale	X	X
Dell Axim X50v	624MHz XScale	X	X
Dell Axim X50	520MHz XScale	X	X
Dell Axim X50	416MHz XScale	X	X
Dell Axim X30	624MHz XScale	X	X
Dell Axim X5	400MHz XScale	No	No
ASUS A730W With built-in camera	520MHz XScale	X	1.1
ASUS A716	400MHz XScale	X	1.1
Fujitsu Pocket LOOX 420	400MHz XScale	X	X
Toshiba e800/e805	400MHz XScale	X	No

Many older Pocket PCs use a special 4C headset connector rather than the typical cell phone 2.5mm headset connector. Finding a headset for a 4C connector will pose a challenge. Your device might have come with a 4C to 2.5mm adapter, as the HP iPaq devices provide. Plantronics makes a headset with a 4C connector (M130i) for Pocket PCs. Learn more at www.plantronics.com/north_america/en_US/products/cat1150057/cat1150057/prod5070003?prodfind=true&mftr=HEWLETT+PACKARD.

Some additional things we found during testing were:

■ Wired headsets worked best.

■ Lowering the volume one setting from maximum helps reduce feedback and echo.

■ Only a few units worked well without a headset (Toshiba and Siemens).

■ Bluetooth did not work as well as wired headsets.

USB Phones for the Mobile Traveler

In Chapter 8, we covered many types of USB phone. We discuss them again here because they are specific to the mobile traveler. USB phones can make it easier to be mobile with Skype when you're working with a laptop or if you borrow a computer to make a Skype call. There are currently two types of USB phone: the typical USB phone and the USB Flash phone. We expect a third type to show up, a Skype-enabled USB phone. *Skype-enabled* means that the display shows all the Skype information that is needed to make a Skype call, including contact names. Most USB phones require you to look at your computer screen when using them to dial your contacts.

Typical USB Phones

The typical USB phone simply plugs into an available USB port and provides a typical phone experience. If you want to be further away than a few feet, you will want to invest in a very long USB extension cable so that you are not restricted to a few feet from your computer—or look into a USB phone that is cordless.

Photo as featured on www.simplyphone.lu

Typical USB phones are perfect for:

- Laptop users
- Businesses that want Skype to act like a regular phone

USB Flash Phones

As we said in Chapter 8, USB Flash phones are perfect for the truly mobile Skyper. I wasn't sure about this clever little device until I got my hands on one. This is a 100MB Flash drive that has a 2.5mm headset jack on the end and a volume button. Loaded on the Flash drive is a full working version of Skype! This device allows you to walk up to any computer with an open USB port and Internet connectivity and use all the features of Skype. Plug in the Flash phone and load Skype from the Flash device; you aren't required to install anything on the host computer! Everything you need is loaded on the Flash drive—even your contacts.

In addition, this device has 90MB of storage space left over for files, pictures, and other data you want to carry with you. This device can use your standard 2.5mm cell phone headset, or it comes with a little earbud headset that will get you by. All of this fits into a little pouch the size of a deck of cards. I have friends who travel all over the world for extended periods of time; they use Internet cafés to check e-mail and send us pictures and even a joke or two during their travels. The USB Flash phone is perfect for them because it is portable, is easy to use, and works without loading anything on the borrowed computer.

As a consultant, I use clients' systems as a part of my projects. If their policy allows the use of instant messaging, I can load up any IM tool that I need to communicate. Using a USB Flash phone, all I have to do is plug it into an available USB port. Since my Skype configuration is on the Flash drive, I don't need to load software onto the client's computer. Learn more at www.mplat.com/eng/productdetail.asp?post=27.

NOTE

This device needs a short USB extension because it is fat and might not fit into many recessed USB ports or alongside another USB device.

Photo as featured on www.mplat.com

The USB Flash phone is perfect for:

- Consultants

- Travelers using Internet cafés

- Stocking stuffers for your Skypers

- People who want to use Skype without loading it onto a borrowed computer

Understanding the Basics... Flash Phone

This device makes a perfect stocking stuffer for a Skyper.

Finding WiFi Hotspots

Being mobile with Skype often means finding a wireless (WiFi) hotspot where you can log into the Internet and surf while drinking your latte and, of course, using Skype. Here we provide many Web sites that will help you locate free or pay-per-use wireless access. In addition, we list several WiFi locator Web sites that cover many countries. If you find more good sites, let us know and we will post them on www.SkypeTips.com for everyone to share.

Skype Zones

Skype has partnered with a large wireless provider named Boingo. You can sign up for this service by the hour or by the month and have unlimited access to more than 20,000 wireless hotspots. For more information on this service, visit the Skype Zones site at www.skype.com/products/skypezones.

Pay-Per-Use WiFi Locators

- www.boingo.com/

- www.ipass.com/

- http://hotspot.t-mobile.com/

- www.wayport.com

- www.telecom.co.nz/content/0,3900,204163-1487,00.html

General WiFi Locators (Free or Paid)

- www.wifinder.com/

- www.wi-fihotspotlist.com/

- www.hotspot-locations.com/

- www.jiwire.com/

- www.surfandsip.com/location_all.htm

Free WiFi Locators

- www.wi-find.com/

- www.wififreespot.com/

- http://metrofreefi.com/

Part III: Implementing Skype in an Enterprise Environment

Chapter 11

Setting Up Skype in the Workplace

Solutions in this chapter:

- A Word about SIP and H.323

- Skype Architecture

- Security

- Performance Considerations

A Word about SIP and H.323

Skype does not use SIP or H.323, but we thought we would cover these two protocols so that you could understand two of the main VoIP protocols used and how they differ from Skype. Session Initiation Protocol, or SIP, is a text-based protocol that uses port 5060 on both UDP and TCP for call setup and teardown. Version 2.0 of SIP has been codified in RFC 3261, where the various details of SIP are included. SIP is a signaling protocol very much like the telco SS7 protocol suite, but unlike SS7, which is very centralized and requires a private network, SIP was designed with the Internet and TCP/IP in mind and the use of many different media types such as voice and video. SIP is also a peer-to-peer type of architecture, similar to Skype. But whereas Skype does not use any central servers aside from the user authentication, SIP does use centralized servers for authentication. Since SIP is a signaling protocol, it offers features such as call waiting, call transfer, and call hold, among many others:

- Call forwarding, including the equivalent of 700, 800, and 900-type calls

- Call forwarding, no answer

- Call forwarding, busy

- Call forwarding, unconditional

- Other address-translation services

- Callee and calling "number" delivery, where numbers can be any (preferably unique) naming scheme

- Personal mobility, which is the ability to reach a called party under a single location-independent address, even when the user changes terminals

- Terminal-type negotiation and selection, in which a caller can be given a choice of ways to reach the party, such as Internet telephony, mobile phone, or an answering service

- Terminal capability negotiation

- Caller and callee authentication

- Blind and supervised call transfer

- Invitations to multicast conferences

Along with the RFC standard, SIP is an official standard of the Internet Engineering Task Force (IETF).

```
Packet:          30  [x]  ⌻    ?
⊕ Ⴠ UDP:            Src=64064  Dst=5060
⊟ Ⴠ SIP - Session Initiation Protocol
    ⦿ Request:           INVITE sip:andymarston@proxy01.sipphone.com 5060 SIP/2.0
    ⦿ Via:               SIP/2.0/UDP 10.222.71.250:64064;branch=z9hG4bK-d87543-331b4876dc598070-1--d87543-;rport
    ⦿ Max-Forwards:      70
    ⦿ Contact:           <sip:17476181145@208.54.15.129:64064>
    ⦿ To:                <sip:andymarston@proxy01.sipphone.com:5060>
    ⦿ From:              <sip:17476181145@proxy01.sipphone.com>;tag=940a2548
    ⦿ Call-ID:           794dc158435e9b318VG1OYW4uY3J1YXRpdmU3b21wdXRlciesSuZXQQ
    ⦿ CSeq:              1 INVITE
    ⦿ Allow:             INVITE, ACK, CANCEL, OPTIONS, BYE, REFER, NOTIFY, SUBSCRIBE, PUBLISH, MESSAGE
    ⦿ Content-Type:      application/sdp
    ⦿ User-Agent:        WinGizmo (Gizmo-s)
    ⦿ Content-Length:    438
    ⦿ CSRN:              242
⊟ Ⴠ SDP - Session Description Protocol
    ⊟ Ⴠ Protocol Version
        ⦿ Version:         0
    ⊟ Ⴠ Origin
        ⦿ Username:        GizmoProject
        ⦿ Session ID:      1
        ⦿ Version:         1590757929
        ⦿ Network Type:    IN
        ⦿ Address Type:    IP4
        ⦿ Address:         208.54.15.129
```

In the following packet sample of a SIP INVITE packet, we can see SIP's basic packet structure:

We can see the destination UDP port of 5060 as well as the request for the invitation, with the caller's information. We can see that the entire request is in plain text, much like traditional HTTP or SMTP.

Understanding the Basics... VoIP

There are many different flavors of Voice over Internet Protocol (VoIP) client, such as Skype, Gizmo, and more, but they all work relatively the same way. In the simplest terms, they run your voice through a codec (coder/decoder) to digitize it, and then they packetize it so that your voice can be sent over the Internet or other network using TCP/IP instead of telephone lines. In the old days and even many times today, the telephone is an analog device and uses dedicated lines that run back to a central office in a star-like pattern. The central offices are tied together using a signaling protocol like SS7, which gives the mechanism access to trunk voice lines and provides the switching of voice circuits around the cloud to make the virtual connection between you and the person you are calling. VoIP gets around all that overhead and equipment requirements by relying on TCP/IP and User Datagram Protocol (UDP) for the transport of your voice. To use a VoIP application like Skype, all you need is an Internet connection, a compatible computer, a speaker, a microphone, and the Skype software.

SIP is the carrier for the encoded data stream that is generated by the codec. This encoded data is carried by the Real-Time Transport Protocol (RTP) stream. RTP carries several key pieces of information for the call. These pieces are like the header that carries the information on how to recombine the codec packetized data. Also included in the RTP data are sequence numbers, payload identification, source identification, and intermedia synchronization. The intermedia synchronization is how the two data streams, video and audio, stay synchronized. SIP has trouble crossing a Network Address Translation (NAT) boundary because it uses RTP and carries the IP address and port information. The details of RTP are covered in RFC 1889. In the following figure, we see the basic SIP signaling at work:

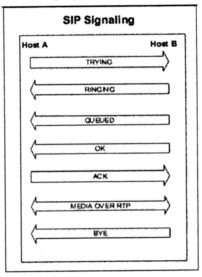

The SIP sessions are considered "peer-to-peer," much like Skype, and do not require a soft PBX (private branch exchange) to function. The two end points can set up their own session by themselves. But to get advanced features and integration with the telephone system, SIP has a high level of support in the Open Source arena with major soft PBXes such as Asterisk, sipX, Yet Another Telephone Engine (YATE), and SIP Express. SIP is also supported as an end point with software such as MSN Messenger, Apple's iChat, and AOL's AIM instant messenger application.

H.323 is a suite of protocols that was designed to move multimedia data streams over a LAN. It has since evolved into of the standards for VoIP and, like SIP, H.323 is an official standard of the IETF. Let's look at how H.323 works:

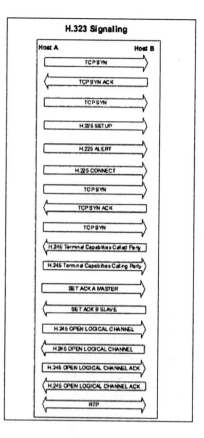

When in use, H.323 references other specifications, such as H.225, which lays out the call signaling and the stream packetization; H.245, which is the control protocol used to open and close logical channels; and H.450, which describes supplemental services. The original specification was based on the ISDN Q.931 specification; thus, it works well at interconnecting IP and ISDN clouds. The H.323 protocol is older and more mature than SIP, but to a large extent, SIP has surpassed H.323. H.323 tends to be a vendor-specific protocol, so although your Meridian H.323 will work fine for all your Meridian equipment, if you bring in a second brand, the odds of it working correctly are low. This incompatibility has been one of the prime reasons, if not *the* reason, that SIP is overtaking H.323 in the marketplace. H.323 is supported by Microsoft's NetMeeting and GnomeMeeting. GnomeMeeting uses an open source version called OpenH323, which can be found at openh323.org.

In deciding between SIP or H.323, you will often find that regarding commercial software, that choice has been made for you already based on the completeness of the support for the protocols. In the case of Cisco, for example, SIP does not have good support, because Call Manager uses a private protocol. By comparison, when you use an open source soft PBX such as Asterisk, you can have very good support for SIP along with the phone-line integration that you have with commercial products.

The difference between protocols like SIP and Skype is that Skype is not open, so you are limited in your understanding of how Skype works by exploring and reverse-engineering the protocol or just using the Skype API calls, as we discuss in Chapter 14 of this book. In the following sections we attempt to document as much as we can about the Skype architecture and how the protocol works.

NOTE

For a much more detailed discussion and list of resources for SIP and H.323 and more VoIP details, try the VoIP wiki at www.voip-info.org/tiki-index.php.

Skype Architecture

The architecture of Skype is very much like Kazaa; some of the same people are involved in Skype that designed Kazaa, so that makes sense. In simplest terms, Skype is a giant peer-to-peer network without data centers or file servers per se. We say "per se" because Skype does use certain servers called *supernodes*, which are described in some detail later in this section. When Skype starts, it opens a random listening port on both TCP and UDP that was chosen during the Skype installation. Skype also uses port 80 (HTTP) and port 443 (HTTPS), unlike SIP, for which there is a given port used for the protocol.

Since Skype is an overlay peer-to-peer network, there is a table of reachable nodes on each client. This table is called the *host cache* and has the IP addresses and port number of a supernode. The supernode is a Skype client that has several criteria to meet:

- Public IP address
- Sufficient bandwidth
- Sufficient CPU power
- Sufficient memory

The idea and use of supernodes have been directly borrowed from Kazaa. The supernode acts as a router for Skype calls and for the client's authorization to have before it is allowed to use the Skype network. If the Skype client cannot make a connection with the supernode, Skype will report a login failure. The Skype client also has to connect to the Skype login server, which keeps track of usernames and passwords on the Skype network.

This is the one constant server in the Skype network. The Skype client cannot "opt out" from becoming a supernode if the client meets the requirements to be a supernode. This is spelled out in the fine print of the end-user agreement that you have to click through to install Skype. Here is an example of the overall Skype architecture:

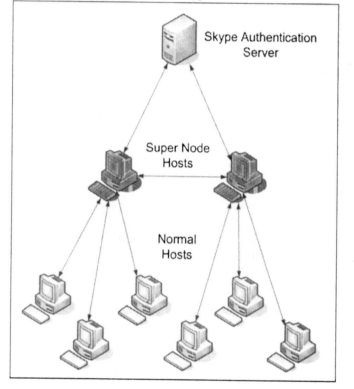

Understanding the Basics... Avoid Becoming a Supernode

For home users and small businesses to avoid being supernodes, just add a P2P-friendly DSL/cable router to your network. For business users to avoid being a supernode, simply make sure you are behind a true firewall device that provides NAT capabilities.

The supernodes play a very important part in the Skype network, since if the Skype client cannot see a supernode, the login will fail after several attempts on the client's part.

Opening Connection

When a Skype client first tries to authenticate to the Skype network, the client opens a connection using HTTP (port 80) to http://iu.skype.com and checks to see if the client is current or not. Here are the results of that HTTP connection attempt:

```
GET
/ui/0/1.4.13.56/en/getlatestversion?ver=1.4.13.56&uhash=13f8c83a6d572d58b59bae2
9b33332147 HTTP/1.1
User-Agent: Skype. (BETA) 1.4
Host: ui.skype.com
Cache-Control: no-cache
Cookie: linkedcampaign=partner-x;
skypeclientinstalled=lastupdated%3D20050913%3Bplatform%3D0%3Bversioninstalled%3
D1.4.13.56; loggedin=1; username=packetattack


HTTP/1.1 200 OK
Date: Mon, 12 Sep 2005 23:46:28 GMT
Server: Apache
Cache-control: no-cache, must revalidate
Pragma: no-cache
Expires: 0
Set-Cookie:
skypeclientinstalled=lastupdated%3D20050913%3Bplatform%3D0%3Bversioninstalled%3
D1.4.13.56; expires=Sat, 11-Mar-2006 23:46:28 GMT; path=/; domain=.skype.com
Content-Length: 9
Connection: close
Content-Type: text/html; charset=utf-8
Content-Language: en
1.1.13.79
```

Once the Skype client has been verified to be using current software and the user has been authenticated, the Skype client attempts several different methods of placing any requested call. Skype does not use a standard port for listening; the port choice evolves from a random port choice made during the installation. The actual communication will depend on whether the Skype client has an open connection to the Internet or has to traverse a NAT-enabled firewall. The use of NAT causes Skype to try a variety of methods to get around it. These methods are partially based on the Simple Traversal of User Datagram Protocol (STUN).

Skype uses the TCP flag called *PSH*. This flag is used when you need to ensure that all the data submitted to TCP was actually sent. And with VoIP, having all the bits is a real plus for quality. The Ethereal trace file shown in the following screenshot shows the TCP side of a Skype connection using the PSH flag.

Dealing with NAT

In the traditional VoIP model using SIP or H.323, NAT will break the connection. Skype appears to use a form of STUN, which is detailed in RFC 3489 and is a method of getting past NAT using UDP packets. The use of a STUN-like protocol has proven very effective for Kazaa in the past and has been migrated to Skype to allow use even behind corporate firewalls. When testing Skype, we were able to make a connection through our Cisco VPN concentrator and then out the Cisco PIX firewall to the United Kingdom without a problem. This ease of use, however, gives corporate system administrators heartburn, since we could conduct a voice call and IM session or even video, and the company has zero visibility into the contents because of use of encryption.

Even if the NAT firewall blocks outbound UDP or restricts outbound UDP, Skype can work around this restriction by using the supernodes as a "relay" point. More on NAT and firewalls are covered in Chapter 13.

Encryption

Skype recently released a Security White Paper by Tom Berson of Anagram Laboratories that outlines exactly how Skype uses encryption. This paper may be found at the following URL: www.skype.com/security/.

Skype uses 256-bit AES encryption for its data stream. The use of encryption also makes it difficult to log the use of Skype, or more precisely, what is being used on Skype or who may be talking using Skype. The use of encryption works for the voice call, any file transfers, and instant messaging.

A potential issue for Skype and virtually any other VoIP messaging application is a set of new rules called the Communications Assistance for Law Enforcement Act (CALEA), which goes into effect in 2007. These rules make it easier for the government to have wiretap access to the media stream. The rules say that any VoIP protocol or company must be wiretap ready, and the list includes SkypeOut, Vonage, Packet 8, and many others. There are crossover worries for other groups offering Internet access, and the Federal Communications Commission (FCC) promises a set of regulations clarifying the first set of rules. The rules can be found at www.askcalea.net.

We highly recommend that any people considering Skype for business use read the upcoming rules and regulations to better understand any impacts these regulations might have on their businesses.

Security

Security on any VoIP network is of considerable importance, given the forensic importance of a phone call. On a conventional VoIP network, as well as on a traditional telephone network, the following information is logged:

- The phone number that was dialed

- When the number was dialed

- When the call was connected

- The duration of the call

- When the call was disconnected

Skype does log some of the preceding information, but only the last 10 records, and a history is not kept as you might see in other VoIP solutions. This raises legal questions if business is conducted over a Skype connection. You need to decide what your security policy is on and whether logging call information is required. Some situations may require logging; others may not. Unauthorized use of Skype on a network can bring the following problems to the network administrator:

- Skype file transfers can cut both ways: unauthorized flow of company data out or the download of files that could be compromised with worms, viruses, and the like that have bypassed your firewalls and scanners.

- Skype file transfers will be caught by an antivirus solution that has an "auto-protect" capability.

- Skype users could consume a considerable amount of bandwidth if unchecked on the network. A large company with a T3 would not notice it right away, but a smaller company with a single T1 or a slower DSL circuit could easily have its WAN link overloaded by excessive VoIP traffic from Skype if all the users performed Skype calls.

- Skype may take over private resources to act as a supernode, even if the user is not actively using the Skype client. This is mitigated by a corporate firewall or DSL/cable router or other NAT device.

- The encryption of instant messaging can lead to exposure of private company data or other legal issues that cannot be monitored by a proactive staff.

Skype is up front about using your computer, or as up front as an end-user license agreement (EULA) can be. What is buried in the fine print of the EULA is the following article:

Article 4 Permission to Utilize

4.1 Permission to utilize Your computer. In order to receive the benefits provided by the Skype Software, You hereby grant permission for the Skype Software to utilize the processor and bandwidth of Your computer for the limited purpose of facilitating the communication between Skype Software users.

4.2 Protection of Your computer (resources). You understand that the Skype Software will use its commercially reasonable efforts to protect the privacy and integrity of Your computer resources and Your communication, however, You acknowledge and agree that Skype cannot give any warranties in this respect.

(© Copyright Skype ELUA August 2005)

Please pay attention to these two sections of the EULA. The first one, Section 4.1 of the EULA, says that to use Skype, you give Skype right to use *your* computer, processor, and bandwidth to help facilitate communication between Skype users. In other words, you give approval to be one of those supernodes that we discussed earlier in this chapter. Your computer can be a supernode only if you are an open client on the Internet and do not have NAT protection.

The next section is also very important to administrators or anyone else with an interest in security. Section 4.2 of the EULA basically says that Skype will use *reasonable* efforts to protect your privacy and the integrity of your computer. This might be acceptable to the average home user, but most chief technology officers (CTOs) or other company management will not be very happy to see an application like Skype sitting on their networks with this type of license in play.

Several key properties are important to any discussion of security with respect to Skype. These properties are:

- **Privacy** How secure is your conversation using Skype?
- **Authenticity** Are you are reaching the person you think is at the other end?
- **Availability** Are Skype users always available when they are listed?
- **Survivability** If the Skype network takes a hit, can Skype keep working.
- **Resilience** Can the Skype user reconnect quickly when there is an outage?
- **Conversation integrity** Does Skype lose bits of the conversation?
- **System integrity** Does Skype work well with other applications?

These points are covered in detail in a security analysis paper written by Simson Garfinkel and available at www.tacticaltech.org/files/Skype_Security.pdf. This paper is highly recommended for anyone with concerns about Skype's VoIP security model and methods.

The privacy of Skype is due to the encryption method Skype uses. Both voice calls using Skype and any instant messaging are encrypted, so there is a high level of privacy. This may change with government agencies looking to have the ability of monitoring traffic in a solution like Skype.

Most of the time, Skype is available when it should be. But Skype and many other VoIP vendors have ongoing issues with availability compared with the "old" telephone service. The telephone routinely has an uptime of 99.999 percent; people have become very used to this reliability, and they depend on this kind of uptime. Even under very adverse conditions, your POTS has a good chance of being up and working.

This is very unlike VoIP, where the connection can fail in a multitude of places. The gateway can fail, servers can fail, the ISP can fail—the list goes on. The telephone companies have had many years to work out how to build a redundant network, and the technology, although old style, is very robust. The VoIP companies are still working out standards, bugs, and billing issues as well as building a robust infrastructure. Being mostly decentralized, Skype has some advantages in terms of robustness, but Skype still has some weaknesses that administrators and users need to be aware of. The primary weakness at this point is the use of Skype servers for the username and password authentication. Without those, the Skype system fails.

VoIP systems such as Skype and others have a distinct advantage in the category of resilience. If the building or location in which you are using Skype loses its Internet connectivity, just go somewhere else with an Internet access point, and you are back in business. No mess, no fuss, Skype will simply work again. This is in contrast to the traditional phone system, where the numbers are generally not portable, so if the building phone system fails, you lose your phone connectivity on that number until the phone company can reprogram switches and their network or you can forward the phone number to a new number somewhere else. Larger companies and corporations may have multiple and redundant Internet connections and allow for rerouting adding to the reliability of a Skype type of solution.

We now know through the analysis by Tom Berson of Anagram Labs that Skype ensures the integrity of the voice call. Administrators or engineers can now compare Skype to products from other vendors to see who provides the best solution.

Skype is a closed protocol, but there has been some documentation on a few parts of the process by which Skype makes connections. Skype's supernodes carry media stream traffic at times, which has the possibility of being a security risk, since the call is traversing an unsecured server. Remember, the supernode is any computer with sufficient RAM, CPU, and a public IP address not protected behind a NAT device.

Understanding the Basics...
Avoid Skype Call Relays and File Transfer Relays

If you do not want to relay your Skype calls or Skype file transfers, configure your network to avoid this.

Blocking Skype

To block Skype on their networks, administrators will, at best, find it difficult, since Skype, like Kazaa, was designed to intentionally get around the normal network security blocks. One of the few ways is to look at HTTP traffic and make sure that the headers and information are really HTTP traffic and not something like Skype just using port 80 to take advantage of the open port on most networks. Some vendors, such as BlueCoat and Verso, claim they can block Skype traffic. BlueCoat and Verso are enterprise-level solutions and therefore very expensive security appliances that are designed for large networks. BlueCoat recommends blocking Skype by preventing download of the Skype application and using protocol filters on the BlueCoat proxy appliance. BlueCoat provides a free white paper titled "Best Practices for Controlling Skype within the Enterprise" available for download from its Web site, www.bluecoat.com/resources/resourcedocs/whitepapers.html.

Verso attempts to block Skype by matching Skype communication patterns referred to as signatures. The Verso appliance has an active client that can receive updates to the appliance's "black list" and algorithms used to block internet traffic, such as Skype. Additional technical information on blocking Skype will be discussed in Chapter 13.

Firewalls

A security best practice to start with is to block the use of the high-numbered ports on your firewall. Also, taking the approach of blocking everything outbound and allowing only what you need is highly recommended, with the understanding that it will mean more work for the security or network administrator. This approach is becoming much more common on firewalls, so if you have problems with your Skype connection, check your firewall to make sure it is not configured to block all traffic unless explicitly allowed on the outbound side.

Downloads

If you have the capability to block certain downloads, you can block the Skype executables (skype.exe) from being downloaded. Using group policies can help prevent the installation of the Skype application on an Active Directory domain or prevent the execution of the executable. Of course, on a non-Microsoft client such as Apple's OS X, Active Directory control is pretty much a nonstarter, so you would need to find another way to lock down the OS X operating system.

We cannot suggest strongly enough that you have a policy in place at the company detailing acceptable software use, spelling out definitions of "good" software and "bad" software. Such a policy provides some cover for the company in case legal issues arise with the unauthorized use of Skype.

Software Inventory and Administration

Another method to block the use of Skype is to use a software inventory solution that is typically found in larger organizations. Companies often scan the systems looking for specific software packages like port scanners and other potentially malicious tools and delete them as a part of a good security plan. You could do the same to control the use of Skype inside a corporation with a software inventory and distribution solution like SMS, Radia, and others.

You could also use a script that attaches to all your remote machines, log on as an administrator, scan for unapproved applications, and delete or disable those applications. This practice would work for smaller companies and those with non-Windows operating systems that may not have a software distribution solution.

Firewalls

Skype uses a modified form of the STUN protocol to deal with security like NAT on a firewall. Restricted ports are dealt with using random ports during the installation and use of HTTP and HTTPS. Between the use of ports 80 and 443 and the random ports, Skype can work around restricted firewalls.

To see if you can pass through your firewall with Skype, you can use a free program called NAT Check, which can be found at http://midcom-p2p.sourceforge.net/. This NAT checking program is not from Skype, but Skype suggests its use to verify your network capability with Skype. The following NAT Check screen is from a typical home network showing a good result:

The following NAT Check test was over a public wireless access point and using a Cisco VPN SSL client showing a good result:

You can also use the Display technical call info option to help troubleshoot your Skype connection to see if it is being relayed or not. For more information on how to Display technical call info, see Chapters 6 and 13.

Proxy Servers

As we touched on in Chapter 6 and will again in Chapter 13, if you have implemented a proxy server on your medium-sized to enterprise network, you can configure Skype to use the proxy server to gain access to the Internet. The address of the proxy server may not be easily determined by setting Internet Explorer's **Connection LAN Settings** option to **Automatically detect settings**. If you would like to determine the actual proxy server name to enter in the Skype configuration dialog, simply type **netstat – v** at a command prompt. You will notice many Internet connections through the same port, most likely 8080 or 8088, from a machine on your network. That machine is most likely to be your proxy server. If you have more than one proxy server on your network, every time you log in, you may get a different proxy server with the automatic configuration. Manually defining the proxy server allows a network administrator to configure a single proxy server for Skype traffic and have more control over Skype traffic. See Chapter 13 for more information on configuring Skype to use a proxy server.

Embedded Skype

Skype has signed contracts with some vendors to embed its client software into various products. These products are phone sets, small office/home office (SOHO) routers, and other network devices. Skype-enabled devices can have adverse effects on the security of your network if you do not know that "hidden" clients are in various pieces of hardware. So the administrator must not only manage the network side but also be aware of the hardware being brought into the network. Be sure to understand the devices on your network and what they do to prevent unauthorized devices being used on your network.

Performance Considerations

Peer to peer is rarely the best choice for VoIP performance owing to potential latency issues. This is not to say that Skype cannot work well because it's peer to peer, but Skype *can* be impacted easily by network or even computer latency issues. Everything about Skype is propriety and closed to tinkering with the exception of the published API calls. Skype's proprietary design makes it difficult to tweak or to tune Skype, and given that Skype works on a P2P model, there is very little you can do to optimize the routing between the nodes. Skype normally uses UDP as its transport of choice, which makes for a low overhead and good performance, but the trade-off is on how much you can optimize it.

The reality of using Skype is that all the user can adjust is the environment that Skype is running in. For example, Windows can kick off the speech recognition engine when a call using Skype is dialed. This results in heavy CPU utilization, upward of 100 percent. So turning off the voice recognition can have a tangible effect on how well Skype can work. By the same token, avoid running any application that utilizes the CPU heavily when you're trying to use Skype or another VoIP application. You can monitor applications that may be using a large amount of bandwidth or CPU by using a bandwidth-monitoring application such as Net-Peeker or Windows Task Manager to watch for CPU utilization. This requires a bit of work on your part to identify Skype and the port being used, but it can help. Placing a firewall between the Internet and your PC with NAT enabled will also disable your system from being a Supernode.

Tweaking the Technology... Bandwidth Requirements

When you decide which encoder to use, remember that Ethernet adds about 32Kbps to the overall amount of bandwidth required for a given data stream. For example, if you use G.711, which compresses your audio stream to 64Kbps, the addition of Ethernet will add 31Kbps for a total bandwidth stream of 95Kbps.

Skype, on the other hand, uses approximately 5Kbps to 25Kbps of bandwidth each direction as long as you are properly protected with a NAT or firewall device, thus eliminating becoming a supernode. This low-bandwidth requirement and the relatively high quality of the voice conversation are among the main attractions of Skype. There have been reports of users becoming supernodes and experiencing impacted performance. These users were on a broadband connection and a cable modem but no firewall or DSL/Cable router. This setup met the requirement of a public IP and apparently included enough CPU and RAM on the users' home computers. These reports point out some of the dangers of using Skype without understanding how to protect yourself and the potential impact on your network.

If you have a firewall in place, and you do not open up ports to allow Skype to communicate effectively, then you will incur more network overhead because of the TCP traffic and relayed calls and file transfers. You can rapidly approach network saturation if a large portion of the enterprise decides to use Skype at the same time. See Chapter 13 for performance tuning information.

Chapter 12

Business Uses for Skype

Solutions in this chapter:

- Help Desks
- WiFi Phones
- Callto: Tricks
- Other Uses
- A Word about Security

Help Desks

Skype has many benefits for businesses calling between offices or calling clients. But another innovative use for Skype—the help desk—has been adopted. Using Skype, help desk technicians are already at their computers, ready to troubleshoot problems and conjure helpful information at a whim.

Here, we examine two major types of help desk support: internal corporate support and end-user/e-customer support. We also discuss some clever humanitarian uses for Skype.

Corporate Help Desks

One major challenge in help desk support systems is the same challenge that businesses often face: location, location, location. Generally, most companies that require more than a few phone lines use a private branch exchange (PBX) system. A PBX is basically a computer that handles incoming and outgoing calls and allows for calls to be transferred and made interoffice, as well as out to the public telephone system. But this setup usually requires employees to be at a station physically connected to the corporate phone network, linked by the copper wires in the walls or a special private point-to-point VPN connection. This is restrictive for employees who want to work from home or satellite offices not connected over a private point-to-point connection to the phone system. Although calls may be forwarded to employees' mobile phones from their corporate extensions, they lose a lot of the special functionality the PBX provides.

But peer-to-peer Skype telephony solves this problem! An office in Mumbai, India, can provide the same support that someone at the corporate office in San Diego or an employee at home in Seattle receives. Company X can provide help desk Skype Me! links on the intranet homepage, and calls can be quickly routed for help tickets. The same is true for IT staff members who travel frequently from site to site. No matter where they are, as long as they have an Internet connection, these employees are able to provide reliable assistance.

Technicians can take advantage of Skype's text-chat option to provide specific documentation or even case-sensitive shell commands to a user in dire straits. Also, a user can copy and paste error messages or logs that may provide essential information to the person dispatched to help. Skype's file transfer capabilities provide a seamless means for technicians and users to exchange files such as software patches, help documentation, and off-site Web links that could offer solutions.

Educational institutions are already beginning to embrace the power of Skype on their help desks. LEARN NC in North Carolina is a K–12 program from the University of North Carolina, at the Chapel Hill Business School. Among many other online technical support resources, they offer Skype-based support. If a user has a question during off-hours or just prefers online contact, he or she can Skype the user learn.nc.help. The Web site is available at http://help.learnnc.org/.

Another company hot on the Skype-desk bandwagon is the Permaworld foundation, "a member-based not-for-profit organization (since 2001) and a trusted, reputable Web hosting provider." Thirty percent of this firm's income is given to environmental organizations. Smart *and* benevolent!

Ruhrpumpen, an industrial pump manufacturer in Tulsa, Oklahoma, started using Skype in the summer of 2005. The company found it the ideal solution to communicate with partners and co-workers all over the world. They regularly use it to call Central America, Asia, and Europe, which would ordinarily cost a small fortune!

And, of course, www.SkypeTips.com helps Skype users with issues and questions on recommendations for hardware and software solutions, and www.VideoCallTips.com assists users in setting up and using video with Skype to make a personal video call. In addition, InternetVisitation.org helps divorced families use Skype and video to keep children and their parents and grandparents better connected.

Virtual Help Desk

But Skype's helpful attributes are not limited to intranet support! Skype is just as effective at Internet support. The folks at biz.konush.net have compiled a directory of businesses that use Skype. Registration is absolutely free, and hundreds of businesses from across the planet have already signed up. At the time of this writing, the listing included 348 entries, and more were being added daily.

A traditional call center or help desk has one or two main dial-in numbers that can ring many desks. Skype can do this, too! Skype supports the capability to have multiple clients on several computers log in to the same account. When an incoming call is received, it first rings every user who is logged in at the time, and the first user to accept the call takes the conversation. Combined with a SkypeIn phone number, this feature gives users and customers a plethora of options to receive support, at a fraction of the cost of a traditional phone system.

But Skype-based help desks need not always be about making money and *customer* support. In 2005, two major hurricanes, Katrina and Rita, struck the United States. Entire cities were devastated by the water and wind, knocking out traditional landline telephone networks. The networks that managed to stay online quickly became saturated as family members all over the world rushed to contact their loved ones in storm-affected areas.

Enter the hero! KatrinaHelp, a grassroots hurricane relief organization, partnered with Skype, SkypeJournal, and Khaos labs (www.khaoslabs.com) to set up a virtual call center. Concerned parties need only Skype *KatrinaHelp*, and they were greeted by volunteers from shelters, emergency rooms, and other emergency services already deployed to the epicenter of the damage. For people who can't or won't use the Skype client, they also enabled a SkypeIn account as well, further lightening the burden on the public telephone network.

Dina Mehta, a researcher and ethnographer based in India, had this to say about her experience helping the victims as a volunteer for the KatrinaHelp Desk:

> I have been taking turns manning the virtual call center we have set up using Skype linked to KatrinaHelp, to help cover 24 hours of the day. I am beginning to understand what it feels like to be a call-center operator.
>
> What amazes me, though, is that I can volunteer my time, sitting in my living room at home in Mumbai, India, and be of use to help those seeking information about their loved ones who are missing on that other side of the world. This morning, I was on a shift for a couple of hours, and I received about eight calls on our SkypeIn number and made a few on SkypeOut. It was really rewarding to be able to point the callers to resources and hook them up with those offering help. And they were so grateful someone was listening to them and that they did not have to figure out how to navigate pages on Web sites and wikis.
>
> Imagine how it would be to have a virtual Skype phone bank. One that is not just virtual, but ad hoc. Just-in-time emergency support. Always on when we have a bank of volunteers from all over the world, and at all hours. Our way of reaching out and helping those in distress.

So we can see that Skype is really beginning to take off in ways not thought of before. The future of Skype business telephony is bright, too! Several companies are currently developing software and hardware solutions to augment Skype's capabilities into a full-fledged business-class telecommunication medium. These devices include hardware applications to simulate operator-based call routing that businesses traditionally use to manage their calls. For example, in a standard business-class PBX system, an operator is able to tell whether an agent is currently on the line assisting a caller or if that agent has been idle for some time, waiting for his or her phone to ring. An idle agent is more prepared to handle a new caller's concerns than, say, an agent who is tied to a call already. Once development on these applications is completed, we can expect to see Skype take a firmer grasp of the help desk business model. See Chapters 7 and 8 for more information on different Skype-based software and hardware applications.

WiFi Phones

Until recently, when users wanted to Skype someone, they would make the call from their desktop computers using a headset or microphone/speaker combo, talking to a monitor. Although practical and cost-efficient, this approach leaves users tied to their desks, limiting mobility and productivity. And, yes, it can sometimes feel a little silly talking to a computer screen. Users demand freedom from microphone cables, liberation from monitors, and all the familiar comfortable benefits of their home telephones. Several different approaches to this dilemma have been devised, offering the ultimate in freedom of choice for Skyping without wires. Several vendors are coming out with WiFi Skype phones. You can read more about this in Chapter 15.

Bluetooth Headsets

The first solution we'll look at is the Bluetooth headset. These headsets are usually designed specifically with telecommunications in mind and are a great, affordable option for cutting the chains that clamp users to their desks. To use Bluetooth with Skype, we need a headset (obviously), a Bluetooth adapter to connect the headset to the computer, and optional software to integrate the headset buttons into Skype.

Plantronics makes an expensive version called the CS50-USB. Retailing at about $299.99, it might be a little out of the price range of the average Skype user, but the superior sound quality it offers makes it an ideal choice for Skype in the office. With a professional Class 3 Bluetooth radio, Skypers are able to wander up to 200 feet away from the base station and still retain an excellence of voice quality. Combined with Plantronics' PerSonoCall software, this device allows you to initiate and end calls at the push of a button. You can read more about the CS50-USB at www.plantronics.com/north_america/en_US/products/cat640035/cat5480033/prod5300004.

Understanding the Basics... Bluetooth 101

Bluetooth adapters can be purchased for as little as $20 at most computer hardware retailers, with prices dropping ever steadily. Software plug-ins often require the use of the Widcomm Bluetooth driver, so make sure to check before you buy one. The headsets themselves tend to cost a little more, with the lower-end models starting at about $30 and ranging all the way to the several-hundred-dollar mark for high-end headsets with advanced features.

This device uses wireless technology similar to traditional WiFi networks and gives a user a personal area network (PAN) with an average range of about 10 meters for a Class 3 Bluetooth device. Class 2 devices have a range of 20 meters, and a Class 1 Bluetooth device has a range of about 100 meters. Actual signal strength depends primarily on the manufacturer and model of both the headset and the adapter.

My headset of choice is the Motorola HS810, which works with both Skype and my Motorola mobile phone. I use a Targus Class 2 adapter that provides more than ample coverage for me to pace frantically around my desk as I chat with my Skype buddies and coworkers. Even when I'm not straying far from my desk, I prefer the headset to a traditional computer microphone/headset combo, because it frees me from my desk and allows me to use my computer as I talk. Of course, Motorola's HS810 is not the only great model of Bluetooth headset. Other manufacturers and models include, but are not limited to, these:

- Jabra's BT250, BT250v, BT350, BT500, and BT800

- Logitech's Mobile Express, Mobile Freedom, Mobile Freedom, Mobile Traveller, and Mobile Pro

- Motorola's HS801, HS805, HS820, HS830, HS850 for cars, and the combination headset/eyeglasses, the RAZRWIRE BT Eyewear

- Nokia's HS-11W, HDW-3, and HS4W

Almost any Bluetooth headset that will work with your current Bluetooth-enabled mobile phone will work with Skype, provided that the necessary drivers have been installed.

SkypeHeadsets

To fully take advantage of a Bluetooth headset's features, we'll want to use the headset's main button with Skype instead of manually intervening with our mouse every time we'd like to take or make a call. Kamal Munir and Stuart John are consultants based in London who specialize in mobile telecommunications. They developed a plug-in for Skype called SkypeHeadset, which changes a Bluetooth headset from an ordinary speaker-and-microphone combo into a complete Skype phone. SkypeHeadset adds many features, including the following:

- Integrated Pairing Wizard

- Quick-dial a contact

- Automatically change Skype status by connecting or disconnecting the headset

- Suspend and resume from the SkypeHeadset popup menu

SkypeHeadset has a few prerequisites to meet before we'll be able to use it. It works with version 1.x, 1.2.0.x, 1.3.0.x, or 1.4.0.x. SkypeHeadset works only with Windows 2000 and Windows XP (SP1 or SP2). The software works only with Widcomm Bluetooth drivers and does not support the generic Windows XP Bluetooth drivers. At this time, SkypeHeadset is not available for Mac or Pocket PC users.

Smart Phones

For the user who is constantly in transit, it's not always feasible to be in front of a computer to use Skype. However, many of the higher-end "smart phones" available today come with the Skype client included. A smart phone is one that combines the functionality of a cellular phone with a handheld computer. See Chapter 8 for more information on Smart Phones that work with Skype. Models known to work with Skype include:

- Audiovox SMT5600

- Samsung I730, which can do either cell or WiFi, but not both at the same time

- Motorola MPX220

- iMate K-Jam, SP5 & SP5m

The mobile phone client is limited to text chat, since the processors in these phones don't usually have the horsepower to use the voice feature and the General Packet Radio Service (GPRS) Internet on these handsets does not provide adequate bandwidth. The exception to this is the SPV M5000, by Orange, which uses the Pocket PC version of the software over 802.11 and is fully capable of voice calls.

Next-generation mobile broadband, such as Verizon's VZAccess, now provides mobile users with access that is more than sufficient for Skype chatting using both voice and text.

VZAccess 3G Verizon uses high-speed Internet access that is fast enough. For more information, visit www.verizonwireless.com/b2c/businessSolutions/mobileProfessional/index.jsp?cm_re=Ho me%20Page-_-Business%20Box-_-Mo%20Pro.

For a user on the road in need of a quick answer, smart phones are the perfect means to stay in touch with the office network. We need to be aware of a few considerations, though. Since Skype is based on peer-to-peer technology, there's a lot of network traffic, even when we are not actively chatting. This is especially important to consider if you pay by the megabyte for your mobile wireless Internet. Skype Mobile edition also requires us to use Windows Mobile 2003.

Pocket PC

For some situations, text just isn't good enough. Skype users on the road or roaming the office want to retain the voice capabilities of Skype's advanced features. For those situations, the Pocket PC client is ideal. To use Skype for Pocket PC, you need to make sure that your device meets the minimum system requirements. See Chapter 8 for more information on Pocket PCs that work with Skype. The Pocket PC must be running the following:

- Microsoft Pocket PC 2003

- WiFi

- 400MHz or better processor

The Skype Pocket PC client enables all the same features we've grown to know and love from the proper client, like SkypeIn, SkypeOut, and as of beta 1.2, Skype Voicemail. The Pocket PC version can participate in Skype Conference calls, but as of this writing it cannot initiate them.

One concern many users voice about the Pocket PC client is the echo they sometimes experience. This echo is because the microphone of the Pocket PC is not designed for telephony use and does not properly damp noise received from the speaker, which creates feedback. Using a headset (wired or Bluetooth) will help to reduce this feedback and provide sound quality comparable with that of the PC client. Some Pocket PCs work well without headsets; some do not. It's best to try out your Pocket PC of choice with Skype before purchasing, if you have that option.

TIP

Turning down the volume from the Max 1 setting reduces feedback. Only a few Pocket PC's do well without a headset, so be sure to test. Also, many Pocket PCs use a 4C connector (see the list of articles in the preceding section) and not a regular headset. Many Pocket PCs do *not* have the Bluetooth headset profile.

Since Skype Pocket PC uses WiFi technology instead of GPRS, it retains all the features of its PC-based bigger brother. Skype Pocket PC can use public hot spots, turning a Pocket PC into a virtual mobile phone! Anywhere there is open WiFi access, we can place calls just as we would with a normal phone. Imagine reading your morning newspaper while sipping a latte at your favorite WiFi-enabled coffee shop. And when you're wandering the halls of your office or home, you stay in touch with all your Skype contacts.

It's important to remember that most modern Pocket PCs have just enough power to make a phone call and nothing else, so some undesirable side effects are inevitable. Many users complain of buzzing noises or weird clicks during calls; many business users will find these quirks unacceptable for calls of a professional nature.

The faster the Pocket PC, the better. A wired headset works best as Bluetooth contends for Pocket PC CPU cycles, which can affect call quality and drain Pocket PC battery life at a vastly increased rate.

Skype Phones

So far we've talked quite a bit about using Skype on the go to stay in touch with the office. But several options appeal to our coworkers who are a bit more static, who don't need as much mobility. These users should consider a Skype USB phone. Many people might be apprehensive about embracing new technology, which might feel unfamiliar and intimidating. A Skype USB phone resembles a traditional landline or cordless phone in almost every way. The feel, weight, and operation are identical to those of a normal phone, offering comfort to users who might otherwise not use Skype. For more details on USB phones, see Chapter 8.

Linksys partnered with Skype to create the CIT200 Skype Phone. This phone is a cordless Digital Enhanced Cordless Telecommunications (DECT) 1.8GHz phone designed not to interfere with existing wireless networks, whereas traditional 2.4GHz cordless telephones can often cause problems. It has a backlit color display that allows us to place calls to other Skype users by selecting a name from the contact list. Of course, we can also use SkypeOut minutes to make a call to the public phone network and gain all the functionality of a regular phone. But the range is one feature that makes this a great solution; Linksys advertises a 300-meter outdoor range and a 50-meter indoor range. With the included belt clip and 2.5mm headset jack, this should be more than ample for most users to work all around the office and still maintain audio clarity. And those oh-so-important poolside meetings in the back yard won't be a problem!

The CIT200 also supports up to four handsets from one USB base station. Each phone can have its own unique address book and extension, making phone-to-phone intercom calls possible. This is ideal for a small business, which can run an entire team of eight people on two USB base stations. And through Skype-to-Skype calls, many offices can stay connected for free. The addition of customizable ring tones allows offices to assign rings to individual departments or offices to distinguish the internal calls from regular inbound calls.

The one thing the CIT200 suffers from is the inability to work as both a Skype phone and a regular landline phone. For this we need a special device, a Skype Gateway or a USB Phone like the DualPhone that can handle both Skype calls and regular telephone lines. Fortunately, many such devices already exist and are relatively inexpensive, about $50 on average. For more information on these options see Chapter 8.

VoSky (Actiontec Skype products rebranded) makes an excellent device called the Internet Phone Wizard, which allows us to connect any regular phone (cordless or corded) and use it with Skype as well as landline calls. The built-in Call Waiting feature allows us to place landline callers on hold to answer a Skype call, and vice versa. One thing to keep in mind is that these Gateways do not provide the Skype Contacts list feature that the Linksys CIT200 or DualPhone offers.

Callto: Tricks

So now we can make and receive calls for free or next to nothing. The cost savings alone are enough to make your company's finance department scream for joy. Now let's look at some clever ways to utilize Skype's *Callto:* feature to make phone calls even easier.

Point, Click, and Call

When Skype is installed, it creates a new Universal Resource Identifier (URI) in the operating system called *callto://*, which enables Skype to be launched at the click of a button. To use this function, simply make a link called *callto://* with a Skype contact name after the URI. For example, we could put some code on the company intranet page for the help desk, which might look something like this:

```
<a href="callto://HelpDesk"><img
src="http://goodies.skype.com/graphics/skypeme_btn_black.gif" border="0"></a>
```

This ordinary HTML code tells our computer to launch Skype and call the HelpDesk user when the link is clicked. Skype tells the operating system to pass all *callto:* requests to Skype, which in turn dials the user specified in the link. Suddenly a Web page can become an automated directory! These shortcuts can be saved on a Web page, in an e-mail, or even as a bookmark within the browser.

Understanding the Basics... Desktop Dialing

Using *callto:* we can create desktop shortcuts to call our favorite contacts. In Windows, right-click anywhere on the **Desktop** and then select **New | Shortcut**. In the dialog box, type *callto://name*, where *name* is the Skype name of the buddy you want to call. Create a name for this shortcut, such as **Bobby's Mobile** or **IT Help Desk**. Then, when you want to call this contact, simply point and click!

The *callto:* URI is great when a Skype user has added a Skype Me! link on a Web site, but what about phone numbers on the Internet that don't have a *callto:* link? If you're a Firefox user, Greasemonkey comes to the rescue! Greasemonkey is a Firefox extension that lets us take user-created scripts and change the behavior of a Web site. Mark Abiuso created a script called Skype Linkify that converts regular text phone numbers on a Web page to clickable Skype *callto:* links. Skype then fires up SkypeOut and places the call, and presto! Point-and-click pizza delivery calls! Combined with Google Local, Skype Linkify transforms your Web browser into a directory assistance switchboard!

To install Skype Linkify, we must first install Greasemonkey, available at http://grease-monkey.mozdev.org.

Remember, Greasemonkey works only with Firefox, not Internet Explorer. You can download the Skype Linkify script from www.questar.it/blog/developer/skypelinkify.user.js.

From the **Tools** menu in the browser, choose **Install User Script** and load **Skype Linkify**. Now any page listing a phone number will have a clickable SkypeOut link! Note that this script is configured for calls within the United States. If you are in another country, you'll have to modify *const defaultPrefix= '+1';* to the country prefix you want to use.

```
// Skype Linkify
// Author: Marco Abiuso
// License: GNU GPL v2 or later
// Modified version of:
//    VoIP Dialer Linkify by Ralf Muehlen
//(http://www.muehlen.com/projects/voip/voip_dial.user.js)
//    Inspired by: UPS Tracking Linkify
//(http://plutor.org/files/upslinkify.user.js) by Logan Ingalls
//
// Match these patterns:
//    800-555-1212
//    (800) 555-1212
//    (80) 555-1212
//    80-555-1212
//    800-555-12123
//    800 555 1212
//    800/555/1212
//    +1 <number>
//    +39 <number>
// Link to "callto://<number>"
//
// ==UserScript==
// @name          Skype Linkify
// @namespace     http://www.questar.it
// @description   Looks for phone numbers in the page and hyperlinks them
//for calling with SkypeOut (www.skype.com).
// @include       *
// ==/UserScript==

//default country prefix
const defaultPrefix= '+1';
```

```
(function () {
        const trackRegex = /(\+\d\d?)?[\-\s\/\.]?[\(]?(\d){2,4}[\)]?[\-
\s\/\.]?\d\d\d[\-\s\/\.]?(\d){3,5}\b/ig;


        function trackUrl(t) {


                if (String(t).charAt(0)!= '+') t= defaultPrefix + String(t);
                return "callto://" + (String(t).replace(/[\-\s\/\(\)\.]/g, ""));

        }


    // tags we will scan looking for un-hyperlinked urls
    var allowedParents = [
        "abbr", "acronym", "address", "applet", "b", "bdo", "big",
"blockquote", "body",
        "caption", "center", "cite", "code", "dd", "del", "div", "dfn", "dt",
"em",
        "fieldset", "font", "form", "h1", "h2", "h3", "h4", "h5", "h6", "i",
"iframe",
        "ins", "kdb", "li", "nobr", "object", "pre", "p", "q", "samp", "small",
"span", "strike",
        "s", "strong", "sub", "sup", "td", "th", "tt", "u", "var"
        ];


    var xpath = "//text()[(parent::" + allowedParents.join(" or parent::") +
")" +
                        //" and contains(translate(., 'HTTP', 'http'),
'http')" +
                        "]";


    var candidates = document.evaluate(xpath, document, null,
XPathResult.UNORDERED_NODE_SNAPSHOT_TYPE, null);


    //var t0 = new Date().getTime();
    for (var cand = null, i = 0; (cand = candidates.snapshotItem(i)); i++) {
        if (trackRegex.test(cand.nodeValue)) {
            var span = document.createElement("span");
            var source = cand.nodeValue;

            cand.parentNode.replaceChild(span, cand);
```

```
                trackRegex.lastIndex = 0;
                for (var match = null, lastLastIndex = 0; (match =
trackRegex.exec(source)); ) {

span.appendChild(document.createTextNode(source.substring(lastLastIndex,
match.index)));

                    var a = document.createElement("a");
                    a.setAttribute("href", trackUrl(match[0]));
                    a.appendChild(document.createTextNode(match[0]));
                    span.appendChild(a);

                    lastLastIndex = trackRegex.lastIndex;
                }

span.appendChild(document.createTextNode(source.substring(lastLastIndex)));
                span.normalize();
            }
        }
    //var t1 = new Date().getTime();
    //alert("UPS Tracking linkify took " + ((t1 - t0) / 1000) + " seconds");

})();
```

Other Uses

We've seen what Skype can do for us in the office and at work. But what are some other ways people have been getting Skype to work for them? After all, business is just the beginning!

Radio Call-In Shows

Radio shows are adopting online simulcasts with increasing frequency. The Internet makes it possible for users outside a radio station's broadcast range to tune in and enjoy the program. Using Skype, radio programs can welcome participation from geographically scattered participants at no extra cost! By setting up a Skype account for the radio show, the show's producers free up traditional analog-based telephone lines for local users to call in while enabling globally scattered callers to communicate with their favorite radio jockeys over the Internet. And because the radio station already runs off an Internet connection, no additional costs are incurred.

The Kingdom of Loathing is an online role-playing game where players take the form of stick-figure warriors who engage in adventures across the Internet. Boasting an impressive fan base with over 20,000 registered users, the Kingdom of Loathing has an Internet radio show that features Skype, allowing fans across the country to participate in the show and in contests. You can visit the Kingdom of Loathing site at http://kingdomofloathing.com.

Scriptschool.com is another online radio show featuring Skype. Scriptschool hosts lessons on programming for the Web, with features on coding in PHP, adding RSS to blogs, and a slew of other content appealing to budding Webmasters. Listeners can call in and request specific help on programming or participate in call-in radio contests by Skyping the radio show hosts such as Skype user TDavid.

Online Pubs?!

Did we hear that right? Online bars? Yes! Robbie O'Connell's Pub (robbieoconnellspub.com) in Daytona Beach, Florida, offers Skype to its patrons, along with a Webcam, free WiFi, and even video game consoles! Skypers can see their favorite barflies on the Web cam and call them up to say hi using the Skype name robbieoconnellspub . People viewing the Web site are even able to buy pints of beer for the bargoers using a PayPal link on the site.

Cyber Sherpas!

At 18,500 feet on Mt. Everest, a Cisco AIRONET 350 crunches away happily, fed by an AAP-1 satellite provided by SES Americom. This setup provides connectivity between the base station Cybercafe, the Internet, and the sherpas at 128Kbps. David Hughes (Skype name: david.hughes) was the network architect who got Internet connectivity to the desolate remotes of Mt. Everest. He needed a voice solution but found that standard VoIP solutions just weren't cutting it. He says:

> So I examined Skype. And after getting it working well across the U.S., I told Tsering to download the code, install it, and try a call to me. He did, taking most of the 64Kbps hour to download the software and 20 minutes to get it up.

> The call was excellent quality from the get-go: loud, clear on both ends, with only two burps in one hour. The only thing we have to do, as we did for the SIP phones, is pause as the bits travel 24,000 miles up, then down, then up again, then down again, delaying about a second and a half as it goes literally to the other side of the world.

And now he is going over to Thame to install Skype on their machine as soon as he gets a speaker phone from Katmandu (there's no corner Radio Shack high in the Himalayas, believe me). As soon as that comes, Mingma will be calling up the kiddies in Thame and teaching both oral and written English, as originally planned.

Tsering will also set up a SkypeOut system, so the trekkers can make their phone calls to dialup phones wherever they are, if they need to. Otherwise, they will talk Skype to Skype.

Tsering will continue to make a living, the kids will learn English, the trekkers will call home after e-mailing their friends, and my investment in time, dollars, and climbing the slopes of Everest will have paid off. And I can put a notch in my Colorado gun belt for racking up another very remote village to the Internet."

Mobile and Remote Users

Employees who travel often find themselves in hotels on the road, many of which offer broadband connections to the Internet as a perk integrated into the cost of the room or at an additional charge. By connecting to Skype, these travelers are within reach of coworkers, regardless of their physical proximity to the office. When the CTO visits the sister office in Singapore, he or she can still conduct business with offices in the United States as though he were making a local call. An employee at a Starbucks equipped with a WiFi Hotspot account or a "Skype Zones" account can make conference calls as though he or she were still at the office. Many airports offer free or low-cost broadband Internet connections that can be leveraged to make Skype and SkypeOut calls.

Users working from home have this same luxury. By virtualizing their telephone extensions, home users can be conferenced in to a call with other Skype users in the field or at the corporate office. This frees up physical stations connected to the phone network for other employees not working remotely. Using Skype could further reduce expenses incurred on cell phone plans that pay on a per-minute use basis or monthly plan and potentially reduce reimbursements for home office telephone bills. Companies must balance the cost of adding the required hardware, implementation, and support against the costs incurred for large cell phone minute plans and home office telephones, to create a communication strategy that both meets their calling requirements and which is also cost-effective and secure.

IP Phone Infrastructures

Many companies have already deployed an enterprise IP phone solution like those from Cisco, Lucent, and others. These systems allow companies to make free calls virtually anywhere in the world within their company network as they route their voice traffic internally over their complex data networks. So for these environments, adding Skype to call an employee internationally is of little value.

However, companies with this kind of infrastructure could use Skype to route a call in the United States to a help desk in India for free by adding one of the Skype PBX gateways that are being developed by several vendors that we discuss in Chapter 15. As we mentioned earlier in this chapter, mobile or remote users could set up one or more accounts connected to the Skype PBX gateway. These accounts would allow remote employees at any location in the world to make free calls to their offices from their hotels or homes . Another way would be to enable a regular telephone user to use Skype or SkypeOut via one of these Skype PBX gateways to make inexpensive local toll or long distance calls or to other Skype users that could be a distributor of a part they purchase for example. So there are ways small, medium-sized, and large companies could add Skype to supplement their existing telephone infrastructures.

A Word about Security

Many companies with an IT staff are or will ask, "Is Skype secure?" While writing this book, Skype released a Security White Paper by Tom Berson of Anagram Laboratories, a well-known cryptographer who outlines how Skype uses encryption. This paper may be found at http://www.skype.com/security/.

Companies that are security aware and have a good security posture will question whether any voice software, or softphone as this technology is often referred to, is secure enough to discuss anything from human resource issues, mergers and acquisitions to participating in conference calls. Berson's paper should calm the fears of many security practitioners. However, many corporations will still wonder about the security of a softphone on a computer that is mobile or in a remote location, such as an employee's home, hotel, or hotspot. For example, corporations will be concerned whether these mobile devices could get compromised with a recording device and record the voice calls and upload them to a Web site to be listened to by the masses or sold to the competition.

These concerns are valid for any company and might be even for the typical home user, but one of the guiding rules of security is to "classify your data." Companies must (1.) decide what data, or in this case voice transmissions, needs to be protected; (2.) determine which devices to use and when to use them; and (3.) set rules or policies that the employees will follow. If you are one of these companies, you should consider developing a policy that sets the classification of voice calls and what the proper device or location should be used when making any voice calls that are "sensitive" in nature and educate your employees to strictly follow this communication policy. Points to consider in this policy include:

- The security of any mobile device capable of voice (cell, Pocket PC, laptop)

- What communication should occur on a landline (e.g. mergers)

- What communication can occur on a soft phone or Skype (e.g. conference calls)

- Where you should or should not be when having conversations on a cell phone or soft phone (airport)

I am amazed at how many people I have encountered in my travels whose companies still do not deploy a personal firewall or encryption on a laptop in today's world of worms, theft, and malicious activity targeted at Microsoft Windows users. It is not Microsoft's fault that these users are compromised; it is the fault of companies that are not practicing defense in depth and securing their assets. Many companies have a "Deny all unless explicitly allowed" policy. Under this policy, these companies do not allow Skype because they have not specifically approved Skype, and yet, they deploy thousands of laptops with very sensitive data without encryption. If I were interested in data about a company, I sure would not be trying to capture Skype traffic. I would go after a laptop, since many companies put asset labels on their laptops indicating the company name or users have business card tags on their laptop bags. Social Engineering 101: Users tell you a lot without saying a word.

Regarding sniffing or capturing a Skype call, only a few governments and companies could afford the amount of storage required to capture the sheer quantity of Skype traffic going through an ISP, for example. The weak point is the client that is the laptop or desktop. If proper security measures were taken to protect these devices and if these measures were assessed frequently, this risk should be minimal. Companies as a regular practice install and monitor antivirus and personal firewall software. Many companies also use an intrusion detection solution on the laptops they issue to employees to protect users from open networks they may connect to (e.g., a hotel or their homes with a DSL or cable broadband connection).

Personally, if I were an IT security manager who had read Tom Berson's Security White Paper and was confident that my laptops were properly secured, I would approve the use of Skype in my corporation as long as I had a "communication policy" covering what I could and could not discuss over Skype or other communication devices. I have overheard some rather interesting cell phone conversations in airports, coffee shops, and airline lounges during which businesspeople discuss very sensitive information. To me, this practice is a greater risk than using Skype.

Besides, if an issue occurred or was discovered with Skype, I could always issue a "Stop using Skype immediately" memo or e-mail to all employees while the issue was under investigation and until the security was reconfirmed. I could also use a software distribution tool or script to disable Skype fairly quickly on all computers that had Skype loaded. A company with valid security concerns could use Skype to reduce its communication costs and enable its employees by adding Skype versus replacing any existing solution like cell phones or landlines. The goals of using Skype in these situations are to reduce the amount of costly cell minutes and lower home office or hotel telephone bill expenses. As long as a company does not replace the traditional way of communicating, Skype could be added with little risk when deployed with a good communication policy.

Chapter 13

Skype Firewall and Network Setup

Solutions in this chapter:

- A Word about Network Address Translation (NAT) and Firewalls

- What You Need to Know about Configuring Your Network Devices

- Ports Required for Skype

- Using Proxy Servers and Skype

- How to Block Skype in the Enterprise

A Word about Network Address Translation and Firewalls

When the Internet began, the creators didn't envision the type of growth that we are experiencing today. During the last 10 years, the number of hosts on the Internet increased by more than a factor of 50.[1] In order for each Internet device, or host, to communicate on the Internet, it must have a unique internet protocol (IP) address. The addressing scheme for the Internet allowed for billions of IP addresses, but now most of them are allocated.

The Internet's popularity results in a maximum number of available IP addresses. Homes and offices around the world are now connecting many hosts at a single location and it is not possible for every single device to have its own public IP address. To increase the number of addresses available, a new standard called IPv6 has been developed. Until IPv6 is finalized, other methods are needed to allow for the sharing of public addresses among more systems. The most effective solution is called network address translation (NAT), defined in the request for comments 1631 (RFC 1631).

NAT is a special type of router that has several different implementations. One popular method of implementation allows for the use of special, unroutable IP addresses on private or internal networks. The private addresses are translated to a public host address, which allows communication over the Internet. Three blocks of the unroutable, or private, IP addresses are defined in RFC 1597 and RFC 1918. The private addresses are reserved by the Internet Assigned Numbers Authority (IANA), the organization that is responsible for all IP addresses. The private addresses are represented in Classless Inter-Domain Routing (CIDR) notation as:

- 10.0.0.0/8
- 172.16.0.0/12
- 192.168.0.0/16

These address blocks cannot communicate directly with public addresses on the Internet and must be translated.

NAT utilizes a mechanism in the Transmission Control Protocol/Internet Protocol (TCP/IP) stack called multiplexing to enable these private addresses to establish communication over the Internet. Multiplexing makes it possible for a single device to establish and maintain several simultaneous connections with one or more hosts using different TCP and User Datagram Protocol (UDP) ports. This architecture allows an implementation where a single public IP address can service the needs of an entire network of hosts, a many-to-one relationship.

NAT routers keep a table of internal address and port combinations, as well as the public (global) IP address and port used to establish the remote connection. External hosts do not see the internal address, but instead use the public IP address to respond to requests. When responses are sent back to the external IP address and port of the NAT router, it translates the response and relays it back to the internal address and port that originated the request.

Firewalls are Protocol layer rules engines. A firewall can be hardware or software based, and many routers include basic firewall functionality as an additional feature. A typical firewall provides a list of rules that are evaluated sequentially against the header data in the packet being processed. As each rule is examined against the packet header, the packet will be blocked, or the next rule will be evaluated. This process continues until the packet is blocked or all rules have been examined, in which case the packet is forwarded.

A proxy server is similar to a firewall, but it works at the Application layer. Proxy servers have packet-filtering features. Packet filtering allows examination of the actual data being transmitted within the packet itself. Packet filters are available on Windows XP, Windows 2000, and Windows Server 2003 products as part of the advanced features of the TCP/IP configuration. However, because Skype encrypts the data it transmits, packet filtering is an ineffective means of managing Skype traffic. Proxy servers handle the requests for each protocol, whereas firewalls merely forward the traffic. If the proxy server is disabled, no traffic is allowed to pass. If you disable a firewall, you are turning off all rules processing and allowing all traffic to pass, which is not a recommended practice.

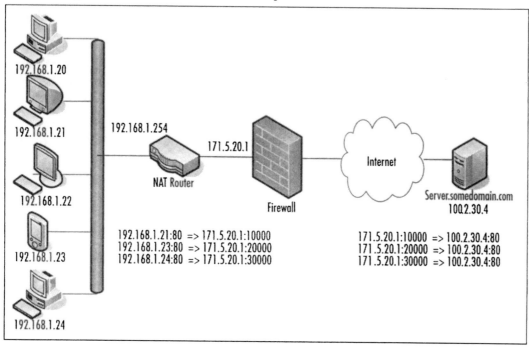

In the preceding diagram, a single external IP address is exposed to the Internet. When hosts on the private network make a request, the following occurs:

1. The host initiates a request for the remote destination address and port.

2. Since the address is remote, the router handles the request.

3. The NAT router adds the entry for the internal host IP address and port to the translation table.

4. The NAT router assigns a new port on the external interface IP address for the internal client and adds it to the translation table.

5. The NAT router then initiates a connection to the remote host on the external network, through the firewall, substituting a new source port and IP address in the IP packet header.

6. The remote host responds to the request to the external address and port.

7. The firewall compares the IP address and port with the list of firewall rules. If the IP address passes the IP address test, the port is checked. For Skype, this would be a UDP port, or if UDP is blocked, TCP port 443 or TCP port 80.

8. The router uses the translation table to translate the response from the remote host from the external address and port to the original internal address and port of the host that initiated the request.

Home Users

We strongly recommended that home users obtain a basic peer-to-peer-friendly, broadband router with firewall capabilities. In addition to a hardware-based router/firewall, you should always use a software-based firewall on each client machine. Windows XP has built-in firewall software that is enabled by default after you install Service Pack 2. Other options for software-based firewalls include products by McAfee, Symantec, and Zone Alarm. Skype should work right out of the gate on most home networks without requiring any further configuration. For home users, no modification is needed.

Later in this chapter, we discuss how to improve the quality of the communication, which could require minor configuration settings on your firewall.

Small to Medium-Sized Businesses

Small to medium-sized businesses must use discretion to determine whether to use a simple implementation, as discussed for home users, or to provide a more robust firewall solution, such as the Symantec Firewall/VPN Appliance, Cisco Pix, or other SOHO solution.

Regardless, we suggest that small and medium-sized businesses use software-based firewalls on each network client to provide an additional layer of security.

Large Corporations

Larger corporations must ensure that the many routers used on the LAN allow Skype traffic over UDP to pass to other clients on the LAN if they want to use Skype effectively.

To better understand how Skype communicates, you need to get a picture of how the Skype network is organized. There are three basic roles in the Skype communication infrastructure. The roles consist of the following:

- Skype client or peer
- Supernodes
- Login servers

A Skype client is your computer running the Skype software. Supernodes are just Skype peer nodes that are not behind a restrictive firewall or a NAT router, and which therefore have unrestricted access to the Internet. Supernodes come and go depending on the needs of the overall network. Any Skype client node can become a supernode if it is not behind a NAT router or blocking firewall and has sufficient CPU and bandwidth capacity.

Understanding the Basics... Avoid Becoming a Supernode

To prevent a Skype client from becoming a supernode, all that is required is for the client to be behind a NAT router or a restrictive firewall (hardware or software).

If a Skype client is behind a NAT router or firewall, the Skype client cannot establish a direct connection to another peer. In these situations, the supernode peers act as relaying agents to help Skype peers behind firewalls or NAT routers establish connections to other peers that are behind firewalls or NAT routers. Skype peers tend to connect to supernodes that are in relative proximity to their locations on the Internet. By connecting to nearby supernodes, Skype reduces utilization and decreases the latency in response times, thus providing a fast and scalable communication network.

Understanding the Basics...
Avoid Relayed Calls or File Transfers

To prevent a Skype call or file transfer from being relayed, the firewall or NAT router must allow a P2P connection.

When Skype starts, it determines whether the client is behind a firewall or NAT router. If there is a firewall or NAT router, Skype determines the best method for communication via the firewall or NAT router using various UDP mechanisms. If no UDP ports are open, Skype will attempt to use TCP port 80, then TCP Port 443. Refer to the basic topology to get a picture of what happens next.

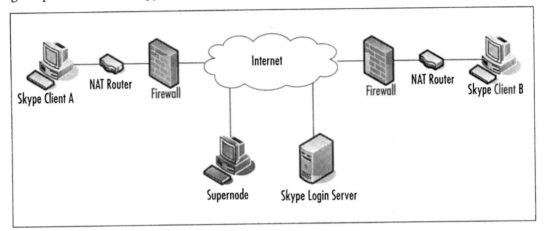

After Skype Client A determines how to navigate the firewall or NAT router, Skype contacts a supernode peer from its supernode list to attempt to log in. If for some reason there are no supernodes listed for the client, the client attempts to log in to the Skype login server. Once the client logs in, the supernode list may be updated with the current active list of supernodes.

Once the connection is established, you can place a call, begin to instant message, or transfer a file. The call starts with a search of the Skype Global Index to locate the target Skype user. Skype Client B will follow the same process to log in. If the target user, Skype Client B, is behind a firewall or non-P2P-friendly device, the supernode acts as the liaison to direct traffic from client A to Client B and vice versa, thus allowing Skype Clients A and B to find and communicate with each other using Skype Clients as relay nodes.

What You Need to Know about Configuring Your Network Devices

We'll now discuss configuring network devices in various environments.

Home Users or Businesses Using a DSL/Cable Router And No Firewall

To use Skype typical home users will not need to configure anything on their DSL/Cable routers with or without wireless unless they have an older DSL/Cable router that is not P2P friendly. Running NAT Check, discussed later in this chapter, and enabling the Technical Information in Skype's Advanced options will help you determine if your router is capable of a Skype P2P connection.

Small to Large Company Firewall Users

To provide the best performance on your network, you will need to tune your network to optimize handling of the Skype traffic. Skype leverages the use of UDP extensively to provide the best possible connection quality with its peers. The NAT translation table is a volatile table that ages old connections to free up room in the routing device's buffer for new connections.

It is important that the NAT routers hold the definition for UDP datagrams sent from the internal network for at least 30 seconds. The delay ensures that there is ample time provided for a response to the original request initiated from the client. The translation table should consistently map the internal host address and port number for UDP traffic in order to be reliably translated from the external address and port used to establish the communication. UDP has very little overhead, but it is prone to loss because it is not guaranteed to be delivered to the destination. Because it has little overhead, UDP is a faster method for communications.

TCP and UDP Primer

TCP requires a threeway handshake to verify that data reaches its destination, whereas UDP just sends that data, and does not require acknowledgment of delivery. Because UDP does not require all of the overhead in the message structure, the messages are smaller, and UDP headers are always the same size. The UDP message structure makes the delivery much faster. Establishing communication sessions over TCP takes three trips instead of the one trip UDP requires. The TCP headers are much larger and vary in size, so there is more overhead to process each TCP message as well.

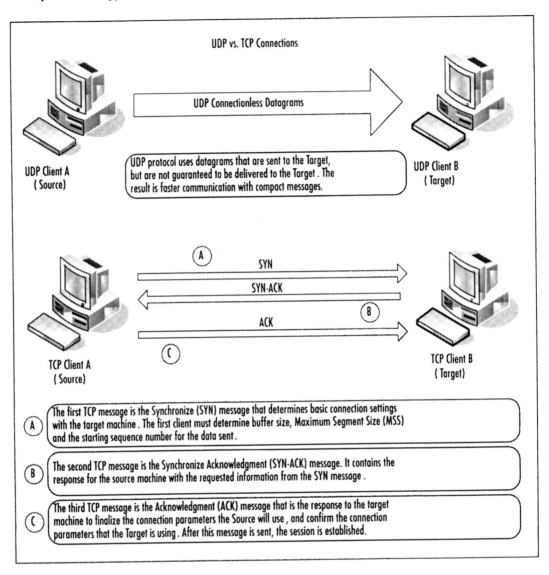

NAT vs. a Firewall

Remember, a NAT device just translates many internal IP addresses to one or more external routable Internet addresses. A firewall can also provide NAT functionality and includes additional intelligence to apply rules to the traffic that passes through the firewall. NAT devices such as a DSL/cable router may or may not have firewall functionality.

Skype also recommends that the firewall or Internet gateway support IP packet fragmentation and reassembly. Fragmenting the packets allows the stream of data to be broken into smaller packets that can be sent simultaneously over multiple ports to the destination. This packet fragmentation can dramatically improve quality and performance by allowing higher throughput, which in turn allows for more effective bandwidth. Some firewalls detect this type of parallel UDP communication incorrectly as port scanning and will block the host traffic. The result could be a degradation of Skype performance.

Skype references a tool called NAT Check by Bryan Ford. The tool can be located at http://midcom-p2p.sourceforge.net.

The tool can be used to determine how P2P friendly your network is. Ford has described the details on UDP communications over the Internet using NAT in an Internet draft. The paper is located at http://mirrors.isc.org/pub/www.watersprings.org/pub/id/draft-ford-natp2p-00.txt.

The following example shows the output from NAT Check for a relayed call:

```
 cmd.exe                                                                  _ □ ×
                   11 Dir(s)   31,289,475,072 bytes free
D:\1dwnload>natcheck
Request 1 of 20...
Request 2 of 20...
Request 3 of 20...
Request 4 of 20...
Request 5 of 20...
Request 6 of 20...
Request 7 of 20...
Request 8 of 20...
Request 9 of 20...
Request 10 of 20...
Request 11 of 20...
Request 12 of 20...
Request 13 of 20...
Request 14 of 20...
Request 15 of 20...
Request 16 of 20...
Request 17 of 20...
Request 18 of 20...
Request 19 of 20...
Request 20 of 20...

TCP RESULTS:
TCP consistent translation:                 YES (GOOD for peer-to-peer)
TCP simultaneous open:                      YES (GOOD for peer-to-peer)
TCP loopback translation:                   NO  (BAD for P2P over Twice-NAT)
TCP unsolicited connections filtered:       YES (GOOD for security)

UDP RESULTS:
UDP consistent translation:                 YES (GOOD for peer-to-peer)
UDP loopback translation:                   NO  (BAD for P2P over Twice-NAT)
UDP unsolicited messages filtered:          YES (GOOD for security)
```

Ports Required for Skype

We'll now discuss the ports that are required to use Skype.

Home Users or Businesses Using a DSL/Cable Router and No Firewall

To use Skype, typical home users will not need to configure anything on their DSL/cable routers or within the Skype software.

Small to Large Company Firewall Users

Skype uses UDP and TCP to communicate with other Skype clients. UDP is primarily used to establish connectivity and perform global directory searches. If the UDP ports above 1024 are open outbound, and you allow UDP replies to return through the firewall, you can improve Skype's voice quality and performance. Opening UDP ports could allow peers on your network to connect more efficiently by providing closer neighbors on the P2P network, thus reducing latency and improving call quality. Allowing more UDP ports also prevents internal contention of port translation in the NAT translation table.

In a perfect world, all outgoing TCP ports would be open through the firewall or Internet gateway. If it is not possible to open all outgoing ports, TCP port 80 should be opened. Using port 80 is a standard practice. When Skype attempts to log on, it first tries to connect using random ports. If Skype cannot connect, it attempts to connect via port 80. If port 80 cannot be opened, Skype attempts to use port 443. There is no guarantee that Skype will work through port 80 if the firewall or proxy server is restricting traffic to the HTTP. By restricting traffic to HTTP, the proxy server or firewall can scan the packets to ensure that the data is actually HTTP data. Skype does not use HTTP and will not function correctly through port 80 if traffic is restricted to HTTP traffic. If you receive errors #1101, #1102, or #1103 the firewall may be blocking port 80.

When Skype installs, it will select a random UDP port to communicate. This port setting is found in the Connection tab under Options and is an adjustable setting and stored in the shared.xml file on each computer and could be set the same for all users of Skype. If you want to avoid relayed Skype calls and relayed file transfers, you can open up the UDP port on your firewall that is specified in Skype to allow for better voice call quality and faster file transfers.

Understand that opening these UDP ports changes the normal corporate security policy, and proper approval and risks associated with opening anything on your firewall should be weighed prior to opening these settings. Discuss this issue thoroughly with your information security team on the impacts and what additional layers of security could be implemented to mitigate any risks, such as enabling a client-side personal firewall solution discussed earlier in this chapter. You could allow TCP and/or UDP inbound on the ports listed in Skype options for all clients internal to the firewall. If necessary, Skype will use TCP ports 80 and 443, respectively, to communicate with other Skype peers, and this will create relayed Skype calls and slow file transfers.

Skype's Shared.xml file

In a larger network, you can control the port for incoming connections by modifying Skype's shared.xml file in the following location:

■   <Drive>\Documents and Settings\<UserName>\Application Data\Skype folder

Using a text editor, *find* the **<ListeningPort>nnnn</ListeningPort>** entry of the shared.xml file, where 'nnnn' is the random port number that Skype chose when it was initially installed. By configuring all users to use the same UDP port, you can improve the quality of Skype conversations by opening a single inbound UDP port, if your network security policy permits this. If the traffic inbound on that port is high, you could logically segment the traffic by setting different groups of users to use a specific UDP port and opening multiple UDP ports inbound, while still maintaining some control over what ports are opened and to whom. Visit Dan Douglass's Web site at the following URL for scripts and utilities to help modify the shared.xml setting in a business environment: www.code-hatchery.com/skype.html.

Microsoft Windows Active Directory

In a typical Windows Active Directory-based enterprise, with clients running Windows XP Service Pack 2, you can set a Group Policy that allows you to enable the Skype traffic through the Windows Firewall on all client machines with little effort. This can be achieved via the following steps:

1. Open the **Group Policy Object Editor** console on the Active Directory Domain controller.

2. Locate the **Group Policy** setting found in **Computer Configuration\Administrative Templates\Network\Network Connections\Windows Firewall\Standard Profile**.

3. Select the Policy Setting for **Windows Firewall** to enable the **Define program exceptions** policy.

4. Next, click the **Show Button** that was enabled by the previous step.

5. Add a definition for a Program Exception as **%PROGRAMFILES%\skype\ phone\skype.exe:*:enabled:Skype** and then click OK.

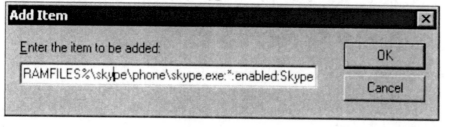

6. Click **OK** to close the Show Contents dialog box, then click the **OK** button to close the Windows Firewall: Define program exceptions Properties dialog box.

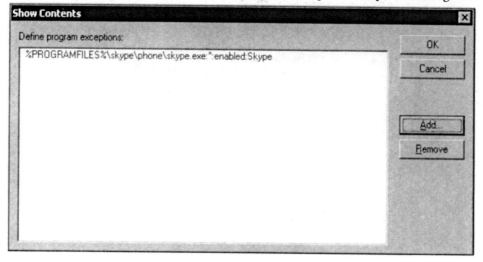

7. Allow time for the Group Policy to be refreshed. The time varies depending on the network settings. Allowing exceptions for Skype and opening up the recommended ports make it easier for Skype to establish reliable communications outside of your network. Other products, such as Norton Internet Security, McAfee Firewall Pro, and Zone Alarm Pro, have similar functionality. Visit Skype's Web site at http://web.skype.com/help_firewalls.html for the specific configuration of your product.

The same option can also be manually configured on each workstation in the enterprise by using the Windows Firewall applet in Control Panel.

1. Open **Control Panel** and double-click the **Windows Firewall** icon.

2. Click the **Exceptions** tab.

3. Tick the box next to **Skype**.

Using Proxy Servers and Skype

Many popular proxy servers are available on the market today. Skype supports HTTPS, SSL, and SOCKS5 proxy standards. Skype can optionally include authentication over proxies if the proxy server requires it. On Windows clients, Skype automatically uses the connection settings in Internet Explorer to identify the proxy settings that may be defined for that user on that computer. It is possible for the user to set Skype to use a manual configuration in the **Tools** menu, **Options**, and **Connection** tab settings. See Chapter 11 "Setting Up Skype in the Workplace" for tips on identifying your proxy server information using the netstat utility.

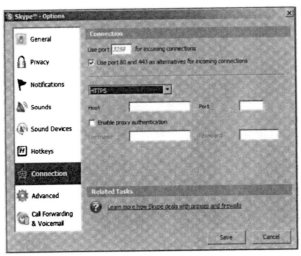

If you are using a SOCKS5 proxy server, it must allow unrestricted connections to the ports discussed in the "Ports Required for Skype" section of this chapter. Most proxy server solutions provide packet-filtering features. As previously mentioned, enabling packet filtering and restricting traffic over port 80 to only HTTP could cause communication problems for Skype.

Wireless Communications

Many companies implement a wireless network, preferably using 802.11G, that directly connects to the Internet. If you want to then connect to company resources, you would VPN back into the corporate network just as you would from home or a hotel over the wireless network. The wireless network could allow for fewer restrictions on traffic for wireless clients while still allowing for stricter security on the wired devices. Refer to Chapters 2 and 10 for more information on wireless communication with Skype. You should also read the benchmark documents located at the Center For Internet Wireless Benchmarks at the following url: http://cisecurity.org/bench_wireless.html. There you will find valuable information on implementing a wireless infrastructure in a secure network enterprise.

If you are experiencing , high latency or poor voice quality with Skype, you can troubleshoot your connection quality by using NAT Check or Skype's Display Technical Call info feature found in the Advanced options tab. To enable the tech support feature or edit the Config.xml file manually:

1. Exit Skype.

2. Locate the **Config.xml** file located in the **<Drive>\Documents and Settings\<User Name>\Application Data\Skype\<Skype user name>** folder and open it with Notepad.exe or a similar text editor.

3. Use the 'find' capability to locate the setting **<DisplayCallInfo>0 </DisplayCallInfo>**

4. Change the value from 0 to 1 and save the file.

5. Launch Skype.

Visit Dan Douglass's Web site at the following URL for scripts and utilities to modify the config.xml file setting in a business environment: www.codehatchery.com/skype.html.

Once you have enabled the **Display Technical call info** feature, you can make a test call to the Skype Test Call user. Once you have established the call, simply hover the mouse cursor over the user's avatar (picture), and you will see a tooltip-style popup with connection information:

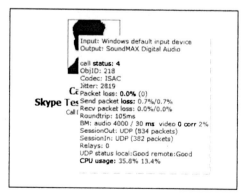

Note that in this scenario, the relays count is 0 and the roundtrip time is 105ms (1000ms = 1 second). Since the Skype answering machine is open, the connection is very clean, and there is very little latency.

Display Technical Call Information

The following is detailed information about the Technical Call Information popup items shown in the preceding and following examples. An overview of this information is provided in the section titled "Using Skype's Technical Call Information" in Chapter 6.

Call Status

- 0 = Hosting conference.

- 1 = ROUTING - call is currently being routed.

- 2 EARLYMEDIA - with the pstn there is possibility that before the call is actually established, the early media is being played. For example, it can be a calling tone, or it can be some waiting message (all operators are busy, hold on for a sec) etc.

- ?? FAILED - call failed. Try to get FAILUREREASON for more information.

- 3 = RINGING - currently ringing.

- 4 = INPROGRESS - call is in progress.

- 5 = ONHOLD - call is placed on hold by you.

- ?? FINISHED - call is finished.

- ?? MISSED - call was missed.

- 8 = REFUSED - call was refused.

- 8 = BUSY - destination was busy i.e. pressed hang up button.

- 10 = ONHOLD - call is placed on hold by other party.

- 13 = CANCELED (Protocol 2)

- ObjID: Ignore this information as it is not important.

- Codec: ISAC is most commonly used (G729 and iLBC are also possible)

- Jitter: Network administrators need to look at jitter. Jitter is the variation in the time between each of the delivered packets of data arriving from the source to the destination. This could indicate a bandwidth bottleneck or heavy traffic from the source to destination causing some packets to arrive sooner than others. The common method for reducing jitter is to buffer data at the destination.

- Packet Loss: Network administrators need to be aware of packet loss. This is the total percentage of the packets of data that don't make it to or from each party in the conversation. This should be low, but will be something if you are using UDP, since delivery is not guaranteed.

- Send packet loss: Network administrators should pay attention to this setting. This indicates how much data is not making it to the destination party in the call. If the Send packet loss is high, it means that something is causing the packets from getting to the remote client.

- Recv packet loss: Network administrators should pay attention to this setting. This indicates how much data is not making it from the other party in the call. If the Receive packet loss is high, it means that something is preventing the packets from getting to you from the remote client.

- Roundtrip: Normal users and Network administrators can get information from this. The higher the number is, the longer it takes for your voice to get to the other party and back. This should be low, and anything about 300ms starts to get choppy, reducing call quality. Look at SessionOut and SessionIN, or run NAT Check to determine why you are relaying.

- BM: This is related to the bandwidth and quality of the audio and is not important.

- SessionOut: Network administrators should look at this if roundtrip values are high. This should say UDP. If it says TCP or RELAY_UDP, then you are not operating at the best performance. In this case look at UDP status remote. If it says remote:Bad, then the remote party is behind a firewall and cannot receive UDP traffic.

- SessionIn: Network administrators should look at this if roundtrip values are high. This should say UDP. If it says TCP, RELAY_TCP, or RELAY_UDP you are not operating at the best performance. In this case look at UDP status local. If it says local:Bad, you could, at your discretion, open up the UDP port as discussed earlier in this chapter to allow inbound UDP traffic.

- Relays: Ideally the relay count is zero (0), and will be when checking Skype voicemail. When relaying is in effect the count will almost always be four (4), but you may see a lower number during the time that the relay connections are being established.

- UDP status: should always be local:Good remote:Good. If either are Bad, look at SessionIn/SessionOut to remedy.

- CPU usage: 35.8% 13.4% Total CPU usage of each processor by all running applications on the local machine. If this is too high, then the machine may be too overloaded to allow Skype to operate efficiently. Other applications will most likely be suffering as well.

The next example is a call to a user on large corporate network where no inbound UDP is allowed back in through the firewall, and there is a very complex network infrastructure.

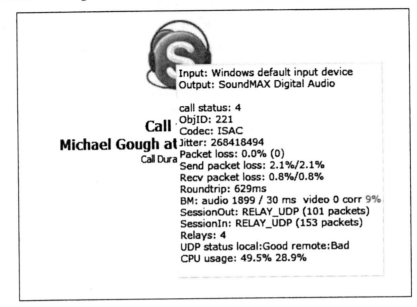

Note the difference in the SessionOut and SessionIn results. *RELAY_UDP*, and the UDP status *remote:Bad* show us that the remote location is the problem, and that a relay node is being used to carry UDP traffic for each of the clients. The result of the relays is the long roundtrip time of 629ms, and therefore, there is a delay in transmitting the voice data to the remote client. Basically, it takes more than half a second for everything you say to get to the remote client, so the conversation is choppy and degraded. To improve this connection, the callers can use NAT Check to see if they are able to use UDP and troubleshoot the connection. If it is possible to open the UDP port inbound to the remote client in this scenario, the sessions can use a direct UDP or peer-to-peer connection, and the communication will be improve almost tenfold. See the following example, to the same caller, without the firewall restrictions:

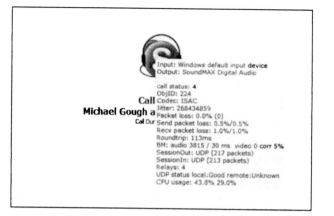

To summarize, if you have a bad connection, each client can run NAT Check and the Display Technical info to see who is having difficulty communicating. The findings can be confirmed with the configuration demonstrated in the previous section. To correct the issue, determine the UDP port the trouble client is listening on. Open that port inbound by defining a firewall rule. The rule should be specific to the client, so it might be something like *Allow: WAN * to LAN 192.169.1.21 UDP: 3259*, which allows all WAN IP addresses to communicate inbound to the private LAN address 192.168.1.21 over UDP port 3259.

Small to Large Companies

In most large companies, this will not be feasible and may possibly be against the corporate security policy and allowable network practices, but this does remain an option for small to medium-sized businesses that desire better communication quality and have the flexibility to modify their firewall rules. Some firewalls allow rules to be enabled during a specific time frame, and outside of that time window, the rule is disabled. If you wish to limit the use of Skype to only off-business hours, this type of feature would provide better security than leaving the port open all of the time. With any modification to your firewall rules, be sure to check your corporate security policy and with corporate security and your network team to gain approval and to understand the potential risks that are associated with opening any ports on a firewall to an internal client. Additional layers of security should be implemented if this configuration is to be used. If any peer-to-peer communication is allowed, it is recommended that the clients have a personal firewall solution to further protect the systems from malicious activity.

How to Block Skype in the Enterprise

From a security or network administrator's point of view, the very same features that make Skype connect reliably through a restrictive firewall present a challenge to preventing or blocking Skype traffic on a network. Skype is very robust and can function with access to only port 80. Most corporations allow outbound Web traffic, so port 80 (HTTP) must remain open. Port 443 is the SSL port (HTTPS), and secure Web sites require this port to remain open. It is not as simple as blocking ports to prevent Skype from functioning.

Several tasks must be completed to block Skype in your enterprise. The first step is to block access to the Skype downloads to prevent the executable from even being installed on your client machines. This practice is referred to as *black listing*. This step is not entirely effective by itself, since some users might already have the Skype client installed or could bring the installation package from home on a CD or thumb/flash drive.

It is good practice to prevent unnecessary applications from accessing the Internet. The best way to achieve that is by blocking all ports on the firewall and then selectively allowing known traffic to pass, the "deny all unless explicitly allowed" mentality. In addition, you may choose to restrict access to all Internet sites except those that have been approved by your organization. This is referred to as *white listing*, and although it requires more maintenance, it is much more secure.

Another method used to prevent communication over the Internet is to use packet filters. Packet filters examine the data inside the headers of transmitted packets. This information can be used to create rules to dump messages that contain headers that meet the filter criteria. Unfortunately, Skype data is encrypted, so packet filters are unable to examine the information in the data packets; therefore, packet filtering is useless. However, a new hardware device is purported to identify the signature of Skype communication and block Skype traffic based on that identification.

In a corporate enterprise environment, you may have other software solutions that allow the use of application filters on the desktops. This is another effective way to block Skype. The method of policies depends on the platform, but essentially, the concept is the same. When a user attempts to execute a program that is defined as disallowed, the process that monitors the client will prevent the program from executing. An example of this would be to use Microsoft Systems Management Server and define a restriction on the Skype.exe executable. Network Associates and Symantec have similar features built in to their groupware products.

Skype is very effective at finding ways to communicate with other Skype peers. There is no straightforward way to block Skype in the enterprise. The most effective method is to prevent the program from running at all or scan for it on all systems that are not approved and delete it from each system.

Endnote

1.   "Number of Hosts Advertised in the DNS." *Internet Domain Survey*, July 2005, www.isc.org (accessed October 4, 2005)

Part IV: Customizing Skype

Chapter 14

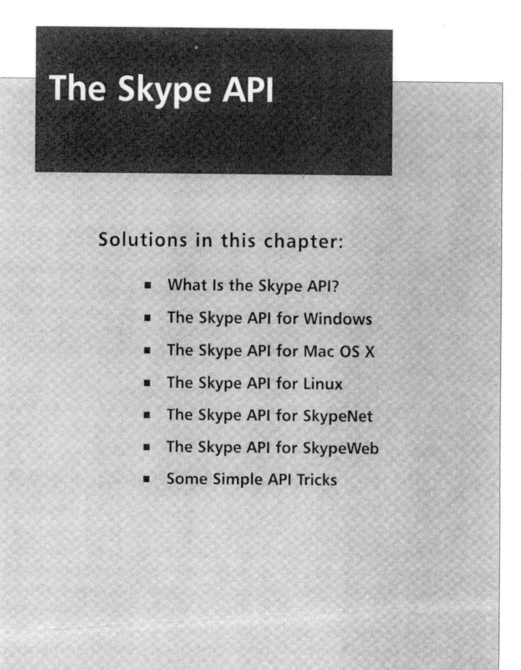

The Skype API

Solutions in this chapter:

- What Is the Skype API?
- The Skype API for Windows
- The Skype API for Mac OS X
- The Skype API for Linux
- The Skype API for SkypeNet
- The Skype API for SkypeWeb
- Some Simple API Tricks

What Is the Skype API?

This chapter is for advanced users and those who have programming skills or who want to develop a hardware or software solution for Skype. So if you are a typical user, skip this chapter. The Skype development team recognizes that you might want to extend Skype in ways that they have not foreseen or add functionality to the Skype program that is not a priority on the Skype feature list. To enable you to write your own external applications that access Skype functionality, the Skype developers have released the Skype application programming interface (API). The Skype API is supported on Windows, Mac OS X, and Linux operating system platforms. On Windows platforms, the Skype API is supported on Windows 2000 or Windows XP. Although it might function on Windows 98/ME systems, it is not supported. There is nothing for the Pocket PC as of yet. On a Mac, you must be using Mac OS X v10.3 (Panther) or later, and the latest version of the Skype Client for Mac OS X. Linux platforms supported are Fedora Core 3, SuSe 9, Mandriva 10.1 Debian; and Gentoo 1.4, all of which require Skype For Linux, version 1.1.0.3 or later.

Simply put, the Skype API allows you to control Skype from within your own applications and to monitor information received about your Skype contacts. The Skype API supports a wide range of control commands and status messages. Some of these commands include allowing you to search for users, create chats, and send messages. Additional commands allow you to make calls to Skype users, leave voice-mail messages, and answer incoming calls from your own applications.

There are many examples of uses for the API, including personalized call forwarding, home security monitoring and control, and integration of the Skype application into enterprise systems such as call center support. To see more examples visit the Skype Developer Zone at http://share.skype.com/share/developer_blog/.

The Skype Phone API and the Skype Access API

The API itself is divided into two main sections, the Skype Phone API and the Skype Access API. The Phone API is an interface Skype uses to connect with hardware devices, such as a USB phone, or virtual software devices, such as one of the many "soft phone" applications available. For hardware devices you find the Phone API implemented as an operating system device driver. This driver exchanges messages with Skype, indicating events such as the handset going off the hook and keypad presses when dialing. Similarly, Skype issues commands through the Phone API, such as instructing the device to mute itself.

The Access API is likely to be of more interest to you as general Skype users because this interface supports the commands to send and receive messages, place and answer calls, and so forth.

An Overview of the Access API

The Access API functionality is fairly consistent across the supported operating system (OS) platforms. You should be aware that using the Access API to control the Skype client differs on each OS platform. For instance, on the Windows platform, the Skype API uses WM_COPYDATA messages exchange to handle commands sent to and received from Skype. On the Mac OS X platform, you use delegates, which are classes that are used to register for and handle events sent from other components. The Linux version uses D-Bus to hook in to the Skype application and exchange messages. D-Bus can be downloaded for free at www.freedesktop.org/wiki/Software_2fdbus.

Information on how to use the D-BUS libraries is located on the Skype domain at:

- http://share.skype.com/developer_zone/documentation/skype_api_for_linux/
- http://share.skype.com/developer_zone/documentation/api_v1.3_documentation/#head-b746aebdc415a9a91c342625313af1dac2a7cbde

The Access API can be broken down into the following smaller API descriptions:

- **Ap2Ap API** Applications attach to Skype, providing a direct connection over the Skype peer-to-peer network to each other. An example would be to use the Skype connection to relay video to the other peers on a call.

- **Call API** Allows you to call Skype contacts, answer Skype calls, or use the Skype Out feature, and access the call logs.

- **Call Forwarding API** This rule engine helps manage redirection of incoming calls to one or more contacts.

- **Chat API** Provides the capability to send and receive text chat messages and search the chat logs.

- **Conference API** Control conference call functions such as joining, leaving, and initiating conference calls.

- **Contacts API** Allows you to add and delete contacts, respond to new client invitations, and set Skype status.

- **Device API** Allows access to manipulate audio devices, such as choosing which device to use for input audio, output, and ringing.

- **DTMF API** Use this to generate and process DTMF tones/notifications through the API. This could be useful for dialing from address books, modems, faxes, and so on.

- **Expressive API** Similar to features on today's mobile phones, this API allows the definition of images and ringtones for different call events.

- **MultiChat API** Allows you to initiate, join, and leave text-based group chats.

- **Profile API** Update personal data on your Skype profile and update presence status.

- **Skype Dialog Control** Provides the capability to invoke built-in Skype dialogs and windows. This capability is very effective in providing your components a consistent look and feel as the Skype client application.

- **User API** Provides the capability to search and view user profiles stored in the global Skype Directory.

- **Voice Mail API** **Provides the capability to** notify users of new voice-mail messages, as well as to play and delete voice-mail messages.

Skype API Plug-ins

Many plug-ins have been developed using the example code provided at the Skype developer site, and you can see these in the Skype Directory published at http://share.skype.com/directory/.

Plug-ins are written by third-party developers. Plug-ins are not supported by Skype; rather, they are supported by the developers of the respective plug-in. Plug-ins can be certified by Skype, and as a developer, that should be a main goal for your design. To identify the criteria your product must meet to be "Skype Certified," visit the Skype Certification Program site at http://share.skype.com/developer_zone/certification/certification_program/.

Note that, even though most of the certification program is focused on hardware devices, a programmer must be involved to write the software that allows the hardware device to interact with the Skype application.

The Skype API for Windows

The implementation of the API for Windows is such that messages are sent between the plug-in application and Skype by using the Win32 SendMessage() function. This standard mechanism for communication under the Windows operating system can be difficult to implement if you are not used to low-level Win32 communications.

There are C++ source code examples provided at the Skype developer site. Fortunately, a number of projects have done the hard work for you, providing an implementation of Windows messaging and leaving you to add your Skype API specific functionality. If you are using C++ and developing for Windows and Linux, you can use ++Skype to greatly sim-plify your development task. ++Skype is Open Source and can be obtained at Ice Brains Software: www.icebrains-soft.com/skype_library_download.

If you are not a C++ programmer, you should take a look at SkypeX. SkypeX, a product from Beesync Technologies, provides a COM library that allows you to use the Skype API from a variety of ActiveX-enabled programming and scripting languages, including Microsoft .Net Framework programming languages. Further information on SkypeX is available at www.beesync.com.

Another extremely comprehensive implementation, ActiveS, is available from Khaoslabs at www.khaoslabs.com. ActiveS does a similar job of wrapping the message-sending layers of the Skype API for you, making it much easier to communicate with Skype. The library is available under a BSD-style license; you can use it within your own application (commercial or otherwise) without having to pay a fee or release the source code.

The aforementioned alternative implementations allow for development of Skype API programs using virtually any of the popular programming languages in use today. Some of those languages include C#, VB.Net, J#, Visual BASIC 6.0, JavaScript, JScript, VBScript, VBA, Java, and ActivePerl for Windows.

As is the standard practice with all free software and add-ins, you should carefully read the copyright, licensing, and distribution documents before you commit to using them as part of you application project.

The Skype API for Mac OS X

The Skype API for Mac OS X provides interfaces for Carbon, Cocoa, and AppleScript pro-gramming languages. You must be running Mac OS X v10.3 (Panther) or later. If you are creating Widgets, you must be running Mac OS X v10.4 (Tiger). First you must download the Skype.framework at http://download.skype.com/share/devzone/example_macosx.dmg.

You must include the Skype framework with your application, and you should abide by Skype's recommendation to include it as an embedded framework. Simply copy the Skype.framework into your application bundle. Once you have the framework in the appli-cation bundle, you can link it to your application.

As mentioned earlier in this chapter, the Skype API for Mac OS X should be imple-mented by creating a delegate class and implementing the appropriate SkypeDelegate inter-face for the language you choose. The delegate architecture is available for only Cocoa and Carbon. AppleScript has only one command. This command allows you to send any com-mand string that complies with the Skype API protocol documentation.

The Skype API for Linux

If you are running Fedora Core 3, SuSe 9, Mandriva 10.1 Debian, or Gentoo 1.4., you should not have any trouble using the Skype API. As previously mentioned, to write to the Skype API on Linux, you must have the D-BUS distributions. Once you have built the D-BUS components, you can update the /etc/dbus-1/system.d/skype.conf and add the following XML code:

```
<!DOCTYPE busconfig PUBLIC "-//freedesktop//DTD D-BUS Bus Configuration 1.0//EN"
  "http://www.freedesktop.org/standards/dbus/1.0/busconfig.dtd">
<busconfig>
  <!-- ../system.conf have denied everything, so we just punch some holes -->
  <policy context="default">
    <allow own="com.Skype.API"/>
    <allow send_destination="com.Skype.API"/>
    <allow receive_sender="com.Skype.API"/>
    <allow send_path="/com/Skype"/>
  </policy>
</busconfig>
```

Once you have completed the configuration file, you will receive a message when initializing to confirm that you want to allow the external program to use Skype.

The Skype API for SkypeNet

The SkypeNet API enables you to access the Skype instant messaging and presence system without having to install the full Skype application on your computer system. This capability allows you to build Skype support directly into your application in a much more lightweight fashion than was previously supported. SkypeNet also greatly simplifies installation and distribution of Skype-aware client applications.

The Skype API for SkypeWeb

SkypeWeb, currently under development by the Skype development team, is touted as being able to allow you to publish your Skype online status on the Internet. You simply copy the HTML code provided by Skype and paste it into the Web site of your choice. Your colleagues and friends are then able to view your status simply by browsing the page.

If you can't wait for SkypeWeb, Skype plug-ins that provide similar functionality are available now. One such example is Jyve, at www.jyve.com, which provides Web presence.

To use Jyve Web presence simply install the plug-in and add the following code to your Web site of choice, replacing SkypeUserName with your user name:

```
<img src="http://www.skypepresence.com/SkypeUserName.png" border="0">
```

Depending on your current online status, or that of the user name you entered, you will then see an image something like one of the following:

Some Simple API Tricks

Before you get started, visit some of the sites referenced in this chapter. These sites include many useful sources of information, including code examples in many different programming languages. The examples, combined with the documentation resources and the free API helper interfaces, will provide you with a good foundation for developing your own useful utilities. Another crucial step in the development of any project is design. It is very important to answer some basic questions before you start the project.

The first question you have to ask is "What platform will I support?" The answer will determine the programming language you will use to write your component. If you are planning to write a component for all platforms, C++ is the best route to take. It is important to note that most Skype users are on the Windows platform, and it just happens to be the OS that has the most code samples, includes the most tutorials, and is the easiest platform on which to build.

The following is an example of a Visual Studio 2003 C# project that uses the ActiveS COM library from KhaosLabs to access the Skype API and open the Sound Devices options page:

```
using System;
using System.Drawing;
using System.Collections;
using System.ComponentModel;
using System.Windows.Forms;
using System.Data;
using SKYPEAPILib;


namespace SkypeSoundTool
{
        /// <summary>
        /// Summary description for frmMain.
        /// </summary>
        public class frmMain : System.Windows.Forms.Form
```

```
{
        /// <summary>
        /// Required designer variable.
        /// </summary>
        private System.ComponentModel.Container components = null;
        private System.Windows.Forms.Button button1;
        private System.Windows.Forms.Button button2;
        private bool m_bAttached = false;
        // Create a Skype Access component
        private SKYPEAPILib.Access m_skype = new AccessClass();

        public frmMain()
        {
            //
            // Required for Windows Form Designer support
            //
            InitializeComponent();

        }


        /// <summary>
        /// Clean up any resources being used.
        /// </summary>
        protected override void Dispose( bool disposing )
        {
            if( disposing )
            {
                if (components != null)
                {
                    components.Dispose();
                }
            }
            base.Dispose( disposing );
        }

        #region Windows Form Designer generated code
        /// <summary>
        /// Required method for Designer support - do not modify
        /// the contents of this method with the code editor.
```

```csharp
/// </summary>
private void InitializeComponent()
{
        this.button1 = new System.Windows.Forms.Button();
        this.button2 = new System.Windows.Forms.Button();
        this.SuspendLayout();
        //
        // button1
        //
        this.button1.Location = new System.Drawing.Point(40, 40);
        this.button1.Name = "button1";
        this.button1.Size = new System.Drawing.Size(296, 23);
        this.button1.TabIndex = 0;
        this.button1.Text = "Open Sound Configuration Dialog";
        this.button1.Click += new
        System.EventHandler(this.button1_Click);
        //
        // button2
        //
        this.button2.Location = new System.Drawing.Point(40, 8);
        this.button2.Name = "button2";
        this.button2.Size = new System.Drawing.Size(296, 23);
        this.button2.TabIndex = 1;
        this.button2.Text = "Connect to Skype";
        this.button2.Click += new
        System.EventHandler(this.button2_Click);
        //
        // frmMain
        //
        this.AutoScaleBaseSize = new System.Drawing.Size(5, 13);
        this.ClientSize = new System.Drawing.Size(376, 82);
        this.Controls.Add(this.button2);
        this.Controls.Add(this.button1);
        this.Name = "frmMain";
        this.Text = "Skype Sound Tool";
        this.Load += new System.EventHandler(this.frmMain_Load);
        this.ResumeLayout(false);
        //
        //m_skype
        //
```

```
        this.m_skype.APIStatusChanged +=new
        _IAccessEvents_APIStatusChangedEventHandler(m_skype_
        APIStatusChanged);
}
#endregion

/// <summary>
/// The main entry point for the application.
/// </summary>
[STAThread]
static void Main()
{
        Application.Run(new frmMain());
}

private void frmMain_Load(object sender, System.EventArgs e)
{


}

private void button1_Click(object sender, System.EventArgs e)
{

        //Attempt to attach to Skype if not attached
        if (true != m_bAttached)
        {
                Attach();

        }

        SKYPEAPILib.UIClass m_UI = new UIClass();
        m_UI.OpenOptions(SkypeOptionsPage.pgSoundDevices);



}

private void button2_Click(object sender, System.EventArgs e)
{
        Attach();
}
```

```
private void Attach()
{
        // The following line will cause the Skype Authorization
        // dialog to appear, prompting the user to allow the
        // application to access Skype.
        m_skype.Connect();




}


private void m_skype_APIStatusChanged(SkypeAPIAttachmentStatus
Status)
{
        if (SkypeAPIAttachmentStatus.apiAttachSuccess ==
        m_skype.APIAttachmentStatus)
        {
                m_bAttached = true;


        }
        else if (SkypeAPIAttachmentStatus.apiAttachRefused ==
        m_skype.APIAttachmentStatus)
        {
                // You will need to use the Privacy settings in
                // Skype Options,
                // click the Manage other programs' access to Skype
                //  and locate
                // the entry that refuses your applications' access
                // and try again.
                MessageBox.Show("The user refused access to the
                application.");
                m_bAttached = false;
        }
        else
        {
                // something else happened
                m_bAttached = false;
        }
```

```
this.Text = m_bAttached ? "Skype Sound Tool Attached" :
"Skype Sound Tool NOT Attached";
```

```
            }
```

```
        }
```

```
    }
```

The source code for this sample project can be downloaded from Dan Douglass's Web site at www.codehatchery.com/SkypeSoundTool.Zip.

With relatively little code, I have utilized the Skype API to provide the user with quick access to a standard Skype dialog to configure settings. It is possible to enumerate all the sound devices and allow the user to define and quickly choose configuration profiles or any number of useful tasks. The seemingly limitless power and potential for this functionality, combined with the Skype Certification program, have made a vast new market open for creative new ideas.

Part V: Skype in the Future

Chapter 15

Future Skype-Enabled Devices

Solutions in this chapter:

- Skype Routers (ATAs)

- Skype-Enabled Telephones

- Skype WiFi Telephones

- Skype-Enabled Cell Phones

- Skype USB Telephones

- Skype PBX Gateways

- A Skype Wish List

Overview

With all the hype about Skype, we can expect companies to continue introducing new products, both software add-ons and hardware that will exploit Skype's existing capabilities and give us even more features and capabilities. In this chapter, we discuss some up-and-coming products as well as some "wish list" items based on hundreds of inquiries from www.SkypeTips.com and our many conversations with vendors that ask us to evaluate their products and provide feedback. We really enjoy doing these reviews because it allows us to recommend the products others can apply to their particular needs.

The Skype community is a close-knit one that shares ideas, testing, comments, and of course, opinions on the growing number of products that are being marketed to work with Skype. These vendors all want you to buy their products. We have included this chapter to not only let you, the reader, know what is coming, but to also spawn new ideas for future Skype-related products.

Skype Routers (ATAs)

One of the most frequent questions I receive as part of providing help to users who visit www.SkypeTips.com is, "Is there is a device that allows you to use Skype without having to leave your computer turned on?" Unfortunately, the answer is "Not yet." What people are looking for is a device similar to what Vonage, Packedt8, AT&T CallVantage, Time Warner Digital phone, and other VoIP providers use to connect you to the Internet without a computer. These devices are called *analog telephone adapters*, or ATAs for short. Vonage refers to its ATA as a *digital phone adapter*. Basically, an ATA is a device you attach to your network that will convert what comes in from the Internet to a regular telephone communication. The following graphic shows a typical VoIP configuration with an ATA.

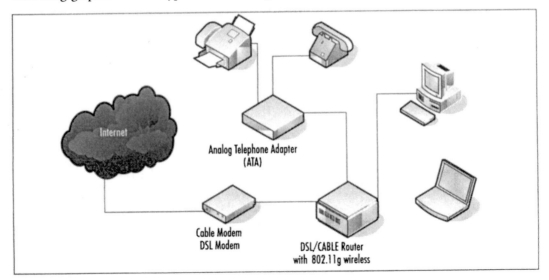

If you have not already purchased a P2P-friendly DSL/cable router that we suggested many times throughout this book, now you have a reason to get one. A DSL/cable router allows you not only to have multiple computers sharing your broadband connection and provides you 802.11g wireless; but you can use it to connect a Skype router or Skype ATA when they become available, without having to change or add anything.

This device for Skype would be a little different than those used for the other ATA products we mentioned; the Skype router will basically need to be a little PC that can be configured with one or more contacts so that it can send and receive Skype calls.

More than likely, this device will either have embedded Linux or Windows running as the operating system, with enough memory to handle what Skype needs. You would most likely configure it using your Web browser.

When a Skype router or ATA is available, it might not have all the functions that you have with Skype on your computer. It will be dedicated to Skype calls only and have basic options as they relate only to Skype calls. It might be able to do call forwarding and other dial-in and dial-out features, as some Skype telephone gateways can.

Potential Users

Possible users of Skype routers/ATAs are:

- Home users
- Small businesses
- Medium-sized businesses

Skype-Enabled Telephones

The term *Skype-enabled* is meant to indicate a device that has all the functions that allow you to use Skype calls without looking at your computer. This means that you can see your Skype contacts on the telephone display and can make and receive Skype calls without any interaction with your computer other than initially plugging in the Skype device. The Dualphone, Linksys CIT200, and VoSky (Actiontec) USB phone covered in Chapter 8 are examples of fully Skype-enabled devices. This is an area that is just now starting to take off. Vendors are shifting from the development and testing phase, in which we have participated for several products, into full-scale production.

A Skype-enabled phone is any type of telephone that has software or firmware that allows you to use it for a Skype call without having to look at your computer. When you look at the display, you should see all your Skype contacts, be able to select one, and then press a button to place the call, just as though you were using a regular old telephone—

it must be so easy that my grandmother could use it! These telephones should have volume-boosting capabilities, necessary to compensate for any signal degradation that could occur.

Potential Users

Possible users of Skype-enabled phones are:

- Home users
- Small businesses
- Medium-sized businesses

Understanding the Basics... Skype-Enabled Telephones

These telephones are perfect for users who do not want to use Skype on a computer. They are as easy to use as any telephone and enable users to enjoy the benefits of Skype.

Skype-Enabled Cordless Telephones

Cordless phones like the Dualphone and Linksys CIT200 will become increasingly popular because they are perfect for the home and small business user. They can come with or without built-in answering machines. Some Skype-enabled cordless phones like the Dualphone will be able to connect to both your computer (for Skype calls), and to the 'regular' telephone company line (landline), or other VoIP provider, so that you can use the same phone for both services. The Linksys CIT200 connects directly to your computer but does not have the option to connect to your existing telephone line. Some devices will allow incoming Skype voice calls to be forwarded to the landline, and vice versa (i.e. to act as a gateway), and others will only interact with Skype.

To use a Skype-enabled phone, you would locate the base unit near your main computer and connect it to an available USB port. The cordless handset can then be located/used wherever convenient. This could be particularly convenient when traveling with a laptop and operating from a hotel room.

Potential Users

Possible users of Skype-enabled cordless phones are:

- Home users

- Small businesses
- Medium-sized businesses

Understanding the Basics...
Skype-Enabled Cordless Telephones

These telephones are perfect for users who do not want to use Skype on a computer, because the devices are as easy to use as any telephone, offer the benefits of Skype, and provide the portability we have become accustomed to with cordless telephones. These are perfect for the traveler with a laptop who doesn't want a USB cable to limit his or her movement.

Skype WiFi Telephones

This is one of my favorite areas for a Skype telephone. A Skype WiFi telephone will look like a cell phone and most likely come in all flavors and colors, very similar to the USB phones we discussed in Chapter 8 or just like your cell phone—or better yet *built into* your cell phone.

The idea behind a Skype WiFi telephone is that so much WiFi, predominantly 802.11b and 802.11g, is available in airports, hotels, coffee shops, trade shows, city centers, and other public hot spots that if you sign up for a service like Boingo that has partnered with Skype, you could easily make free Skype calls from any wireless hot spot. Locators for many WiFi hot spots, including Boingo, are included in Chapter 10 for your convenience. See "A Skype Wish List", later in this chapter, for a description of my ultimate Skype WiFi device.

Companies that have large factories and are WiFi enabled could use Skype WiFi telephones much like the Sprint Nextel two-way phones to reach anyone at the location, with a potential cost savings.

Home Users

The home user who has a broadband router with 802.11g wireless would be a good candidate for a Skype WiFi phone. If you already have a cordless telephone unit at home, why would you replace it with a Skype-enabled version until it broke or became obsolete?

With Skype WiFi phone, you could just add one or two of these units around the house if your wireless coverage was good enough to make and receive Skype calls or anywhere wireless is available with a decent signal. I have a daughter, and although she is only six now, I see her one day having one in her room so she can roam freely and keep my phone line open for normal home use.

Small Businesses

Small businesses can utilize a Skype WiFi phone in much the same way a home user does, with the added benefit of significantly reducing long distance phone bills and enabling employees to travel or roam about WiFi hot spots, like the world-famous Starbucks or your nearest airport.

Many small businesses struggle with controlling costs, and if they need to call suppliers or do telemarketing to potential clients, they will rack up significant phone bills. One of Skype's best benefits is reducing long distance calls for small businesses.

The key is to have a flexible phone that can be placed anywhere in the small business and work well. Of course, here is another promotion for using 802.11g wireless: a Skype WiFi phone that can be placed on your desk, next to your regular desk telephone.

Medium-Sized to Large Businesses

Medium-sized businesses would benefit from using Skype WiFi phones. Building on the examples we used for the home user and small businesses, medium-sized businesses would have more applications and large cost benefits due to the sheer volume of users.

Warehouse, shipping departments, guard shacks, collections, and telemarketing departments could all benefit from reduced local toll and long distance and cell phone costs. The larger the company, the higher its cell phone bills.

There is a definite need for cell phones—I could not live without mine—but with a Skype WiFi phone, I could attend conference calls, make calls from the airport or hotels and, of course, Starbucks, and in turn reduce my cell minutes, allowing me to get a less expensive plan. I do business worldwide and had a recent experience in Canada with my cell plan not covering calls from Canada—I spent a bundle on calls.

Of course, there is a major requirement in that you must have access to a wireless network to use a Skype WiFi phone, but WiFi is virtually everywhere, and if you had one of these Skype WiFi phones, you would soon know and use WiFi hot spots. Check out our extensive list of WiFi hot spot Web sites in Chapter 10.

Skype-Enabled Cell Phones

If you are like me, a dedicated and addicted cell phone user, you read the Skype WiFi phone section and said, "I don't want another phone." Well, what if your cell phone has wireless built in and could operate in either cell or WiFi mode, or both?

You would have the best of both worlds and would not have to carry an additional device to make Skype calls, instead using your cell phone even when you do not have wireless access. I can tell you that several vendors already have or have in the planning a Skype WiFi/cell phone.

The i-mate PDA2 and PDA2K and JAM Pocket PC phones are the first examples of a cell phone/WiFi Skype phone combination. These are Pocket PCs, but Skype comes with the device. (We discuss the i-mate devices in Chapter 8.) Motorola has also announced a VoIP-enabled WiFi cell phone. This is perfect for those who use a cell phone over a Pocket PC device and want to be able to use Skype over WiFi.

Many cell phone providers offer high-speed Internet offerings for their cell users for phones that have mini-browsers, downloading movies, news, sports clips, and the like. These services are also capable of good Skype calls; several users have called me and the calls sounded fine, but this high-speed Internet option for cell phones is much more costly than WiFi hot spots. So just be aware that they are not the same service, and charges may vary. Decide what is best for your needs.

Potential Users

Possible users of Skype-enabled cell phones are:

- Home users
- Small businesses
- Medium-sized businesses
- Corporations

Skype USB Telephones

USB phones in their current state are missing many of the functions that they need. I know from talking with the vendors of several USB phones that improvements that I recommended during evaluations are already in the works. VoSky USB phone is truly Skype-enabled. The Linksys CIT200 is also Skype enabled as well as USB connected and cordless. Generally speaking, the typical USB telephone is inexpensive and has a cord.

Most importantly, USB telephones have cords, and, like many people, unless I am working at my desk, I prefer the freedom to roam around, multitasking as I see fit. So as far as I am concerned the cord has got to go. So look for more companies coming out with devices similar to the Linksys CIT200 and Siemens Gigaset M34 adapter. USB phones will become more Skype-aware, with their displays showing you all your Skype contacts, allowing you to make and receive Skype calls without using your computer or interrupting your work.

In addition, it would be advantageous if USB phones included a built-in speaker phone which would free up the user's hands to take notes while in a conference call, for example. Many of my clients' conference rooms have computers to control the display system, and connecting a USB conference telephone to such a computer would also be practical for medium-sized business and corporate users.

Potential Users

Possible users for Skype USB phones are:

- Home users
- Small businesses
- Medium-sized businesses
- Corporations

Skype PBX Gateways

Here is the true device that small to large businesses want: Gateways between Skype and Private Branch Exchanges (PBXs). Several vendors are developing Skype PBX gateway devices which will permit a user on a PBX to make Skype or SkypeOut calls, and which will allow an incoming Skype or SkypeIn call to be routed to the PBX user's phone.

These devices would connect to an open PBX Foreign eXchange Office (FXO) interface and then to the Internet in a way that is similar to a Skype ATA or Skype router, and as discussed in Chapter 8. The following picture depicts a typical PBX setup.

The Skype gateway always sits between the PBX and the Internet, and provides a method for routing incoming Skype calls via the PBX directly to the phone on the user's desk phone. Normal functionality of the PBX and the way it interacts with the existing telephone services would not change. The capability to use Skype would be added as an additional telephone feature. The following picture illustrates a Skype gateway with this type of configuration.

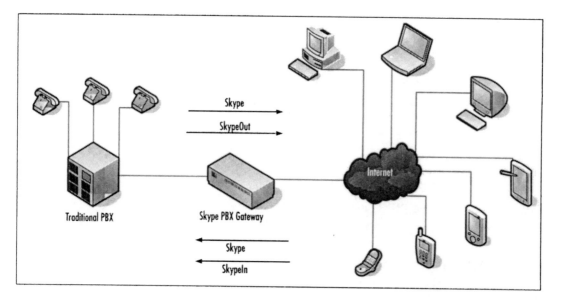

A Skype PBX gateway would provide a company bi-directional Skype voice-call capability which would mimic calls to and from the regular telephone network, and which would avoid quality issues, delays, and relays that would most likely be associated with Skype calls over a complex, firewalled, corporate data network (see discussion in Chapter 13). The corporate user would typically dial a single digit number (e.g. 7) to access Skype, thus employing the same familiar sequence already being used to access an 'outside' telephone line (i.e. by dialing 9). Then the user would be able to make free Skype-to-Skype, or inexpensive long-distance SkypeOut calls. Speed-dialing would be fully supported, and this could be used to easily access a Skype user who is acting in a standard Help Desk capacity, as was discussed in Chapter 12. Additionally, a company could set up several Skype accounts, 'Company_XYZ_Support' for example, which could provide Internet users using Skype the ability to be routed to the Help Desk for Company XYZ without incurring long-distance fees. Also, this type of gateway could be used to for inter-branch calls, conference calls, or calls to any number of locations around the world, either for free or less expensively than using traditional 800 services or long distance plans.

A Skype PBX gateway would provide these common features:

■ Connect to your company PBX and take advantage of Skype, SkypeIn, and SkypeOut services.

■ Employees can use SkypeOut for low-rate calls.

■ Customers can use regular phones to call your SkypeIn number for local call service.

- A Skype user on a computer can call customer service for free.

- Integrate with PSTN switches; no need to change existing telephone systems.

- No need to change the firewall or the network.

- Independent host; no need to use another computer.

- Scalable; directly plug in another one to expand the capacity.

Potential Users

Possible users of Skype PBX gateways are:

- Small businesses

- Medium-sized businesses

- Corporations

A Skype Wish List

In addition to those described previously in this chapter, the only product I would like to see is the SkypePod.

SkypePod?

I have suggested to all my Apple/Mac-user friends that Apple should release a Skype-enabled iPod with wireless capabilities and a headset jack, so all of us iPodders can make Skype calls when we are near a WiFi hot spot. Plug in a speakerphone and imagine how cool it would be to use an iPod in your home or business to participate in a conference call.

If you took the new iPod Nano and placed it in the form factor of the original iPod, it would be perfect for a SkypePod—or easier said, a "SkyPod" device. If Apple used the iPod Nano or iPod Shuffle electronics in the larger iPod body, there would be room for a wireless card and the additional microphone/headset components. So, Mr. Jobs, if your people read this and you develop the SkyPod, I get ten of them for *free*! Every Skyper I know who also uses an iPod would buy one of these in a heartbeat. So would every teenager and young adult who is a hardcore iPod user. You heard it here first ... I coined the terms *SkypePod*, *SkyPod*, and *SkypePodders*.

SkypePod Video?

Of course, with the iPod now supporting video clips, you could add a small camera like the ones we see in cell phones. With the upcoming addition of Skype Video, Apple could add the Skype Video add-on to the SkyPod, allowing for SkyPod-to-Skype video calls. Then these little devices like a Pocket PC could make video calls as well. So add *SkyPod video* to our coined terms. Your teenagers and "hip" young adults and us true Skypers would love this type of device—and be able to have our iTunes to boot.

Potential Users

Possible users of SkypePods are:

- Home users
- Businesses
- Travelers

Index

Syngress: *The Definition of a Serious Security Library*

Syn·gress (sin-gres): *noun, sing.* Freedom from risk or danger; safety. See *security*.

CPSIA information can be obtained at www.ICGtesting.com
Printed in the USA
LVOW071625180712

290619LV00007B/126/P